DEAR Lord and Father of mankind,
  Forgive our foolish ways;
Reclothe us in our rightful mind;
In purer lives, Thy service find,
  In deeper reverence, praise.

In simple trust like theirs who heard,
  Beside the Syrian sea,
The gracious calling of the Lord,
Let us, like them, without a word
  Rise up and follow Thee.

O Sabbath rest by Galilee!
  O calm of hills above,
Where Jesus knelt to share with Thee
The silence of eternity,
  Interpreted by love!

With that deep hush subduing all
  Our words and works that drown
The tender whisper of Thy call,
As noiseless let Thy blessing fall,
  As fell Thy manna down.

Drop Thy still dews of quietness,
  Till all our strivings cease:
Take from our souls the strain and stress,
And let our ordered lives confess
  The beauty of Thy peace.

Breathe through the heats of our desire
  Thy coolness and Thy balm;
Let sense be dumb, let flesh retire;
Speak through the earthquake, wind, and fire,
  O still small voice of calm!

                              J. G. WHITTIER.

REPTON

TO THE END

REPTON

TO THE END

EDITED BY JOHN PLOWRIGHT

III THIRD MILLENNIUM
PUBLISHING, LONDON

Repton to the end
© Repton School and Third Millennium Publishing Limited

First published in 2007 by
Third Millennium Publishing Limited,
a subsidiary of Third Millennium Information Limited.

2–5 Benjamin Street
London
United Kingdom
EC1M 5QL
www.tmiltd.com

ISBN: 978 1 903942 55 0

British Library Cataloguing in Publication Data
A CIP catalogue record for this book is available from the British Library.

Edited by John Plowright
Designed by Susan Pugsley
Production by Bonnie Murray

Reprographics by Asia Graphic Printing Ltd
Printed by Butler and Tanner, Frome, Somerset

Previous Page: The Arch.
Right: By 'staid and silver Trent'.

CONTENTS

EDITOR'S FOREWORD

No matter how critical and exciting History may be in schools – and Repton certainly has a good record in this regard – the typical school history is incestuous, anecdotal, parochial, sentimental and smug. Lacking in real authority because burdened by its 'authorized' status, the typical official school history reads, not surprisingly, like an extended prospectus. In short, blue pencil and rose-tinted glasses combine to drain true colour from the past by presenting it as a mere prologue to the apotheosis that is the present or, at least, the present Headmaster. How much greater are the dangers of sanitized self-congratulatory myth at a time when even the most prestigious schools are obliged to think in terms of marketing!

However, let it be stated here that the Editor has not been censored in any regard, having been left entirely free to choose what to write, whom to solicit for material, what to include and what to omit (although there is an obvious bias in favour of the fifty years since the last school history). The Editor can also attest that although provided with a list of subscribers he has not – however foolishly – paid any attention whatsoever to the demographic data contained therein to tailor this book to its guaranteed audience. In short, this book has not been written for 'gentlemen of a certain age' but for all Reptonians past, present and future – or at least until 2057 when one assumes the present volume's shelf (or coffee table) life will be ended by a 500th anniversary volume.

What then do you hold in your hands? It is not, it must be admitted, a scholarly history of the school, although it rests upon the scholarship of others, most notably Alec Macdonald's *A Short History of Repton* (1929) and *Repton 1557–1957* (1957), which was edited by Bernard Thomas. More than any man alive, the Editor can appreciate their labours and acknowledge the extent to which they have diminished his own. A book of this nature is, moreover, the work of many hands, and the Editor is deeply indebted to the many people who have provided the text and/or photographs for what it is hoped you will agree is a handsome and fitting celebration of the school's 450 years.

Special thanks are due to Robert Holroyd, Edward Wilkinson (C 1946), Chris Charter, Cathy Twigg, Sarah Tennant and Paul Stevens. Equally heartfelt apologies go to those whose contributions had to be edited or omitted because of the constraints imposed by the book's word limit.

Lastly, a word about the title: it came with the invitation to edit this work and has been followed by correspondence from several generations of Reptonians who have pointed out its shortcomings, not least the fact that in the days when the school song was regularly sung the last line was amended to 'Repton, Repton, Repton *is* the end'. If anyone can suggest a better title or spot inaccuracies in the present text, please drop the Editor a line and he'll have great pleasure in placing this in the archives for the edification of his successor fifty years down the line.

John Plowright

Reflections.

SIR JOHN PORT AND THE FOUNDING OF THE SCHOOL

The Founder.

*R*epton school was founded in accordance with the wishes of Sir John Port, as expressed in his will. Comparatively little is known about the school's benefactor, including the precise date of his birth, which was c1505–8.

We do, however, know that the Port family made its fortune as merchants near Chester and that 'our' Sir John Port's father, also Sir John Port, was a very distinguished lawyer, who by 1525 was a judge for the King's Bench. Sir John Port senior was also a philanthropist, who made Brasenose College, Oxford, the particular object of his charity. In 1522, for example, he gave the college £200 for the maintenance of two scholarships, of which his son, our founder, the youngest child and only son of Sir John senior's marriage to Joan Fitzherbert, was one of the first recipients.

After Brasenose John Port was admitted to the Inner Temple (without fee 'because the son of a judge'), but he appears not to have practised the law. One of the 40 Knights of the Bath created at the time of the coronation of Edward VI on 20 February 1547, he sat in the first parliament of Mary Tudor as one of the Knights of the Shire for Derbyshire, in which county his father had bought various lands, including the manor of Etwall.

When he came to make his will on 9 March 1557 Sir John Port had no son and heir, his first marriage, to Elizabeth Giffard, having produced two sons who died young, and three daughters, whilst his second marriage, to Dorothy Fitzherbert, was without issue. As the son of his father and as a father without a son, it was natural for Sir John to think in terms of putting some of his wealth to charitable purposes. There are, however, additional reasons why this might have occurred to him.

As Sir John contemplated his life and how it would be judged in the afterlife he might well have had doubts regarding the fate of his soul for not only had he engaged in the spiritual somersaults natural for a public figure in an age of religious flux (having lived through England's Reformation and brief

The School crest in the School Library.

10

In 1545, as part of the Reformation, chantries (private chapels where masses were sung for the donor's soul) were suppressed. Sir John – like many others – circumvented this by stipulating in his will that at the school founded in accordance with his wishes the masters and scholars were to pray daily for his soul.

It is not clear at what point in the school's history that this daily observance became a weekly ritual, although Macdonald (published 1929) refers to 'our weekly remembrance of our Founder' representing 'the direct fulfilment of his own injunction'. Again, it is not clear when this weekly invocation of Sir John was dropped, but now he is formally remembered only once a year at the Commemoration of Benefactors' service in Chapel.

Sir John Port should be remembered as our founder, and we should continue to pray for his soul, bearing in mind that he was no saint – but then, saints have no need of our prayers.

John Plowright

Sir John Port Window in Pears School.

Counter-Reformation) but he had also acted as an instrument of persecuting orthodoxy and is thus commemorated in John Foxe's *Acts and Monuments* as amongst the merciless judges who at Derby condemned Joan Waste, a blind girl aged 22, to the stake for heresy.

In short, Sir John Port might, with good reason, have feared eternal damnation and sought any means by which he might avoid or alleviate that fate. His charitable bequests should be seen in that light.

The Death of St Guthlac: stained glass window in the School Library.

The School's Coat of Arms

Repton school adopted the Port coat of arms, which was originally granted to Sir John Port senior. It comprised 'Azure, a fesse engrailed, between three birds each having in his beak a cross formée fitchée, Or'. The Heralds' College records these birds as eaglets, but Macdonald believed them to be pigeons, on the grounds that 'with its suggestion of the Carrier, it can be read as an allusion to Port'.

John Plowright

 # The School Motto

The current motto is certainly a play on the name of the founder. Originally – or rather, unoriginally – it was Floreat Repandunum. *However, the Rev. William Johnson picked up the phrase* Porta vacat culpa *after the Rev. Joseph Gould told him that he had jokingly told his Upper Third that the phrase referred to Sir John Port and the Arch, after a boy had used the phrase when construing a line in Kennedy's* Palaestra Latina *from Ovid's* Fasti *(II, 204).*

Macdonald tells us that the date of this incident is not recorded, but given the two masters involved and the fact that by 1882 *Porta Vacat Culpa* replaced *Floreat Repandunum* in accompanying the coat of arms on the Reptonian, it must have occurred at some stage between 1858 and 1882.

Repton is unique amongst schools in possessing a motto that originated in a play on words and that anticipated the Trade Descriptions Act by at least 86 years.

John Plowright

REPTON IN THE BEGINNING *1557–1854*

*T*hou has most traitorously corrupted the youth of the realm in erecting a grammar school

SHAKESPEARE, *Henry VI part 2*

It is commonly assumed that the Old School – Repton as it existed between 1559, when it opened its doors, and the advent of Steuart Adolphus Pears in 1854 – was fundamentally

Fisher strides out from the Pillars of Hercules.

different from the New School as it developed in the later 19th century. In some respects this assumption is patently correct: there were no boarding-houses in the old days, few masters, no organized games, no Science Block, no Cadet Corps. But essentially it is over-drawn. The history of Repton through 450 years has been one of marked fluctuations and, at times, of great changes, the admission of girls as pupils in our own time being perhaps the most revolutionary; but continuity has prevailed too, and the school has always had the same social function in the eyes of teachers, parents, pupils and governors. In this respect Pears brought in no radical change. He was a deeply traditional Headmaster, a truly conservative reformer. My purpose in this essay is to describe the tradition, in its strengths and weaknesses, its ups and its downs, as it operated for nearly three centuries, so that Pears' work can be seen in its proper light and proportions.

Repton was not founded as a public school: that concept was almost unknown before the reign of George III. Sir John Port, the Founder, was quite explicit in his will. His executors, he said, were to set up a hospital (almshouse for indigent old men) at Etwall, and were to find 'a priest well learned and graduate and of honest and virtuous conversation freely to keep a Grammar school in Etwall or Repton from time to time for ever' [spelling modernised].

And the school's Charter, issued by James I in 1621, after referring to the Free School of Sir John Port, Knight, lays it down (evidently confirming existing practice) that the foundation should support a master, two ushers, and four 'poor scholars'. Every such scholar was to be the son of some poor man, 'such as is not able to maintain his child to learning'; and each was to receive a stipend of five pounds a year for his

The Old Priory from the Arch.

Repton Priory from the South West, c 1800.

maintenance. The rest of the income from the Port estate, deeded to the Corporation, went on the expenses of the hospital and the school, and on a £5 annual payment to Port's old college, Brasenose at Oxford.

Repton, then, was planned as an endowed grammar school of the sort that was founded far and wide in Tudor England. 'Grammar' meant Latin: a grammar school, Dr Johnson was to state in his *Dictionary*, was 'a school in which the learned languages are grammatically taught'. 'Gramarye', in the Middle Ages, meant grammar or learning, but also magic, necromancy, occult knowledge. This was not so far-fetched as it may seem. Grammar schools were originally intended chiefly to fit likely boys for careers in the Church; by the time Repton was founded their scope had broadened to train boys also for service to the State, for the competent administration of local government and for the management of their personal estates, trades and professions. These aims were to be achieved by a rigid curriculum of Latin lessons and the Protestant religion. A Reptonian, then, might well be held by the ignorant to have mastered a form of magic, which could bring with it power, riches and a superior status.

Except for the Protestantism, the idea was not new: such schools had been springing up ever since the 14th century in steadily increasing numbers as the pressures of a rapidly developing society made themselves felt, though something like an explosion of foundations occurred under Henry VIII and his children. The King and his gentry helped themselves liberally to the lands of the dissolved monasteries, but assuaged their consciences by devoting some of the loot to the furtherance of education. Rent from land underpinned, indeed made possible, the creation of 'free' schools of the sort devised in Sir John Port's will and many other instruments. So the schools were all charities, but they were not charity schools. Sir John, for example, sought to win merit in the eyes of God and posterity by his endowments; but he intended his school for the general furtherance of education, not simply the education of poor boys. The school would charge no fees, but the students (or rather their families) would have to pay for clothes and books and, sometimes, coaching, unless they were among the few poor scholars. Boys who came from a distance (nearly half the total in 1622) would have to 'table out' – that is, board and lodge in the village, and pay for the privilege. These costs were high enough to debar all but the sons of the prosperous – gentlemen, farmers, professionals, tradesmen. It is the pattern which we associate with the 'public school' system of later times. It is unlikely that it would have vexed Sir John Port. He knew what he was about. He cannot possibly have intended to found a school where only four boys were taught by three masters. He was thinking on a larger scale, and expected Repton (to the extent that funds allowed) to follow the already well-established model of such foundations as Winchester and St Paul's. It is not even certain that he was interested only in boys from his own locality. As a practical matter he must have expected many recruits from the Trent valley, but he was a Knight of the Bath and Member of Parliament. He may well have been thinking nationally as well as regionally.

The definition of the grammar schools by the teaching of Latin, which looks so peculiar today, needs explanation. To some extent it was a legacy of the Middle Ages, but it was also a matter of common sense. Latin was still the language of the law; it was still required for a career in the Church, though the Reformation was giving England a vernacular Bible and Prayer Book, and sermons in English; it was still the *lingua franca* of Christendom, the language of science and scholarship. No one could claim to be educated who was not competent in Latin. But the extent to which Latin was allowed, indeed required, to exclude almost all other study, once reading, writing and ciphering had been mastered, went far beyond common sense. In principle the only permitted modification to its sway was the teaching of Greek to those boys who were interested in a university career, and, occasionally, instruction in Hebrew, such as Thomas Whitehead (Headmaster 1621–39) gave to a few boys who perhaps hoped to be theologians; and even this modification, though it had a vocational justification, was, we may think, in the wrong direction. Mathematics, history, modern languages, natural science – the list of excluded subjects is long.

An ideology was at work. The great humanists of the Renaissance, in their excitement at recovering much of the Greco-Roman civilization, were convinced that only through mastering classical literature could young men attain 'virtue', the object of all education: wisdom, self-control and mental discipline; only so could they realise their full potential value as servants of the State. Cicero and Demosthenes, Livy and Xenophon: through these and a hundred other authors, only through these, could statesmanship and good citizenship be attained. It was a faith, and not without reason. Before the invention of the printing press such an education for more than a handful of literate persons was inconceivable, but that did not make it any the less valuable; and when the press arrived, what could it print but (mostly) Latin and Greek? The great vernacular literatures were largely yet to come (Shakespeare was not born until seven years after Sir John Port made his will); the translation of the Bible, let alone its general dissemination in printed form, was only just begun.

The Renaissance ideal, then, had a good deal of justification in its day, and during the 16th century it carried all

before it. In its name small boys (admission to Repton apparently began at the age of eight) were kept to their hornbooks every day of the week (one half holiday excepted) and were birched, often cruelly, when they made mistakes. They were allowed to run around their playgrounds twice a day, and there is no reason to doubt that on the whole they were adequately fed, lodged and clothed; but during daylight hours they were mostly being drilled in grammar and vocabulary, in translation from Latin and into Latin. They were supposed to converse only in Latin, and spies among them ('monitors') were given the job of reporting when they did not. (As a result schoolboy slang was for centuries peppered with Latin words and phrases). The results, in Repton at least, seem to have been spectacular. There were sometimes as many as 200 boys in the school, in the years before the Civil War, a number that was not surpassed until the later 19th century. Then as now the chief test of an elite school was its ability to get its pupils into Oxford and Cambridge (a test even more important then than nowadays, for they were the only two English universities). Here too Repton succeeded. Some of its boys were going up to Cambridge when the school was barely ten years old, and by the early seventeenth century the connection with both universities was flourishing: the Lady Margaret colleges at Cambridge, Christ's and St John's received particularly large numbers of Reptonians. As in later times, boys came from all over the kingdom, and some from Ireland, including a boy called Oliver Cromwell, a distant cousin of the Lord Protector; but as already mentioned, the preponderance came from the Trent valley. When in 1621 James I issued the school's Charter it was to an institution which had succeeded to a degree exceeding, probably, its founder's rosiest hopes.

We know almost nothing about precisely how this success was achieved: even the names of the earliest headmasters are uncertain. It can at least be said that the times favoured the school and the dozens like it which flourished under Elizabeth and James. The grammar school model gave general satisfaction. The causes of Repton's swift decline in the later 17th century are rather clearer. First may be mentioned the Civil War. There was no fighting in Repton itself, but there was fighting nearby in all directions – at Bretby, Swarkestone, Ashby de la Zouch and Burton upon Trent, and the village joined many neighbouring parishes in sending a bitter petition of protest to the authorities in Derby against the depredations of the parliamentary army of the area, commanded by the high-handed Sir John Gell. The impact of the war can also be discerned, somewhat vaguely, through the careers of several Old Reptonians: we know of one who was a colonel in the New Model Army and three who served as Presbyterian ministers during the Interregnum and were ejected from their parishes at the Restoration of Charles II. For the triumphant Church of England was resolved to break with radical Protestantism decisively; assent to the Thirty-Nine Articles was now to be obligatory for all clergymen, and the penalties for nonconformity were severe. This had a disastrous effect on Repton, for one of its missions was to train boys for holy orders, and now a large number (it is impossible to guess exactly how many) who might previously have entered the school for that purpose went elsewhere.

Repton was too much bound up with the Established Church, the traditional monarchy (the boys celebrated Oak-Apple Day until well into the 19th century) and the existing legal system to do other than let the dissenters go, and it became a rigidly, sometimes bigotedly, Anglican school. Another misfortune which was also damaging, was outside its control, and was entirely local.

Under Sir John Port's will his executors had established his school in the 'large, great and high house' at Repton which had survived from the Augustinian Priory that had been dissolved by Henry VIII. The executors bought the building (formerly the guest house and Prior's lodging) from its owners, the Thackers: a family notable, it seems, for hereditary bad temper and bad judgement. They lived in what became Repton Hall – another survival from the Priory – and found that they had acquired, as permanent neighbours, a pack of noisy schoolboys whose chief playground lay right outside the Hall. In 1651 Gilbert Thacker, who had just inherited the estate, began a campaign of vengeful harassment, which went on for nearly 20 years. In an early battle he ordered his bailiff to put up posts and railings ('stoops and rayles') to keep the boys out of a least half of the schoolyard nearest his front door; but the brave Reptonians pulled out the only post which the bailiff managed to set up and filled in the hole with earth (the yard was not then paved; one Headmaster grazed a cow there and stalled her in the Priory undercroft). On another occasion Thacker and his wife, possibly drunk, assaulted the Headmaster's wife as she stood at her own front door. The row went on, with suit and counter-suit until 1670, when a division of the land was at last agreed and executed, on terms which Thacker could have had 10 or 15 years earlier, had he been so minded: a wall was built to mark the lower end of the playground, and in it Mr Thacker inserted a triumphal gateway, soon and still known to the school as the Pillars of Hercules.

Repton had certainly suffered in the affair. At one point Thacker threatened to arrest and sue for trespass any boys he could catch; it was feared that he might attack them physically; as he had the Headmaster's wife. It is hardly surprising that many parents, it seems, decided to keep their boys at home, or at least not to send them for their education to Repton.

This need not cause any difficulty, for many other schools, non-grammar schools, were now flourishing. Unlike Repton and its fellows they were not constrained to teach only, or mainly, the 'learned languages'; they could offer subjects which, in the eyes of many prudent fathers, were much more useful in what was becoming the modern world. The times, or perhaps it was only the fashions, were changing, and Repton, like many other grammar schools, was prevented, by the terms of its Charter, from changing with them; and the universities would not admit boys without Latin. Yet Latin's comparative uselessness (or what was now thought to be such) became part of its power: only gentlemen could afford to devote many years and much cash to its study; Latin, therefore, became peculiarly a mark of genteel status, which encouraged one sort of entrant; but those who wanted to make their fortunes before they aspired to gentility drew away, and the school's numbers shrank some more. Another issue, which never quite subsided, was that of caning and birching. The *Children's Petition* of 1669 was the first important printed protest, but not the last; the grammar schools' well-deserved reputation for savagely unreasonable punishments was another disincentive to parents.

As a result the grammar schools reached their nadir during the 18th century. On top of everything else, many of them rotted from within. As with so many other aspects of the English *ancien régime*, the process began even before the Civil War, but it accelerated after the Glorious Revolution. The social order which emerged from the struggles of the 17th century lived by place and patronage, and the possibilities of the great scholastic charities did not escape the notice of men looking for sinecures. The warden and fellows of Winchester siphoned off half or more of the college's income, spending as little as possible on teachers, pupils and the buildings. As early as 1635 boys at Eton were complaining that they were being robbed of 'breakfast, clothing, bedding and the commonest necessities of life, while the college income is divided among the few'. In 1746 the Headmaster of Harrow, overwhelmed by debts and drunkenness, fled the school and had to be dismissed. In his life of Dr Arnold Lytton Strachey accurately summed up the 18th-century school system as 'anarchy tempered by despotism'. Boys were regularly flogged for mistakes in their Latin (savagely or gently according to the temperament of the usher); otherwise they were left to themselves, with lurid results. Occasionally there were full-scale revolts, as at Winchester and Rugby in the 1790s, which regular soldiers had to be called in to repress. Snobbery completed the picture of educational disaster: because most of the ruling oligarchs either hired private tutors

The Church and Arch in Early Victorian days.

spot where Pears School steps now rise, and there, presumably, the smaller boys were herded until they were literate enough to proceed to Latin. It was a rational enough arrangement in the first decades of the school; but eventually it foundered on the rocks of the emerging English class system. Middle-class parents, anxious to protect their investment in gentlemanly education, objected to their sons sharing the old school bench with mere country boys and poor scholars; and the locals began to question the value of Latin to their own offspring, who on the whole were no longer interested in the prospect of a career in the Church or the universities. The Writing School furnished all the education they required; and there was increasing resentment at the way in which the benefits of what, understandably, they regarded as their own educational charity were being appropriated to the advantage of 'foreigners'. 'We make a countryman dumb, whom we will not allow to speak but by the rules of grammar,' Dryden had observed. So the countrymen felt humiliated. Yet by the Founder's will as well as the Charter the school was obliged to teach grammar.

In these circumstances almost everything would depend on the leadership of the headmasters; and here it cannot be said that during the 18th century Repton was fortunate. Sir John Port's Charity was administered by a Corporation consisting of the master of the Etwall Hospital, the Headmaster of the school, the two ushers, and three of the Etwall pensioners. The hereditary governors (descended from Sir John's daughters) appointed the masters of school and hospital and filled vacant places among the pensioners and poor scholars. They were, it appears, conscientious, but had very little to do with the day-to-day running of the Charity. Their appointments to the Headmastership varied from the excellent to the disastrous to the run-of-the-mill. The worst appointment was John Doughty (1681–1704) who was so scandalously negligent of his duty that at last he was dismissed. His successor, Edward Abbot (1705–14) was perhaps the best, but he died too young and too soon. Of the rest there is not much to say except that they leave the impression of being less concerned with earning their living than with keeping their place.

Dr William Prior (1767–79) saw that at least some changes were necessary. Soon after his appointment he persuaded the Governors to take a lease on the Hall (from which the Thackers had long since departed) and make it the Headmaster's official residence; and also to charge every boy, except the poor scholars, a fee of two guineas a year, one of which was to go to the Headmaster, the other to be divided between the ushers. The first of these improvements would allow the Headmaster to increase his income by taking in more paying boarders, and the second, by improving salaries, would make jobs at Repton

or sent their sons to a handful of schools in or near London, the idea took hold that these schools were in some sense better than other grammar schools; they were certainly more fashionable. Eton, Harrow, Westminster, Winchester began to be spoken of as 'public' schools – national schools – schools for the training of statesmen, generals, bishops and bankers. The prestige of all other schools suffered proportionately.

Repton was not spared the effect of these tendencies, but because it was provincial and its endowment comparatively meagre it avoided the worst consequences; however the state of affairs was quite bad enough. A famous tale says that a Derby auctioneer boasted more than once that he had been Captain of the school in Dr Stevens's day (1779–1800); when his friends had done congratulating him he revealed that it was because he was then the only boy in the school. The tale seems to be a legend, but it might well be believed: Shrewsbury, when Dr Butler took it in hand in 1798, had only twelve, or one, or two boys in it (depending on which authority you believe); and some other schools were so depleted that they had to close.

Such conditions could not be allowed to continue, if the traditional system of elite education in England were not to collapse entirely; but first the system's contradictions would have to be faced, and then reform would have to be thorough; and neither logic nor reform were attractive to the many conventional minds of 18th-century England. In Repton's case the root of the difficulty relates to a provision in the Charter, according to which the master (Headmaster) and first usher were to teach 'Grammar' and the second usher 'to write, read, cipher, and cast accompt'. A 'Writing School' was built on the

Dr William Prior, 1767–79.

High Master of St Paul's. With this background it is not surprising that William Sleath succeeded in temporarily reviving Repton on the old lines. He was a genial, middle-aged man, who did not take school discipline too seriously; he was also a good teacher, as the number of Reptonians going from the school to the universities attests. He had quite wide cultural interests, of which the most important was archaeology: it was Sleath who first stimulated serious Reptonian interest in the Anglo-Saxon and medieval remains by which the school was surrounded, initiating an antiquarian tradition which has been almost continuous since his day. But he stayed in his job too long; as he aged applications for admission fell back; and he did not even attempt to resolve the tension which had developed between the two sides of the mission which Sir John Port had laid on the school.

John Heyrick Macaulay (1832–40), who followed Sleath, was a cousin of the great historian, and displayed the Macaulay family traits almost to excess. He always knew that he was right; a big, bullying, good-humoured man, a strict disciplinarian and ferocious flogger – perhaps the most brutal of all Repton's

more attractive to qualified men; but there seems to have been fierce consumer resistance (no doubt chiefly local) to the ending of free schooling, and the fees were abolished after Prior's death. Yet the number of admissions, which had fallen when fees were introduced, did not recover.

William Bagshaw Stevens, Prior's successor, was in some ways the most interesting of all the Headmasters, but he was also one of the least successful. He was a capable poet, kept a first-rate diary (in which he never mentioned any of the boys in his charge), and was a valued preacher, but he so detested his trade of teacher that during his 20 years as Headmaster he was constantly in search of other employment, whether as a country parson or as an officer of his college (Magdalen, Oxford). In 1800, the year that he finally succeeded, he died of an apoplectic fit, said to have been brought on by laughing at an Italian organ-grinder's monkey in Repton High Street.

Stevens' tenure, in retrospect, seems to be no more than a hiatus in Repton's stumbling course towards renewal. His successor, William Boultbee Sleath (1800–32), certainly reanimated the place: in his very first year some 80 boys were entered on the register; but no more than Stevens did he begin the process of adapting the school to the needs and opportunities of a new epoch. He was a thorough professional, who had taught at Rugby, his old school, for 20 years; his younger brother was also a master at Rugby before becoming

WILLIAM STEVENS D.D.

Willam Bagshaw Stevens, 1779–1800.

William Boultbee Sleath, 1800–32.

Thomas Williamson Peile, 1841–54.

headmasters. Just before Christmas 1840 he fell fatally ill. Order at once collapsed: the boys rioted and fought among themselves; they broke bounds in order to get hold of cakes and ale; hearing that Macaulay was beyond hope they invaded his rooms, smashed his furniture, and burned it on a bonfire outside. Macaulay died in the night, and the next day the boys went home. The episode may be held to mark the real, final end of the Old School.

Thomas Williamson Peile (1841–54) took the decisive steps which turned Repton from a country grammar school into an embryo public school. Unlike Macaulay he took out a hot temper on his colleagues, not the boys; he was a fine scholar, who had been a Fellow of Trinity College, Cambridge, and an experienced parson and schoolmaster. In his day the simmering dispute about the school's function and future at last came to a head, in a lawsuit, the outcome of which was in favour of Dr Peile and his regime – which amounted to this, that in order to fulfil one side of Sir John Port's intentions, a 'commercial school' was founded at Repton, to teach reading, writing, arithmetic and 'sound scriptural education' to the boys of Repton and Etwall, while the grammar school (referred to in the documents as 'the Free School') continued to dispense a classical education to those who could afford the fees (between 60 and 90 guineas a year). Peile insisted that 'no obstacle had ever been thrown by me in the way of any boy coming to the

Free School instead of the said Commercial School, or of leaving the said Commercial School, for that purpose,' and we may believe him: the poor scholars (now referred to as Foundation Scholars) continue to figure in the Repton register. But it is clear that from 1852, when the case was settled, Repton's identity as a public school on the new model was certain; from now on it would simply be a matter of following the blueprint fashioned by the early 19th-century reformers, of whom Arnold of Rugby was the most important.

Peile seems to have had his own clear idea of how Repton should proceed. It was to be of no great size, perhaps (only 34 names are registered at Repton in the year of his retirement) but of real distinction, sending a steady stream of well-educated youths into the professions and into business as well as to the universities. He was remembered for his unbending dignity, his courtesy and kindness, and above all for his exceptional scholarship. But his way was not to be that of the future. In his day a school cricket-club was founded, and the first cricket field laid out (on the site of what is now the Square): an epochal moment. Peile was long gone before the full consequences could be felt. Ill-health forced his retirement. It would be for his successor to carry his policies further, and modify them, and win for Repton the status, so vague and yet so desirable, of a Victorian 'public school'.

Hugh Brogan (O 1949)

21

HEADMASTERS *1854–2003*

DR STEUART ADOLPHUS PEARS, 1854–74

Dr Steuart Adolphus Pears is widely regarded as Repton's second founder, and it is easy to see why. In 1854 when he was appointed Headmaster, at the age of 39, there were fewer than 50 boys on the register and the school occupied only the Old Priory and the Hall (which was still held on short lease), yet by the time of his retirement in 1874 there were 260 boys (nearly all of whom were boarders), seven boarding houses, and Repton had achieved a national reputation as a leading public school. If anything, this bald summary of the facts underplays Pears' achievement. In effect, he completely transformed the character of the school.

Repton was not, of course, alone in changing out of all recognition in these years. It was part of a revolution in public school education that is traditionally traced to the reforms of Dr Thomas Arnold of Rugby. Arnoldian influence on Repton came via Messiter, Pears' Second Master, who had been Captain of Rugby under Arnold, and Dr C.J. Vaughan, a former pupil of Arnold's, under whom Pears had served as an assistant master and housemaster when the latter was Headmaster of Harrow. Five years before the threat of exposure of his having had an affair with one of his boys forced his resignation, Vaughan wrote privately to the Chairman of the Repton Governors to sing Pears' praises in the following terms:

Steuart Adolphus Pears, 1854–74.

Some men have a genius for the office, which raises them at once to a rank far above men of three times their University distinction. [Pears, a scholar of Corpus Christi College, Oxford, had graduated with a second class degree in Literae Humaniores.] Mr Pears has indeed proved himself to be one of those born Schoolmasters. With a most refined & cultivated mind, remarkable skill as a composer & preacher and true originality, he combines wonderful power as the manager of Boys …
I need not add that he has the basis of all other qualifications, in a truly Christian piety, free from all oddities and peculiarities, but fervent and genuine.

Overton's Tower.

The Chapel.

The Arch in need of a trim. Note the absence of the Marshal's Lodge.

It was Dr Vaughan's remarks on the importance of a school chapel, made in the course of his sermon to mark Repton's 300th anniversary, that provided the spur that led to Pears being able to open the Chapel in 1859, and it was Pears' evangelical sensibilities that ensured that it was severe in style.

Pears' additions to the school buildings also included the Orchard, the Trent Garden Schools (a two-storey block of classrooms in what is now Hall Yard), a two-storey block of classrooms facing the Paddock and the school's first fives courts (where the Marshal's Lodge now stands). He also provided half

the funds for the lease of a house on the west side of the Hall Orchard, which became the first school sanatorium (the Housemasters collectively providing the balance).

However, Pears' greatest contribution to Repton was to reorganize its management so as to make it a public school. This he did by severing the connection with Etwall Hospital and placing control of the school in the hands of the Headmaster, who was responsible to a public governing body of 13 (albeit one leavened by four hereditary governors who owed their position to their relation to Sir John Port). The Scheme of the Endowed Schools Commissioners of 7 July 1874 also placed the whole teaching staff on an equal footing under the Headmaster's control, fixed ten as the minimum age of admission, broadened the curriculum (while keeping Classics as its core), and fixed the number of scholarships at eight (four 'Poor Scholarships' nominated in rotation by the hereditary governors, and four awarded by open examination).

Repton was already a member of the Headmasters' Conference (HMC), Dr Pears having attended since its first meeting at Uppingham in 1869, but with the new Scheme Repton truly became a public school.

By 1874, however, when Dr Pears retired, his health was broken. His last gift to Repton was to insist that his memorial fund be devoted to some building at Repton, where he himself was buried against the north side of St Wystan's on the last day of the Michaelmas term (15 December) 1875.

HENRY ROBERT HUCKIN, 1874–82

Henry Robert Huckin DD was 32 years old when he was appointed as successor to Pears in 1874. Seven years younger than his predecessor when he entered the post, he was a better scholar (with a double first in Mods and a second in Greats at St John's College, Oxford), had two years' more experience of schoolmastering (at Haileybury and his old school, Merchant Taylors') and was equally concerned to reform Repton, addressing his concerns to the new governing body in a long, printed letter shortly after his arrival.

His greatest concerns focused on the size and nature of school property. Too much was held on lease, and Big School, 'when the whole school is assembled, as it is at least once every day, and on three days in the week several times', was already too cramped, whilst Huckin had a vision of raising school numbers from 260 to 400. However, Huckin's specific proposals, which would have involved using the Pears Memorial Fund, were vetoed by the Governing Body. Huckin was thus not only stymied in his plan of reform but had to deal with the increasing impatience of those who had subscribed to the fund and yet seen nothing for their money. This was not the only difficulty

Henry Robert Huckin, 1874–82.

Interior of Pears School, 1896.

The Hall, smothered in ivy.

with which Huckin had to contend, as Macdonald suggests that he was also subjected to sniping by some members of Common Room who were so enamoured of the memory of Pears that they experienced difficulty in transferring their loyalties to Huckin.

In 1880, when Sir Francis Burdett succeeded his cousin Sir Robert to the Burdett estate, there was a brief ray of light insofar as it was hoped that he might prove more amenable than his predecessor to selling some of the land currently leased to the school. Unfortunately, an injudicious remark of the Headmaster's at a village dinner so offended Sir Francis that he refused to have anything further to do with 'that man Huggins' [sic].

The Rev. William Johnson was acting Headmaster from May to December 1882, during Huckin's terminal illness (he died on the first day of the summer holidays) and the interregnum before Furneaux was able to take up his appointment as Headmaster.

The above is bound to give the impression that Huckin's Headmastership was a time of missed opportunities. In fact, it was not entirely barren of achievement as it was during these years that the modern side was born. To be precise, in the Lent term of 1878 17 boys, under the Rev. A.F.E. Forman, became the 'Modern Form': a small but significant loosening of the stranglehold of Classics over the curriculum. Nevertheless, the overall impression must be that under Huckin Repton, not for the first or last time, was merely marking time.

WILLIAM MORDAUNT FURNEAUX, 1883–1900

Appointed Headmaster at the age of 34, William Mordaunt Furneaux was a force for change at Repton. As Lionel Ford, who was Head of School when Furneaux arrived in January 1883, later wrote:

> He was … no respecter of established customs just because they were old … [and he] knew immensely clearly what things wanted doing, and what he meant to do … It was all very novel and upsetting to us, as we discovered it was also to some of his more conservative colleagues. But the net result was that things began to move.

William Mordaunt Furneaux, 1883–1900.

Repton's very own fire brigade, formed by Furneaux, with Vassall placed in charge.

Furneaux had been educated at Radley (briefly), Marlborough and Corpus Christi College, Oxford, where he obtained a first class in Classical Moderations and graduated with a first in Greats before teaching at Clifton (briefly) and Marlborough, which he left as Sixth Form master in order to come to Repton. He found that Repton's standards of discipline and scholarship fell short of those to which he was accustomed, and he strove, successfully, to raise them. However, the most enduring aspect of his legacy, as that of any Headmaster, was his improvement of the school's buildings.

The *sine qua non* of progress in this area comprised rebuilding the bridges to the Burdetts that Huckin had unintentionally burnt. Relations were at an all-time low when Furneaux arrived on the scene. In 1882 Sir Francis had demanded a more than tenfold increase in the £30 rent for the Hall, and when the Governors balked at this, the school was given notice to quit at Michaelmas 1883 and contemplated decamping to the Haskey Field, on the side of Askew Hill facing the Milton Road. However, a compromise was arrived at in 1883 whereby Burdett sold to the school the site of the Headmaster's kitchen garden and granted the school a 60-year lease of the other land, including the Hall, for £375 a year.

At his first Speech Day Furneaux therefore explained that it was proposed immediately to rebuild and extend the boys' side at the Hall and to build a large Pears Memorial Block with classrooms, staff common room and large assembly hall, on the site of the kitchen garden. A building fund was launched, and Furneaux led by example with a subscription of £500. He also sought to tap ORs and to that end, in March 1885, started the *Terminal Letter*.

The Pears Memorial Hall, to give it its full original name, was declared open on Speech Day in 1886. The Pears Memorial Fund amounted to nearly £3,700 by this time but the total cost, including that of the classrooms beneath the hall, came to over £9,000, the balance being found from school funds.

No sooner was Pears School completed than work began on the two-storey Chapter House Block, while some old cottages at the foot of Boot Hill were replaced by a carpenter's shop and a music room.

A sign of improved relations with the baronet was that within two years of his arrival, Furneaux had cajoled Sir Francis into joining the Governing Body. However, Sir Francis remained reluctant to part with what he regarded as the oldest part of his family estates. The most valuable piece of historical research ever undertaken at Repton cleared this logjam because Furneaux was able to satisfy Sir Francis that the Burdetts had owned their property at Bramcott in Warwickshire some 150 years before they acquired Repton and thus, in 1891, Sir Francis sold to the school the Hall and all of the remaining land within the Arch for £15,000.

Furneaux's improvements continued apace, including red-brick classrooms (with a 'Chemical and Physical Laboratory') overlooking the Upper Paddock in 1895; the Marshal's Lodge (paid for by Furneaux himself) in 1896; and the Hall Orchard, levelled and ready for games by 1899. Mrs Furneaux was responsible for the fund that paid for the enlargement and embellishment of the Pavilion, and it was under Furneaux that games at Repton enjoyed their first golden age. The school's expenditure on plant was partly financed by rising numbers of boys, reaching the record number of 318 in 1893 before falling back below 300 in Furneaux's final years.

In matters of the curriculum Furneaux was not a great innovator insofar as it remained overwhelmingly classical, although a more specialized curriculum for army candidates was now offered on the Modern side in a special Army Class, and an engineering workshop, the Stephenson School of Engineering, was opened on Askew Hill in 1887.

W. J. Stephenson-Peach, who helped to produce the first Morgan automobile, helped spread the name of Repton, as, to an even greater extent, did another development under Furneaux, namely the foundation of the Repton Club in London's East End.

However, generally as the 1890s progressed Furneaux and the school lost vitality. Discipline as well as numbers dropped away. In the Christmas holidays of 1899–1900 Furneaux broke his ankle whilst skating in Switzerland and was out of school for the first month of the Easter term. He appears to have enjoyed the experience to such an extent that he retired in July of that year. He went on to become an energetic Dean of Winchester (1903–13) and lived until 1928. He remained a great friend of the school, and one of the last acts of his life was to send a donation to the fund for extending once more the Chapel to which in his time he had added the south aisle. He deserves to be better remembered.

Hubert Murray Burge, 1900–01.

HUBERT MURRAY BURGE, 1900–01

In 1900 Hubert Murray Burge was elected to succeed Furneaux as Headmaster. He came to Repton with a reputation for liberal Anglicanism, sound if unspectacular scholarship, a love of cricket and outdoor pursuits, and the ability to put people at ease. However, after just two terms he became, to the chagrin of the Repton Governing Body, the first headmaster of Winchester to be appointed by open competition and the first non-Wykehamist to hold that post. The full extent of Repton's loss only became fully apparent as Winchester entered into a golden age under Burge's leadership.

Lionel Ford, 1901–10.

Speech Day. Note the moss on the Arch and the ivy on the Old Priory.

LIONEL FORD, 1901–10

Lionel Ford (P 1878) was the first (and to date the last) OR since William Asteley (1741–67) to become Headmaster of Repton. Indeed, he came from one of the most famous Repton dynasties: all seven Ford brothers were in the Cricket XI, six of whom captained it; three held the position of Head of School; six of the seven went to Cambridge, of whom it was commonly said that three got cricket blues but not a First and three got a First and no cricket blue. In fact, in 1887 Lionel got a Part 1 Class 1 Division 2 in Classics in a year when no one was placed in Division 1. He did not proceed to Part II at all but instead taught at Eton (where he also took holy orders) before returning to Repton as Headmaster.

There appears to have been only one other candidate, perhaps reflecting unease over Burge's hasty departure and the rather down-at-heel character of the school. During his nine years at Repton Ford restored discipline and raised the standard of worship, both of which had become rather lax; improved numbers (which had declined from 318 in 1893 to 280 in 1901); and improved both the buildings and the grounds.

Repton being Repton, these changes were not always welcomed (some letters to the *Reptonian* were signed 'One who does not wish to be an Old Etonian'), but Ford's determination, dynamism and ruthlessness allowed him to steamroller opposition, accomplish a great deal and attain widespread respect, if never universal affection. In the words of S.S. Jenkyns: 'When he had set his heart on some alteration or

Speech Day. Ivy also clings to the main classroom block.

reform he … would invite opinions of the Staff at a Masters' Meeting, and when the Die-Hards had blown off steam … he would thank the masters for their valuable expression of opinion and say quietly: "Well, I think I shall start this next term"; and it was so.'

Of particular note was his introduction of the OR Society, the School Shop and the prefect system, the enlargement of Chapel, the replacing of morning prayers in Pears School by

daily service in Chapel, the abolition of the distinction between Classical and Modern forms in the lower school, and ending the system by which most forms did Maths at the same hours (thereby ensuring that Mathematics was taught by experts). He also created the School Library in its modern form, commissioned new songs for the school's 350th anniversary; built the Science Block, Gymnasium, Armoury and shooting range and made miniature rifle-shooting compulsory for all boys of 16 and above.

> *I got a very strong impression of a sort of simplicity, freshness and purity about these boys. Last night their attention and courtesy were marked; there was no sort of discipline kept – it was all spontaneous and unaffected courtesy. Today the manner of the boys in chapel was ideal. I did not see a single whisper, a single act or sign of irreverence. Yet it all seemed natural and spontaneous not drilled – like the well-born boys of a good, virtuous and well-bred family. The perfection of manner – better than Eton, because more simple and less superficial. Perhaps it is hard to judge, but they also gave me a feeling of great manliness and good tone. I would send a boy there with great confidence.*
>
> A.C. Benson, *Diaries*, 9 December 1906

Last but not least, Ford began the process of buying and enlarging the boarding houses outside the Arch. In 1904 Brook House was bought and a new wing added to it, in 1906 the Mitre and the Orchard were purchased and extended, and in 1909 New House was built and opened in the following year.

It is fitting that under Ford electric light was installed in all the school buildings for he was a veritable human dynamo as Headmaster. He is not an altogether sympathetic character but clearly deserves to be ranked alongside Pears and Furneaux as one of Repton's greatest Heads.

WILLIAM TEMPLE, 1910–14

William Temple was probably the most left-wing of Repton's Headmasters and Canterbury's archbishops, although the competition in both categories is hardly fierce.

The 28-year-old Temple was in Aden, en route to a Students' Christian Movement meeting in Australia. when he received news of the offer of the headship of Repton. After three hours in prayer he decided to accept and arrived in Repton a fortnight after the Michaelmas term had started.

Filial devotion appears to have been taken so far by Temple that his life closely followed the template laid down by his father, Frederick – that is, Balliol, a double first, an Oxford fellowship, ground-breaking theology, a spell of headmastering and then a steady ascent of the Church hierarchy from diocesan, to archdiocesan, to primate. There were, however, crucial differences.

A sight that stirs mixed emotions in the light of what was to come.

William Temple, his mother (left) and Speech Day guests.

Whereas his father at Rugby had been 'a beast, but a just beast', William at Repton was 'Billy' to the boys: chubby and cheerful (despite gout) but largely ineffectual (despite the quality of his preaching and teaching) because he lacked the will to enforce discipline. On learning that boys had been stealing from the School Shop, for example, he appealed to the culprits' 'sense of honour', and on hearing that Reptonians had pelted the Liberal candidate with eggs in the course of one of the two general elections of 1910 he merely observed that, 'Gentlemen do not throw eggs'.

Temple adored Repton but was simply not cut out for headmastering, and did not stay long, becoming the third shortest serving Head in the school's history (after Dudson and Burge). Even while in post he was often called away to sit on committees concerned with social and Church matters.

The only physical mark of his time at Repton was a new cricket pavilion, which is ironic given his view of cricket as 'organized loafing'.

Temple eventually escaped from Repton in 1914 to become Rector of St James's, Piccadilly, in London's West End. This marked an uncharacteristic departure from his father's path (Temple senior having never had a parish). He would have gone even earlier but the offer of a canonry at Westminster Abbey had had to be withdrawn at the end of 1912 because he had not yet been ordained for the requisite six years.

As principal preacher at a Cambridge University mission, one of the undergraduates Temple greatly influenced was the young Michael Ramsey, who was ultimately to follow Fisher, after Fisher had followed Temple as Archbishop of Canterbury, so that the archdiocese had a Repton connection for 45 consecutive years (1929–74).

> ‘ *The spirit of this School and of its members … simple, homely, natural … draws daily from the long past of our forefathers … yet lives ready to shoulder the burdens of the present and give itself in service for that which is yet to be.* ’
>
> **The Rev. G.F. Fisher, 9 June 1928**

Geoffrey Fisher, 1914–32.

The Cross c1914.

GEOFFREY FISHER, 1914–32

If Temple followed his father's footsteps, then Fisher followed Temple's, succeeding him at Repton in 1914 and at Canterbury in 1945.

Although Geoffrey Francis Fisher, at 27, was a year younger than his predecessor on appointment, he slipped into the role of Head much more easily, not least because he had previously taught at Marlborough, whereas Temple had had no previous schoolmastering experience.

Whilst Temple confessed to having been in 'a blue funk' when he arrived at Repton and invited the assembled school to pray for him, Fisher approached his Headmastership with natural authority and a well-founded belief in his own abilities, as symbolized by his response to a query regarding a new set of rules. The first commandment was 'Any breach of commonsense is a breach of these rules'. When asked who decided what was commonsense, Fisher replied that he alone did.

A strong hand on the tiller was certainly necessary given Temple's legacy of lax discipline, the strains imposed by the war on staffing and finances and the fact that, in the words of Charles Smyth (H 1916), 'at least three of his housemasters (who in those days could hold office until they retired …) were, in their different ways, an embarrassment, if not a liability'.

Fisher's greatest test in his early years was the Gollancz–Somervell affair, which, like Roald Dahl's posthumous attack on his reputation, is dealt with elsewhere.

Brigadier the Rt Hon. Sir John Smyth Bt, VC, MC. The School's only recipient of the Victoria Cross (to date).

The War Memorial completed. Notice the gable to the right, since removed.

The Headmaster at ease with his pupils, Speech Day, 1928.

Four Headmasters (photographed in 1922): (left to right) seated, Furneaux and Ford; standing, Fisher and Temple.

Space is too limited to do more than provide a brief review of the reforms wrought by Fisher in his 18 years as Headmaster. Most notably an increase in numbers was facilitated by building the Gallery in Pears School, by enlarging the Chapel, playing fields and games facilities, and by expanding classroom and boarding house accommodation (including the removal of two houses to new quarters). In addition, much property in the centre of the village was acquired by the School. Academic organization and the curriculum were overhauled for both the Sixth Form and Lower School, and an embryonic careers department was established. Subsequent generations of Reptonians also owe thanks to Fisher for the brilliant reconstruction of the Garth and the creation of the War Memorial.

By 1932, however, Fisher had determined to resign because, as he told Temple: 'I have been here long enough … and I know this: *when a boy is seriously ill in the San, I can no longer stand the strain.*'

Described as 'the greatest schoolmaster – AND the greatest schoolboy – who has ever sat upon the Chair of Saint Augustine', Fisher was also clearly one of Repton's greatest Headmasters. Not only did he occupy that role with distinction for 18 years, he was also a Governor between 1938 and 1972 (and Chairman of Governors, 1938–59). Nor did Fisher's influence end there as two of his sons taught at the school, namely, Francis Forman Fisher (1946–54) and Richard Temple Fisher (1953–69),

Those who came after Fisher, such as John Thorn, sometimes found his legacy – and the forceful expression of his advice – oppressive, but there can be no doubting Fisher's love of Repton, as one might expect given not only his length of service but also the fact that his wife was the daughter of a Housemaster (Forman) and granddaughter of a former Head, (Pears).

Fisher is remembered by all as a superb administrator and an individual who managed to enforce discipline without, by and large, exciting rancour. One story illustrates why. Learning that a boy had departed for the holidays on a motorcycle, Fisher telegrammed the boy's home: RETURN TODAY OR NEVER. Back came the boy on his motorcycle. Fisher caned him soundly and sent him home again – on his motorcycle. Fisher combined efficiency, moral strength, a sense of decorum and a sense of humour.

John Traill Christie, 1932–7.

JOHN TRAILL CHRISTIE, 1932–7

J.T. Christie came as Headmaster to Repton after a scholarship at Winchester, a spell in the Coldstream Guards (in which he was commissioned but didn't see active service), a scholarship and double first at Trinity College, Oxford, six years teaching Classics as a Sixth Form master at Rugby and four as a Fellow and Tutor at Magdalen, Oxford.

Repton's first lay Headmaster, he was, nevertheless, a deeply religious man, describing himself as 'a late-Victorian Evangelical'. Although conservative by nature he found much to reform during his five years at Repton.

The shape of the schoolday and the shape of the school pupil changed with, respectively, the removal of the first lesson and chapel before breakfast and the Eton jacket for younger boys. Boarding facilities were upgraded with washing rooms modernized and the movement of the Mitre from the Old Mitre to its current venue. The financially crippling practice, from which Christie himself suffered in the Hall, whereby the incoming Housemaster had to buy all the furniture on the boys' side from his predecessor, was brought to an end, and the per capita food allowance was altered, with any overspend being met by the Housemaster from his own resources, while any surplus was ploughed back into the school.

Christie had a fine intellect and a quick wit, as illustrated by the following exchange between himself and a Housemaster at the end of a staff meeting:

'I hope Headmaster, that you will be giving a half holiday so the School can watch the Derbyshire Friars' [cricket] match?'
'Excellent idea!' replied Christie. 'The only time a Repton boy ever reads a book.'

This symbolized a fundamental clash of values as Christie was concerned that games were paid excessive deference compared to matters of the mind. The Housemasters were identified as the high priests of the cult of the athlete, and Christie took steps to reduce their influence by limiting their tenure to 15 years and by introducing house tutors. However, so unhappy was he at Repton that he jumped ship to become Head, at a reduced salary, at Westminster, which he found much more congenial.

John Plowright

H.G. MICHAEL CLARKE, 1937–43

If every headmaster is required to be something of an actor, the Rev. H.G. Michael Clarke was our Sir Henry Irving. Tall, with aquiline features, a resonant voice and a quaint turn of phrase, he made Repton his stage and the boys his players. He insisted on taking a part – preferably the lead role – in any theatricals that were going. He would swoop on a rehearsal, reshuffle the cast, make daring emendations to the text, order the scenery to be repainted and depart. Then he sent us on tour to mining villages with *The School for Scandal* and *Lady Precious Stream*.

H.G. Michael Clarke, 1937–43.

'Goodbye Mr Chips', filmed in part at Repton in 1938.

T.L.T. and Head Prefects, Spring 1955.

He liked to tease. 'I got it first hand from somebody who had heard it,' he smiled when we protested at a too-improbable anecdote. The boys, although puzzled by his excursions into metaphysics, liked and respected him. The staff and governors did not. He arrived at Repton in 1937 and was gone by 1943.

Kenneth Rose (O 1939)

THEODORE LYNAM THOMAS, 1944–61

When T.L. Thomas assumed the responsibilities of Headmaster in April 1944 (S.S. Jenkyns having been acting Headmaster since Clarke's departure) the situation resembled that which faced Fisher during the First World War. T.L.T. was even more experienced than Fisher, having already been teaching for 21 years and a housemaster for ten. In at least two respects, however, the problems confronting him were even worse than those that had faced Fisher. First, a larger number of regular staff were serving in the armed forces. Second, although by 1917 the War Office had issued regulations under which boys who were recommended by their COs as likely to make efficient officers were to remain at school until they reached

Clarke was without self-consciousness or self-esteem. His tour de force was as Lady Macbeth in a modern-dress production that owed something to Shakespeare, but not much. Wearing a tweed skirt and clutching a shooting stick, he bore down on a cocktail cabinet, selected a bottle and declaimed: 'Yes, here's a spot. Out, damned spot, out I say. One, two. Hell, it's murky! The Thane of Fife had Black & White, where is it now?' We had travelled a long way from the Repton of Dr Pears.

In the classroom, in Chapel and at his own table he mesmerized his audience with arabesques of language. 'The Pope and the Emperor were the two eyes which guided the path of the Church. In the Middle Ages those eyes unhappily began to squint!' He extended the boundaries of geography, too. 'Florida sticks out like a tail to cover the entrance to the Spain Main,' he said, and 'The Baltic Ocean is like a sausage carried at the slope.'

Professor C.E.M. Joad, a bearded, bouncy man in a hairy green suit who had acquired an ephemeral reputation as a philosopher on the BBC *Brains Trust*, was at breakfast one day. Having delivered the Leather Lecture the evening before, he continued to instruct us over boiled eggs. Clarke was unpersuaded by homespun radicalism: 'Do not drink deeper draughts of freedom than your delicate political stomach can stand,' the Headmaster admonished him.

'*The school was adept ... at bringing out the best in everyone of us, regardless of our latent abilities and talents ... Only now, 50 years on, do I fully appreciate how fortunate I was to have been there, and the extent to which it equipped me, despite the ups and downs of childhood, to deal with and make the best of adult life.*

Tim Scorer (O 1954)

'*Repton taught me many things but the greatest lesson was common courtesy and good manners.*'

Brian Marshall (L 1957))

A Study.

A Bedder.

the age of 18, in the Second World War many senior boys left young to join the forces, which not only seriously depressed numbers and finances but also weakened the crucially important Upper Sixth and body of prefects.

However, T.L.T. tackled the problems of wartime and reconstruction alike with enormous energy. He was assisted by the fact that he was a shrewd judge of character and made many excellent appointments. Among the last was Stuart Andrews, who recalls T.L.T. in his last year as Headmaster 'as venerable, benign and formidable. (He never could understand why he inspired such awe in the boys – or in young masters.)' It is a tribute to T.L.T.'s ability to spot talent that when Stuart Andrews in due course became a new arrival at the Headmasters' Conference he found that 'no fewer than ten of my fellow headmasters had been Lynam's appointments to the Repton staff'. The final tally was 14.

The numbers of staff expanded as the roll increased by about 150 within a few years of T.L.T.'s arrival, allowing the reopening of the Cross (1945) and Latham (1947), while the preparatory school migrated to Foremarke. As the spouses of both Repton and Foremarke headmasters were sisters, relations between the two schools could hardly have been closer.

T.L.T. also (like Ford) had a keen understanding of the importance of good relations with Old Reptonians, as symbolized by his organizing a reunion attended by about 500 ORs in 1946. By the time of his retirement roughly a quarter of the school were the sons of ORs.

T.L.T. was also no slouch in promoting the school's name, notably through the 400th anniversary celebrations in 1957, with the visit of Her Majesty and Prince Philip occasioning press speculation that Prince Charles might attend Repton.

The chief changes to the fabric of the school under T.L.T. are obviously those connected with the anniversary. In 1957 as a result of the 400th Anniversary Appeal Fund reaching approximately £107,000 and a grant of £17,500 from the Industrial Fund, work began on the 400 Hall, the Chemistry Block and the workshops in the Precinct, which were formally opened in 1959.

Over the course of 17 years T.L.T.'s safe pair of hands saw Repton placed back on an even keel. However, by the time of his retirement the Governors were looking for a successor who would be prepared to rock the boat in the pursuit of greater academic honours.

John Plowright

JOHN THORN, 1961–8

In terms of age, Lynam Thomas could have been John Thorn's father. Thorn was appointed when he was 35 years old, and

John Thorn, 1961–68.

suitable for monks at all. But Benedict decided that 'because in our day, it is not possible to persuade the monks of this, let us agree at least to the fact that we should not drink to excess, but sparingly'. I'm sure that several Reptonians of my day would have endorsed the tribute of one of their number, who recently told me gratefully that J.L.T.'s 'General Studies' course on wine, which included sampling rival vintages in the classroom, provided one of the most important of the life skills that his generation took from Repton. And once, when heads of department were invited to the Hall to discuss General Studies over supper, we were presented with a dinner menu that printed the food in the margins and the wines in the centre, ending with Château d'Yquem. We never did get around to discussing the curriculum on that occasion.

Not all pupils or staff could respond to the liberality implied in such metropolitan sophistication. One of my 1960s pupils, who went on to read History at Cambridge, recently admitted to me that he found it disconcerting that so many boundary-stones were being removed simultaneously. As he put it: 'Everything seemed to be up for grabs.' Academically and culturally speaking, that certainly seemed to be true, with

his youthfulness was a considerable culture shock. Even more shockingly, the Thorns announced in advance that they wished to be known as John and Veronica. That was regarded as revolutionary by so determinedly traditional a Common Room. But the first day of J.L.T.'s collective encounter with that Common Room was memorable for quite a different reason. As was the Repton custom then, the staff met for a short service in Chapel before the initial staff meeting in the Library. The first words of the new headmaster came from the 6th-century Rule of St Benedict:

> *Whenever matters of importance have to be dealt with in the monastery, let the abbot summon the whole congregation and himself put forward the question that has arisen. Then, after hearing the advice of the brethren, let him think it over by himself and do what he shall judge most advantageous.*

Repton Priory had been a house of Augustinian canons rather than Benedictine monks, but there was something about J.L.T.'s Christian liberalism that was almost Benedictine.

St Benedict had ruled that 'in view of the weakness of the infirm we believe that one pint of wine a day is enough for each one'. He admitted that some authorities held that wine was not

School Roll Call for the whole school (every Sunday at 5pm).

Inter-House Boxing Competition, 1955 - 'the annual tribal blood-letting' abolished by John Thorn.

the Headmaster providing the pre-eminent role model. John Thorn made sure that we knew Wilfred Owen's battlefield poems and introduced us to Britten's *War Requiem*, and he acted in a staff production of Chekhov, together with Veronica, who transfixed the audience with the suppressed malice she brought to 'What pretty flowers!'

Above all there were the Thorn sermons in Chapel. I particularly remember his conjuring up of the vision of Emperor Constantine before battle, a flaming cross in the sky with the command, 'In this sign conquer'. And then there was the Remembrance Day sermon that began with a wine-lover's tour of the pre-1914 vineyards of France, so soon to turn into wildernesses of mud and blood. Nor shall I forget the atmosphere in Chapel when almost the entire school voluntarily turned out to mourn the newly assassinated President John F. Kennedy. Thorn, like Kennedy, had been 'born in the 20th century'. But after entertaining Geoffrey Fisher and his wife, it must have been galling for even so young a headmaster to receive a bread-and-butter letter from Lady Fisher referring to 'a number of points in your sermon'.

More of a Temple than a Fisher, Thorn founded the William Temple Society, where the more serious-minded Reptonians could engage in philosophical and cultural discussions, irrespective of their particular academic disciplines. He admittedly showed a young man's impatience to change the pattern and tone of Chapel services, just as John Christie had tried to do in the 1930s. A generation after Christie, it was inevitable that Repton would reflect the tensions and turbulence in an Anglican Church provoked by Bishop Robinson's *Honest to God* and by the prototype new liturgy,

later to become the *Alternative Service Book*. When J.L.T. eventually got the chance to appoint his own chaplains it sometimes seemed to housemasters that the Chapel was trying to subvert Repton's house-based pastoral system and its well-established traditional values, which seemed somehow to be bound up with the survival of the *Book of Common Prayer*. (One Housemaster's advice to a new house tutor on how to take house prayers was meant in jest, but only just: 'When we've won on "League" we use the General Thanksgiving, when we've lost, the General Confession.') Christianity at its best is always somewhat subversive, but there were times in mid-1960s Repton when it seemed that upsetting housemasters had become an end, not merely a means.

Thorn, who had been educated as a day boy at St Paul's, and whose housemastering experience at Clifton had been of a Town House, found Repton's housemasters difficult to deal with from the beginning. Repton's houses, scattered throughout the village, had developed as feudal fiefdoms more than was the case at Clifton. And Clifton houses had been uprooted by war-time evacuation to Bude, where long-standing traditions were exposed to the scouring buffetings of Atlantic gales. At Repton there were faults on both sides, but on one occasion at least I was able to sympathize with headmagisterial frustration. There had been an informal meeting of teaching staff in the OR Room one evening for a wide-ranging discussion of various changes that might be made in the life of the school. The meeting broke up in apparent general agreement, but several housemasters went back to their houses and wrote to J.L.T. expressing their opposition to what had seemed a consensus view. St Benedict would not have approved.

The demise of some long-standing traditions went unlamented. One was Sunday call-over of the entire school, when the duty-master calls the roll in the Yard and each boy gives the traditional Repton salutation of the 'tick' as he passes the Headmaster. I was the last Repton duty-master to perform the call-over ritual, and I can testify to the general relief at its discontinuance. Nor was the disappearance of the cases of stuffed birds from the staircase to High Chamber much mourned. More controversial was the abolition of inter-house boxing. Thorn was himself a Cambridge Boxing Blue, but one year's experience of the annual tribal blood-letting persuaded him to drop the competition.

John Thorn was too much of an historian to want to flout all tradition. He quoted the Duke of Cumberland's maxim: 'When it is not necessary to change, it is necessary not to change.' Repton's strong tradition in art, drama and music was meanwhile cherished. He did not feel the need to be as pro-active in these areas as he would later be at Winchester. Dennis Hawkins, a practising artist, who had long been able to run the Art School untrammelled by the demands of public examination syllabuses, was now assisted by staff skilled in ceramics and other three-dimensional work. Drama and music were brought together in the musicals written by William Agnew and Michael Charlesworth, while the traditional staff production of the Pedants, first staged in the 1930s, was not allowed to languish. William Agnew (N 1945) and Michael Salter, successive directors of music, were among the best of J.L.T.'s appointments.

Cricket was one of Repton's proudest traditions, as I learned to my cost when I committed the sacrilege of marching my drill squad across the First XI square. The Thorn years could not expect to rival the excitement of Richard Hutton's 1,000 runs in a single season, but the frequency with which we lost the Malvern match was harder to bear. Yet in other sports, the record of wins and losses was not much different from the seasons of the 1950s and 1970s. And in spite of erring drill squads, a particularly well-run CCF was a far cry from the screen parody of Lindsay Anderson's *If* ... .

Individual masters undoubtedly felt confident that they would be supported in any sensible new initiatives which would widen their (and their pupils') experience. My seven

weeks' leave of absence in the United States, under the auspices of the US Information Service, changed for ever the balance of my historical interests. And when I came back, a convert to team-teaching, I was at once allowed to introduce it into Repton's history sixth.

What were J.L.T.'s relations with the staff as a whole? Considerably better than they were made to seem in his *Road to Winchester*, where Hawkins and Charlesworth were singled out as the only kindred spirits. Part of the common room was indeed implacable in its opposition, but there were those of us in the middle who sought to build bridges between rival clans. Peter Wills, the Chaplain, and Barry Downing, later Second Master, who escape mention in J.L.T.'s account of his Repton years, deserve to be included among the loyal and constructive critics.

Yet creative tension can be surprisingly productive, and I believe this was true of Thorn's Repton. Much of his attempted liberalization was resisted by the same individuals who would soon accept it at the hands of John Gammell, former Winchester housemaster and a reassuringly unrevolutionary-looking figure. The parallel with the comparative civil rights achievements of Kennedy and Lyndon Johnson was drawn at the time, and is too striking to ignore. Thorn's emphasis on the liberalizing and civilizing virtues was accompanied by an undoubted rise in academic standards. He inherited a 'Blue Book' in which forms were listed in order of individual merit rather than in alphabetical order. More objectionably, in order to arrive at a monthly order of merit, marks had to be rescaled to reflect the comparative status or presumed difficulty of, for example, Classics and Chemistry. It was thus hardly possible for good scientists to outclass good classicists. It was not only housemasters who thought that J.L.T.'s abandonment of such statistical manipulation would spell academic disaster. Yet in one vintage year there were four Oxbridge awards in Bill Blackshaw's Modern Languages department alone, while Keith Workman's classicists continued to excel, James Fenton among them.

Whatever reservations there may be about Thorn's stewardship at Repton, I am

public school ... [is] not designed to make you cleverer or more likely to succeed. It's all about ensuring your children have the happiest possible childhood. Mine was.

Jeremy Clarkson (P 1973)

John Gammell, 1968–78.

personally grateful to have had the chance to serve under him. His civilizing influence and his sense of fair play helped to promote a sense of balance between science and the arts, between the examination curriculum and more general education, and between academic and sporting success. My guess is that J.L.T.'s most enduring legacy will be his impact on individual Reptonians and on individual members of staff. He had a passionate concern for the individual and acted at times like a housemaster without portfolio in his fostering of individual talent and his concern for seeming misfits. Similarly, Veronica played an important role, which does not feature in Speech Day reports. Apart from the formal hospitality expected of a headmaster and his wife, she supported staff wives with the crèche held at the Hall and often averted a personal crisis by lending a sympathetic ear to a boy or master who felt himself at odds with the Repton ethos.

Such individual contacts, remembered with gratitude down the years, perhaps provide the only kind of immortality worth coveting.

Stuart Andrews

Opening of the new tennis courts, 1972. Left to right: Bryan Valentine (O 1921), former England test cricketer, Jonathan Collings (B 1967), John Gammell and Richard Grew (Master i/c Tennis).

JOHN GAMMELL, 1968–78

Stuart Andrews has already referred to the fact that John Gammell, war hero, 'former Winchester housemaster and a reassuringly unrevolutionary-looking figure', was able to persuade those who had jibed at Thorn's proposals to accept comparable or even more sweeping changes. Given that the most revolutionary of these – the admission of girls – is described elsewhere by John himself, this brief appraisal will focus on the other aspects of his headmastership.

When Mrs Thatcher entered 10 Downing Street for the first time in the aftermath of the 'winter of discontent' she uttered the prayer attributed to St Francis of Assisi, which seeks, amongst other things, to replace discord with union and darkness with light. After the storm clouds of the Thorn years John Gammell might have been permitted to utter a similar sentiment. Had he done so he could have spoken with greater sincerity than Mrs Thatcher and ultimately have looked back with a greater sense of achievement that he had indeed calmed troubled waters.

Gammell not only gave his support to all aspects of school life but took the common-sense steps of allowing greater access to parents and ORs by the introduction of, respectively, parents' meetings and gaudies. The year 1973 not only saw the first of the latter but the launch of a major appeal, the fruits of which included greatly improved study conditions in all houses, an all-weather sports area on the Tanyard and the new Art School (freeing the Tithe Barn). It was typical that Gammell personally acknowledged in writing every contribution to the appeal.

Having felt that he had achieved all he might reasonably expect to achieve after ten years at Repton, Gammell left to take up a post with the Cambridge University Appointments Board. A big man in all respects, Gammell presided over a decade of steady, civilized progress befitting a gentleman of the 'old school', whose instincts were conservative but who was unafraid of innovation.

John Plowright

DAVID JEWELL, 1978–86

David Jewell came to Repton as Headmaster at Christmas 1978, just as the first snow of the 'winter of discontent' was falling. His first impression was one of sheer beauty – the snow falling on the ancient buildings in the lamplight – and the second was of discomfort – burst pipes, freezing fog, leaks in the roof and biting cold. In that icy winter there were no outdoor games for half the term and everyone hurried from one warm place to the next. No one told him about meeting between lessons in the Yard, a vital part of Repton life, and, having moved his study to the front of the Hall to be more

David Jewell, 1978–86.

those who disapproved of any but comprehensive education during the 1970s made him realize that no school could be self-sufficient. His links with the outside world – the press, HMC and politicians – started as a reaction to the threats to the public schools, but he disliked the idea of a school as a closed community and fought against it all his life. For him, the independent schools were a part of the national educational provision and needed to play their full part. He believed not in total equality, but in equality of opportunity and fraternity. He fought for the Direct Grant Scheme and then was instrumental in establishing the Assisted Places Scheme.

He knew, moreover, that, if you wanted a school to be successful, it had to be full, otherwise there would be economic constraints on everything you did, and to achieve this a good reputation was vital. This meant social and professional contacts with the wider community, bringing people into the school and getting staff and pupils to go out and meet people. There was no place for arrogance or an ivory tower. The feeder schools – preparatory and primary schools – were to be cultivated and the views of their heads sought. The Old Reptonians, too, were both a source of knowledge and of possible future parents.

The Governors had appointed him in order to make use of his wide experience in education and for his administrative abilities. As the ideological 1970s gave way to the meritocratic 1980s, academic standards had to rise. Learning was not only desirable for its own sake but also essential for success. This was agreed by everyone at Repton – Housemasters (many of whose children were in the school), Heads of Departments, parents and preparatory schools and the Governors. That standards did rise was the result of the efforts of all the teachers and the taught. The Oxbridge results achieved post-war records in those years. How it should be done was not always agreed, and Housemasters and the Head clashed over priorities. David Jewell was never a man to shirk a row, and he felt that sometimes he was opposed, not over principles but over power. He was fortunate in having the firm backing of the Governing Body and of men like Professor Geoffrey Dawes, Sir Desmond Lee, Frank Fisher, Alan Bemrose and, later, Sir Charles Pringle, all Old Reptonians. He was also fortunate in having, in Nigel Spurgeon, a Bursar who shared his aims and ideals for the school and never thought that he was running a commercial business or a stately home.

The 1980s were also a time of change in the style of schoolmastering. The comfort and happiness of the pupils became paramount, and most parents were determined that this should be so. David detested corporal punishment and abolished it – not without difficulty – in every school he headed. He also loathed bullying and did all in his power to

accessible to all, he waited … in vain. However, his natural optimism was justified, and Repton eventually thawed.

David Jewell was a large, generous man. 'Ebullient' was the word used by the press, but his cheerful, confident manner concealed an anxious and often nervous personality. He was always aware of the responsibilities of his position, and, moreover, his life was a constant struggle with poor health as he suffered with high blood pressure and rheumatic illness. His pride never let him take a day away from his work but the strain was there.

He had come, at the age of 44, from Bristol Cathedral School, where he had been Headmaster for nine years. He had taken it, a small, artistic grammar and choir school, to membership of the Headmasters' Conference (HMC) and to independence after the abolition of the Direct Grant. His previous experience had included being Head of Science at Eastbourne College, on the Winchester College staff, where the birth of a Down's syndrome son profoundly affected his values and ideas, and Deputy Head at a large state comprehensive and community school on a Bristol housing estate. His own education was at Blundell's School and St John's College, Oxford.

His breadth of experience, backed by studies at Bristol University and Bristol Polytechnic, gave him a wide knowledge of education. The battle to save Bristol Cathedral School from

David Jewell (left), at the start of a Charity Run.

stamp it out when it reared its ugly head. He found the young endlessly endearing and entertaining:

> *'Sir, I broke my arm when I fell off an ostrich.'*
> *'You're joking!'*
> *'No, sir. I really did.'*

He lived in Kenya and he really did. We last met him there flying planes to refugee camps in the Sudan and prayed that he was no longer accident prone.

David enjoyed the international character of the school – the serious hard work and subtle mischief of the boys from Hong Kong. (We still have a set of ivory wise monkeys that one of them felt was a suitable gift for a Headmaster.) There was the occasion when one boy was asked by a parent, 'Do you have a drug problem at Repton?' 'Oh no! You can get anything you want.' The openness and bounce of some of the Europeans was refreshing. 'Sir, I *like* being called Kraut,' was the answer to attempted political correctness. And the night when Noah's Ark was washed up on the cricket pitch was a masterpiece of Teutonic organization. In contrast, serious bad behaviour, though comparatively rare, made him genuinely angry. Drug supplying, bullying, loutishness, particularly against the girls, were severely punished, after an extremely unpleasant tongue-lashing.

He felt that as Headmaster he had to support the teaching staff, and the sickness and premature death of Chris Parker affected him greatly. Much of his time was spent listening to, and trying to help, his colleagues with their personal problems.

Appointing new staff was something over which he took great pains, consulting widely and telephoning referees and employers. However, poor teaching (in his view boring eager young people was inexcusable), corruption or violence were dealt with angrily and sometimes summarily, and sometimes he was never forgiven. His decisiveness could lead to impetuous and sometimes mistaken decisions, which he came to regret. He could put the wrong man into a job but, on the other hand, no one said of him, as they did of some of his colleagues, that the last person he spoke to was the one who got his way.

The artistic and spiritual life of Repton mattered enormously to him. He restored daily morning chapel, and in a surprisingly short time it became accepted as a normal start to the day. His own strong personal faith made him anxious to support the work of the chaplains. As he said in an interview for the *Reptonian* in 1985, he saw the New Testament as a code of conduct that has never been bettered. In the arts he was used to high standards, and the school's drama, music and art fulfilled his hopes. The sheer fun and the splendid parties that went with them were among the highlights of Repton life. The staff revues by the Pedants had him crying with laughter.

Games were vital to the health, happiness and self-esteem of both staff and pupils, and he saw no conflict with academic work. The winter of 1979 made that clear. They were also part of the image of the school in the wider world. Though cricket was his first love, he backed Roger Thompson's tennis scheme to the hilt. It brought many talented and intelligent children to the school, as well as the Youll and Aberdare Cups.

Games were also a valuable link to the Old Reptonians, especially through the Cricketer Cup and the Arthur Dunn Cup. He greatly enjoyed their company, both at the school itself and all over the country at their meetings and dinners. When the 1982 Appeal was launched their support was invaluable. This appeal, with its meetings of former pupils and parents and staff, was a great rallying point for Repton, even if it meant attending the same speeches and dinners rather too often. Everyone came together for a common purpose. The proceeds resulted in the transformation of the old sanatorium into the beautifully designed Robert Beldam Music School (named after the major donor), the Tanyard and its pavilion, and the refurbishment of Pears School. There were also, I believe, bursaries established to enable less well-off pupils to come to Repton. It culminated in the opening of the buildings by the Duchess of Kent in 1985.

In 1986 he accepted the post of Master of Haileybury and left Repton at Christmas after eight years. He felt that he had accomplished all that he could there and that, for him, 16 years in one school would be too much. Haileybury welcomed him, and he enjoyed nine years there, becoming HMC Chairman in

1990 and travelling widely on their behalf. He missed many things at Repton – many friendships and occasions. He retired in 1996 and was still active, particularly as a school governor. He died suddenly of a heart attack in 2006.

David Jewell's philosophy as a Headmaster could be summed up in his own words, quoted in the *Terminal Letter* of May 1987 from a speech he made thanking the Old Reptonians at his last annual dinner in London:

> *We should seek to discover whatever talent a pupil has, and to develop it to the full. We hope they will learn to enjoy work for its own sake and not for the reward it brings ... [and develop the ability to] give up short-term pleasures for joy in long-term achievement.*

Katharine Jewell

A BOSS'S EYE VIEW

I have always taken the view that a headmaster is the leaseholder of a school; the former pupils are its freeholders, and they can rightly feel umbilically attached to the institution that shaped their early years. During his tenure a headmaster must be the guardian of the heritage but also an instrument of change. He steers that precarious course between the Scylla of fossilization and the Charybdis of upheaval. The danger is that staff and former pupils can often see relatively minor adjustments as shaking the foundations. One immediate objection to my announcement of the planned reduction in the size of the Hall to more manageable numbers was an interesting example of the parochialism (and perhaps gamesiness) of a school – 'But there won't be a stopping-out house to do the refereeing'.

One important decision was to become co-educational throughout the school, which, given a co-educational preparatory school and the Abbey for sixth form girls, had an inherent logic. There was also the wider argument that we should be preparing pupils for a world of university – and ultimately work – that was clearly no longer predominantly single sex. A number of leading independent boarding schools had already gone in that direction, and it was important that Repton was seen to be doing it as a positive step, as evidenced by the need to build one, and then another, new house to accommodate the increased number of girls. The longer term repercussions of full co-education could not be predicted but would prove to involve some potentially painful changes. Since there was no wish or capacity to increase overall numbers, the increase in girls meant that there was slack in the boys' houses. There was a logic in the amalgamation of Brook House and the Hall, but, given the tribal loyalties of the Repton house system, not a move that was easy to sell to the pupils. The

Graham Jones, 1987–2003.

morning after the announcement there was a brief demonstration by Brook on the steps of Pears School, but any problem was lanced by the Head of the Hall leading his men to cheer for Brook in the House Match Final in the afternoon. The next reorganization was not needed for some years but was easier in that it allowed for the Cross to be closed for much needed refurbishment before the Mitre boys moved in, vacating the Mitre buildings for conversion to the fourth girls' house.

At the heart of Repton has always been the concept of community, born in the house but spreading into the school as a whole. Traditionally that was a community built up by living together, a boarding community. When day pupils were introduced they maintained fundamentally a boarder's day and were thus fully integrated into the school. There was

Remembrance Sunday.

constant pressure, particularly from a number of Foremarke parents looking for convenience rather than conviction boarding, to reduce the length of the school day and to introduce weekly boarding. The danger is that some, particularly if local and vocal, were attempting to demand the product on their own terms even if those terms would profoundly alter the nature of the product they wanted to buy into. Many schools yielded to such parental pressure, and over the years their boarding withered and has frequently disappeared. Repton made a

Wilkinson, Walker, Workman, Grew and Charlesworth are legendary names that both my father and I had the good fortune of being taught by. But there were many other great teachers at Repton. As far as I remember there wasn't a dull master. And there was never a dull moment. Thank you for everything Repton. People who say they are the best days of our lives are not far wrong.

Harry Newbould (C 1989)

conscious decision to put clear blue water between itself and these other schools by protecting the boarding ethos. The length of a day pupil's day remained, but it proved possible to get greater weekend flexibility without ever emptying the school to the disadvantage of those who could not get away at the weekend. The result was, by the end of my time, a resurgence in boarding and the preservation of an ethos that all wanted to protect.

The favourite image of a headmaster is of a duck serenely floating across a pond, with few realizing that it is paddling like hell underneath. Those Speech Day addresses, newsletters to parents and former pupils, and interviews with prospective parents all tell of the successes of the school and of the carefully crafted plans for future developments. They inevitably gloss over the real problems that exercise a headmaster and which he is desperate to shield from the public gaze, certainly from the press and sometimes from the staff. People can be critical or curious, but often the head is the one in full possession of the facts but not at liberty to reveal them. These are the secrets that can be known only to your Chairman of Governors and perhaps your Deputy, and they are what make headmastering at times an

Graham Jones, Speech Day.

unexpectedly lonely life beneath the surface, but nonetheless absorbing.

Repton has been fortunate to attract governors with a wide range of expertise and a willingness to devote a lot of their time to the school. They were extremely supportive throughout and certainly never baulked at some of the most expensive investment projects imaginable – new houses, refurbishing boarding houses, Chapel and the Old Mitre, a sports hall, the studio theatre, an enlarged art school, two all-weather pitches and an indoor swimming pool. A major strength was the presence on the Governing Body of members who had had first-hand experience of headmastering and the teaching world and who well understood the problems and ethos of independent schools. At my very first interview the presence of Frank Fisher was a great reassurance, and it was a sadness that he had died before I took up post but thankfully there were others there with similar experience and wisdom. A congenial staff also sets the tone for a school and its pupils, and the high quality of the staff and their good relations with pupils was a major theme of both inspection reports in my time. What inspectors don't see – and often nor do the pupils and parents too – is the sheer fun that a staff can have. At Repton it was at its

most public in the Pedants, but what went on behind the scenes of the 400 Hall was even better, as was the banter between the 'Yard Set' between lessons or the announcements over coffee in the Hall – often giving the prefects a surprising insight into common room life.

Over all those years, what does one really value? What actually matters? The answer is, unequivocally, the boys and girls. And it is not just the achievements that are rightly recorded in the annals of the *Reptonian* or on the honours boards, but the informal contacts with individuals whether in the Yard, on the touchline, in the Art School, over lunch each day or in the classroom. There is a rich bran tub of memories to be dipped into. Which is the boy who told me, apropos the communion service, that he 'preferred the 1066 version'? Who was it my wife visited in the San to be told, of his sister's career, that 'she wasn't planning anything too erotic'? There was the never-to-be-forgotten 'sink' set to which I taught Economics for a year, a Sisyphean labour in itself. They, my 'Magnificent Seven', could have won hands down at any sport, but the fact that few had much hope of even passing A level (cost curves had to be explained in terms of the shape of a hockey D) did not deter one of them from telling me, with a twinkle in his eye,

'Let's face it, sir, none of us is aiming to get anything more than a B.' There were the individuals in disciplinary trouble. Two occasions I remember vividly when sections of the staff were baying for blood and the school as a whole expected little else than expulsion, but such were the particular circumstances that I decided on less draconian action. In neither case was I let down, and one of those pupils kept up a correspondence long after he left. There was the last night of term when the Second Master had been chasing round the school with his torch trying to persuade a group of revellers to go back to their house. It was hard to contain the grin the next morning at the banner flying from chapel: 'Boys 2–Bearded Monster 0.' Well played New House leavers. It is of such events and such people that the real memories are made.

There were many changes over 16 years, some thrust on the school by the outside world, others the school's own initiatives. A number may have seemed revolutionary at the time but are now lost in the mists of time. When I arrived the bell at the Arch was rung at the end of lessons, something no one actually needed reminding of. Punctuality for lessons was appalling, so I had the bell rung when lessons should begin – the mosaic of the real Repton consists of a host of such small, mostly unrecorded, changes. Looking back, being Headmaster of such a school was a stimulating and enjoyable experience, and like, I hope, its former pupils one can look back with many fond memories of people and events. In 1987 I arrived from my previous incarnation with the nickname 'Whale', and when I left Repton in 2003 I really meant my final words at Lists: 'For the last 16 years the boss has had a whale of a time.'

Graham Jones

‘During the last decade of the 20th century, when I served on the Governing Body, Repton took not a leap into the dark but a steady and thoughtful jump into the future. The task of school governors, especially of a great and historic school like ours, is not to dwell on the past, but to reflect on history while determining to extend it. Governors are by nature cautious: they feel it is not their money they are spending, but the parents', and they are always acutely aware that future generations will judge them. I feel confident however that the remarkable advances which I witnessed and supported ... will stand the school in good stead for many years to come.'

Edwina Currie Jones (Governor, 1993–98)

Jacob's Ladder.

45

THREE COMMON ROOM PORTRAITS

*I*n his autobiography Leon Trotsky wrote: 'The percentage
of freaks among people in general is very considerable, but
it is especially high among teachers.' Had Trotsky had the
opportunity of studying the Repton Common Room over the
centuries, with grotesques such as the misogynistic Wall and the
narcoleptic Exham (Percy not David), he would doubtless have
seen little reason to review this thesis.

However, few students would trade in the colourful teachers of
their youth for grey technocrats, for, as John Stuart Mill
reminds us: 'Eccentricity has always abounded when and
where strength of character has abounded; and the amount of
eccentricity in a society has generally been proportional to the
amount of genius, mental vigour, and moral courage, which
it contained.'

The following pen portraits remind us that teachers can
make their marks in numerous ways, but for better or worse
their influence over their young charges can last a lifetime.

John Plowright

In the winter of 1981–82 Mike Charlesworth seizes the moment to treat an English set to Chaucer on ice.

LAURENCE ARTHUR BURD (1863–1931)★

The publication in 1891 of the first fully annotated edition of
Machiavelli's *Il Principe* established its editor as the foremost
English authority on Machiavelli and a scholar of European
reputation. Laurence Arthur Burd (1863–1931) was aged
28 and had completed only five of the 37 years he spent
teaching the Classical Sixth Form at Repton. The book was
much praised by newspapers as well as by academic journals.
But the congratulations of colleagues were tempered by
resentment at the last sentence of Burd's Preface: 'For the
many shortcomings of the present edition, I can only plead that

it has been written under many difficulties, in a remote village,
during the *moments perdus* of a very busy life.'

Burd, modest and self-effacing, had not intended to offend
'those grumpy, ill-paid, rather feeble and discontented men', as
A.C. Benson called them. He merely wished to record how
distant from Repton were the great libraries of Europe from
which he had quarried his sources in seven languages.

At Clifton and at Balliol Burd had shown promise, taking a
First Class in both Mods and Greats, but without the
encouragement of Lord Acton he might never have embarked
on his magnum opus, much less completed it to acclaim. The

The Common Room.

Laurence Arthur Burd.

Young Mr Burd towers above his colleagues, 1889.

Nestor of European historical studies had been impressed by the young man who tutored his son for a year. Thereafter Acton discussed with him the progress of the work at every stage, lent him essential books from his own library of 60,000 volumes, read and corrected the 480 pages of *Il Principe* in proof and himself contributed an Introduction of dense erudition.

Burd repaid his mentor by writing a chapter on Florence and Machiavelli for Acton's *Cambridge Modern History* but published little else in the 40 years that remained to him. His first duty was to his pupils of the Classical Sixth. He taught them not only the Classics but the place of art and literature in the history of Europe and how to express themselves in precise, elegant English. Sometimes, however, he seemed to stretch young minds beyond what they could appreciate and absorb. In spite of his rusty clothes and spectacles held together by a twisted pipe cleaner, Burd inspired awe in the classroom – and in the common room, too.

For 20 years he was the school's librarian, creating almost out of nothing one of the best libraries of any public school. He bought many books out of his own pocket or gave them from his own library. Hanging there today are the saturnine features of his portrait by William Rothenstein to which generations of pupils subscribed; it captures the austerity but conceals the kindliness of the man whom the boys called 'The Auk'.

Burd's generosity to the library and to other good causes was made possible by his financial independence. The son of a Shrewsbury solicitor and land agent, he married a first cousin, the daughter of the leading consultant physician in Shropshire – 'the little Burd with the long bill,' as he was known. The young Burds were affluent enough to commission Edwin Lutyens, already a fashionable architect, to build them a 12-bedroom house in the Pastures set in 10 acres of garden.

It was not the only advantage he enjoyed over his colleagues. The historian D.C. Somervell wrote that Burd's 'timetable was of enviable brevity; he never had to attend the before-breakfast period in those days; he was never called upon to face the barbarians of the middle or lower school.' Nor would he accept the responsibilities of being a housemaster.

> *... the Lower VI Classical [was] presided over by Mr L A Burd ... We did a lot of our work in the school library where ... we were accustomed to lure the Auk's Scottish terrier, who frequently accompanied him, away from his master, to pursue balls of paper bowled along the length of the library, and to see how many times this could be done with impunity!*
>
> **G.H. de B. Wyllys (C 1916)**

So he had more leisure than most to read Plato, play the 'cello, practise portrait photography and study the history of the Penny Black postage stamp that brought him an invitation from King George V to inspect the royal collection.

Burd held aloof from the frictions of the common room and the suffocating shibboleths of public school life. One colleague was amazed to discover that the man who knew so much about Machiavelli did not know the name of the current captain of the Cricket XI.

Kenneth Rose (O 1939)

★ *The author of the above is much indebted to Dr Russell Price, of the Department of Politics at Lancaster University, for his recent researches into Burd, Acton and Machiavelli.*

ALDOUS HUXLEY (1894–1963)

Appointed by Geoffrey Fisher to fill a sudden vacancy, Aldous Huxley arrived at Repton in the summer of 1916 on the eve of his 22nd birthday. He came of an intellectual dynasty with a reputation of his own. He was a great-grandson of Dr Arnold of Rugby and grandson of T.H. Huxley, exponent of Darwin's theories of evolution. Aldous, a King's Scholar of Eton who had taken a First in English at Balliol, felt himself wasted teaching small boys Latin and History.

That they 'behaved very nicely' was a tribute both to them and to himself. Six feet four inches tall, with the untidy limbs of a young giraffe, and half-blind since suffering a severe eye infection at Eton, he was made to be persecuted. But his lively mind and good humour earned attention and respect.

He called his colleagues a set of Calibans and the Head-master 'a hearty parson'. When the future Archbishop of Canterbury prayed for the Almighty to restrain the covetousness of the workers and to make their masters holy and good, 'I could hardly restrain my derisive laughter'. He had to send away for his favourite pipe tobacco. 'The village is too small to provide a decent shop and the boys evidently don't smoke enough.'

The letters of a lonely, impoverished young man need not be taken too seriously. He was released from Repton in August 1916 and moved into Garsington Manor, near Oxford, Lady Ottoline Morrell's retreat for the Bloomsbury set: writers and artists, genuine conscientious objectors, shirkers posing as agricultural labourers and other assorted hangers-on. It inspired him to write his first novel, *Crome Yellow* (1921).

Driven to find a job, he returned to schoolmastering, this time to Eton, where he taught George Orwell and won the regard of David Cecil and Harold Acton. As a disciplinarian, however, he had a harder time than at Repton.

Both those treadmills contributed to the satirical opening chapter of his second novel, *Antic Hay* (1923). The anti-hero, a

Aldous Huxley.

public school master called Mr Gumbril, thinks subversive thoughts in chapel. He is then required to mark 63 essays on the Risorgimento, each of which dismisses Pope Pius IX as 'a kindly man of less than average intelligence'. Mr Gumbril has had enough and resigns in mid-term.

Kenneth Rose (O 1939)

JOHN DAVENPORT (c1910–66)

John Davenport made his bow in 1941 with stately panache. Seated in an old-fashioned Bath chair borrowed from the Boot Inn where he lodged, John Davenport progressed from classroom to classroom escorted by a rabble of excited small boys. He said that he had fallen at Waterloo – the railway station, not the battlefield. We thought he was suffering from gout.

Davenport was in his early 30s, short and stout, with the physique of a pugilist (he had boxed for Cambridge) and the head of a dissolute Roman emperor. He was softly spoken with an incongruous lisp. His talk was an education in itself. He knew everything and everybody, had read everything and had been everywhere. He had feasted with the current deities of literature, music and painting; he had translated Mallarmé in Paris and written scripts for Sam Goldwyn in Hollywood. All this and more, he assured his pupils, he would share with them.

We were fascinated and amused but had our doubts. Could he really be the friend of T.S. Eliot and of Augustus John? And if, as he mentioned lightly, he had recently collaborated with Dylan Thomas on a novel called *The Death of the King's Canary*, why had the school bookshop not heard of it?

It took a generation posthumously to vindicate Davenport's truthfulness and to shame the cynics. Ten years after his death in 1966 a sale of his papers at Sotheby's confirmed that he had indeed been the intimate correspondent of titans. That same year, 1976, there appeared *The Death of the King's Canary* by Dylan Thomas and John Davenport, an ingenious but scurrilous book about the murder of a poet laureate. Fear of libel had long delayed its publication until most of the characters savagely caricatured in its pages were safely dead.

Davenport cared nothing for administration, for mark books and form order, rewards and punishments. His end-of-term reports, however, were works of art; but before they could be sent off to parents, higher authority insisted on removing veiled insults and psychological speculation.

He took trouble over boys of every age and ability, encouraging them to argue on equal terms. The promising ones never forgot his broad command of history and literature, embroidered with anecdote, allusion and paradox. The less clever, who showed no interest in either the substance or the style of his discourses, were allowed to doze through those humid Trent Valley afternoons.

Candidates for awards and places at Oxford and Cambridge – other universities were scarcely mentioned at Repton in those days – remembered his tutorial skills with gratitude. In his spidery italic hand he wrote out reading lists for each of us, for we had a splendid library and the leisure to use it. I recall George Otto Trevelyan's life of his uncle Lord Macaulay ('the second-best biography in the English language'), William James's *Varieties of Religious Experience*, Kenneth Clark's *The Gothic Revival*, Eckermann's *Conversations with Goethe* and G.B. Shaw's musical criticism written under the pseudonym Corno di Bassetto.

All were designed to stretch and stimulate the minds of his pupils, to catch the eye of a bored examiner and, as with Aldous Huxley's novels, to annoy my housemaster. Davenport was fun; but he was also subversive. The common room resented his disloyalty, his mimicry, his menacing outbursts over the dinner table. After one, or possibly two terms, Repton dispensed with his services. He turned up soon afterwards at Stowe, where again he was mistrusted by the staff but adored by the boys. He lasted two terms.

Kenneth Rose (O 1939)

Causey graffiti.

The Cloisters, students and the ubiquitous mobile phone.

DEEPER AND WIDER:
THE CHANGING STUDENT BODY

*W*hen an OR returns to Repton in the holidays the most obvious changes to the school are those in what one might term its 'capital plant' or what others would call the fabric of the school. Some facilities have sadly ceased to be a part of the school (like Brook House) or disappeared entirely (like the open-air pool), whilst new buildings have figuratively taken their place (like the covered pool or the Garden and Field), and yet others have completely changed in character (like the Old Mitre and the Mitre).

However, the OR visiting during term time might be struck even more by the changes to the student body, as the bounds of the school in the 20th century have been extended in terms of age (especially if one looks at Foremarke), in terms of gender (with girls now comprising roughly 40% of the school) and

geography, with the Hong Kong community providing the oldest and strongest international component to a school whose reach is now truly global.

The section which follows examines these processes whereby the student body has changed shape, offering the Repton experience to more and for longer.

John Plowright

REPTON'S PREPARATORY SCHOOL
In September 1939, just after war was declared, there arrived in Latham House a small boy, aged just 11. This boy, M.D. Spring (L & M 1939), loved to play yard football and frequently there would be a cry of 'Give Spring a kick', which unfailingly duly occurred. Seven years later he became Head Prefect, a reward, no doubt, for long service and good conduct.

This illustrates the possible need to consider the founding of a Repton preparatory school. H.G.M. Clarke, Headmaster of Repton, was strongly in favour of the idea, and B.W. Thomas was invited to be Headmaster of the preparatory school, which opened in April 1940 with eight boys. At the end of the first year numbers had reached 50. So Clarke's enthusiasm had been fully justified. For the first two years the Cross provided bedders and classrooms, but when Latham House closed in 1942, the prep school moved up there, although lessons continued in the Cross. When that house re-opened in 1945, teaching moved to the Old Mitre.

In 1947 the demand for places at Repton had increased so considerably that is was decided to re-open Latham, and this meant that a new home was needed for the prep school. Fortunately, Foremarke Hall, an elegant Georgian mansion, some 2 miles from Repton, had recently been released by the Army.

An early aerial view of Foremarke.

Observers observed at Foremarke

Heads down. A Foremarke class, 1963.

B. W. Thomas remained at Latham as Housemaster, and he handed to his successor a school built on sound foundations and with high standards, particularly in the classroom and on the games field.

Foremarke's first headmaster, K.L.T. Jackson, was an inspired choice. A pre-war Oxford Cricket and Rugby Football Blue and a Scottish Rugby International, he had taught at Wellington College before joining the Army and achieving a distinguished war record. His relationship with T.L. Thomas, Headmaster of Repton since 1944, gave rise to a story that Jackson told against himself. He was driving the old school bus when the boy sitting next to him suddenly said 'Sir, if your wife had not been the sister of the Headmaster of Repton's wife, do you think that you would have got this job?' While Jackson paused to consider his answer, the boy said 'Well, I don't think you would.'

Ken and Betty Jackson had a tremendous gift of friendship and fun and the determination to make Foremarke a fine, all-round school, but for this to happen a first-class teaching staff had to be recruited. Some of the early masters were somewhat eccentric, ranging from one who kept his bicycle in his room at the top of the building, up three flights of stairs, to a retired colonel, who was much respected by his regiment. The small boys, however, became riotous, driving the colonel to shout at one boy: 'You are expelled.' This did the trick, as he had only meant 'sent out of the room', but the boys took it to be the ultimate punishment and hurriedly calmed down.

The Officer Cadet Training Unit (OCTU) had left plenty of Nissen huts in the grounds, and many of the slogans were still in place. 'Kill to live' greeted a somewhat surprised Latin class in September 1947. The solidly built red-brick dining hall and classroom block were splendid and are still to be seen, in a slightly altered form, today. Fortunately, Health and Safety Inspectors had not been invented and the annual bonfire party was extraordinarily dangerous, with horizontal rockets whizzing about in all directions, many of them fired by parents not long out of the Army. Miraculously there were no casualties. The Georgian building had hidden dangers, too. It was not built to hold masses of soldiers and even greater masses of energetic small boys, and one day, just after 7 a.m., two stone stairs in the top flight came loose and fell onto the middle flight, taking two more and thence to the bottom flight, so that six stairs lay in a heap at ground level, leaving gaps above them. A few minutes later the stairs would have been full of boys hastening from their bedders to the washrooms. For the next few weeks, while the necessary repairs and reinforcements were carried out, boys and staff had to make their way out down a ladder that led into the Jacksons' flat.

St Saviour's Church made the perfect setting for the Headmaster's first sermon in the September term of 1947. Unfortunately, the main door was left open and in pranced a goat. The animal could be seen only from the pulpit and by some of the staff. The boys, in their box pews, were blissfully unaware of its presence and rather surprised at the preacher's sudden loss of concentration. This church became a wonderful school chapel and made a deep and lasting impression on generations of Foremarke boys.

A.C. Baxter and J. Grosvenor Hill ('Hillie' to everyone), pre-war masters from Amesbury School, Hindhead, and the only staff with prep school experience, soon made their mark. Both were Scouters, so Scouts and Cubs became an important part of the life of the school. Hillie, who had been crippled by polio as a boy, was inspirational, running an active scout troop from his wheelchair and even taking them to camp. The Cubs were somewhat military and were frequently involved in night ops, complete with thunder flashes, borrowed from the Repton Corps.

Foremarke cricket and football flourished, encouraged by our games-playing Headmaster, and First XI fielding practice during break became a daily occurrence. One summer term, the cricket season being over and only sports week remaining, the Master i/c Cricket repaired to the Common Room for his first-break cup of coffee. There was a knock on the door and in came the Captain of Cricket, who said, 'Sir, what about our fielding practice?' The master replied, 'But the cricket season is over,' to which the skipper answered, 'Well if you're not going to take it, we'll have to take it ourselves.' So take it the master did, and they all enjoyed it more than ever.

While I was on sick leave in 1945–6 I taught at the prep school in Repton. I then went to Oxford, where I read History until 1949, when on my return to Foremarke Ken Jackson greeted me with the words: 'Carr, the History is all yours. I shall not interfere, but I will be most interested in your results.' What a challenge! Two years later Dominick Spencer, one of the original Foremarke staff of 1947, returned from Cambridge, also with a History degree, and Jackson said, 'Well, Spinner. Carr has got the History, so you can do the Geography.' And quite brilliantly he did it, making full use of his artistic talents and covering acres of blackboard with wonderful maps. The Common Entrance results were excellent, and the staff eagerly awaited the marks or grades, comparing each subject in the most competitive way imaginable.

After 13 years at Foremarke, Ken Jackson was appointed Headmaster of Cargilfield, a leading Scottish preparatory school. He left behind him an exceptionally happy school, where not only the boys but also the masters had learned a huge amount about life in general and had developed considerable mutual respect for one another.

So well did some of the staff learn that they soon moved to headmasterships: the Carrs went to Yarlet Hall in 1960, the Spencers to Oswestry Junior School and then to Amesbury, and the Tullos to Westminster Abbey Choir School.

Such fun did Foremarke life become and so happily did the growing community develop that a number of the children born to staff during our Foremarke years thought that Mum and Dad enjoyed life so much that they became prep school masters themselves. As I write, Robert Spencer and Philip Carr and their families are neighbours in a well-known Berkshire school, to which they were appointed by John Hare, one of Ken Jackson's outstanding Foremarke student masters.

Donald Carr (L & M 1940)

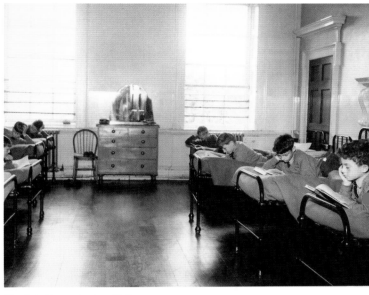

Temple bedder at quiet time, 1963.

FOREMARKE HALL, 1960–85

My wife, Peggy, and I arrived at Foremarke in September 1960. I had started teaching at Haileybury and was then a housemaster at a residential school for physically disabled boys. So, at the age of 32 I started my first prep school job, and I think the experienced staff made allowances for that! There were eight teachers, 3½ matrons, ½ a secretary and a part-time groundsman. DIY was essential. We had 106 boarding boys and one day boy (son of staff). A cheering message from a Governor said that they were sorry but fees must rise to £100 a term and they hoped the school would survive.

As term started, re-roofing and re-flooring work on the red-brick classroom block was unfinished, and all the desks were piled up outside in the rain. I think my first decision as Headmaster was that each form should have lessons in an allotted bedder. For four days the boys were taught there, and they seemed unsurprised and unfazed. The routine of school life, with its ups and downs, successes and disasters continued.

In 1965, having made a unilateral decision, I advertised that the school would select five day boys a year to be chosen by competitive exam. Five, possibly more, duly arrived in September 1965. Day boys were not universally popular on principle, but no one argued with the quality, and the system began to bring dividends. Numbers grew, nudging up year by year, and soon the day system blended in.

Money was a problem. We had built two temporary classrooms in about 1964 – I was delighted to see them still in full action in 2005! – but we needed more, and the dining room had become cramped. An appeal was launched to enable us to build a dining room extension and the 'New Block', which became habitable in 1968. But the way had to be cleared: we could not build on land we did not own. A wonderful deal was negotiated by which the Church Commissioners agreed to sell the Hall and two cottages, with 45 acres for £20,000.

By the end of the 1960s the school was big enough to allow streaming in the top three years, and academic scholarships began to be a regular feature. Boarding places were full, and demand for day places was strong. This time also saw the end of exciting episodes of running away – some caused by individual worries, some by sheer bravado.

One character reached home near Uttoxeter in four hours. One left his sick bed and marched doggedly for 17 miles on a dark Sunday night before being retrieved. One father rang me at 9 am and asked how his son was. I explained that all was going well and that he was immersed in his studies in first lesson. 'That's odd,' he said, 'I can see him from my window, walking up the drive!'

A sure winner was the boy who, in any free moment, would stand at the school gates and politely ask every motorist to 'kindly ring this number and tell my parents I am unhappy'. We could not keep him. Another winner was a boy who accepted so many bets that he cantered off and was found having a picnic at Tutbury Castle before being returned in triumph. There was a losing group of four who escaped with maps and compasses, planning a cross-country trek. Three hours later they burst through their final hedge, in front of my car, as I came back from Milton!

Any lengthy period produces changes, and the prep school world was changing. Young parents, especially mothers, began to question the need for boarding, science became more important, and Latin and its overriding importance came under scrutiny and attack. Change for its own sake was resisted, but there were gradual surrenders on all fronts. The pressure of numbers introduced cafeteria-style lunches, which had the benefit that pupils could eat in ten minutes and release a chunk of relaxing free time. Against the change was the feeling that table manners declined. The great advantage was the real rise in food quality – three choices of each course became the norm, replacing the dull, monotonous food of previous decades.

The whole system of games began slowly to alter. In the 1950s and 1960s the normal afternoon, all year, consisted of an organized team game for everyone, every day. In darkest winter games in the afternoon were followed by lessons, whereas the lighter months followed the reverse pattern. Thus everyone played a compulsory game six days a week. Gradually 'activities' came in and with it a mix of games rather than the whole school playing the same game. I never managed to get

School's out! Foremarke, 1963.

junior hockey in the summer term when pitches were fast and dry – maybe I was wrong.

It was clear by the late 1960s that many parents were less anxious for their offspring to board at the weekends and were rather opposed to having sons and daughters in different schools. Co-education was clearly going to come, by popular demand, and we were eager to provide it. There was real resistance from the School Governors and from many senior Repton staff but after three years of arguing we admitted nine girls in 1972. It needed money and there were some worries but soon the numbers flourished. Many prep schools made the change but we were ahead of the pack.

The school has been extraordinary lucky in that the church stands near by. A gem of a place, it was built in 1657, one of the few erected during the Commonwealth. Its triple-decker pulpit and box pews give it a flavour of simplicity and snugness, and pupils probably enjoyed the shelter from oversight that the pews provided. The school service was compulsory, lasting 40 minutes on average, and it followed a set pattern of the Book of *Common Prayer*, somewhat shortened. Evening service was always rather special in winter, and it is probable that for many the simple, special surroundings had an effect that was beneficial and memorable. The church was undoubtedly an integral part of school life, and all would have been the poorer without it.

The strength of any school is determined by the quality of the teaching and auxiliary staff and the school was well served by a procession of people who injected their knowledge, enthusiasm and skills into the school and most of the pupils. It is easier to remember the visual moments – the plays, exhibitions, cricket matches and fierce athletic contests. Behind all the successes, however, the hard work carries on out of the public gaze: noses to the grindstone in the classroom, exhausting work in the kitchens and the care and concern of the matron's staff. All these areas are the backbone of a school, and Foremarke would have had no success without the efforts of the staff involved.

Music at Foremarke reflects much of the change in the prep school scene in the 1960s and 1970s. At the beginning of the period concerts were fairly agonizing events, but at the end they were ambitious and enjoyable, as they were across the national independent school scene. The requirements were taking the decision to go for it and having the right staff and the commitment. All these gradually came in to place – not without argument and not without grief. A confrontation took place one morning break when the same boy was required for choir practice and fielding practice. The argument was about to be solved either by a swift thrust of a conductor's baton or a heavy blow from a cricket stump, but the headmagisterial decision was that choir practice should take precedence! In many meetings the cry was 'Music is taking over the school'. Music did grow inexorably and was speeded by the decision to offer entrance scholarships for eight-year-olds of real talent. They came along, and all parties benefited.

The system was that Repton music staff helped us, instruments were acquired, and standards rose. There were orchestras, bands and groups. Foremarke gained a huge reputation for music, and the chapel choir reached a sound of real quality. From the end of the 1970s Foremarke became the venue for the Prep Schools Concert Band, at which over a hundred of the best from all over the country rehearsed for six hours a day for six days in the holidays before giving a stirring and enthralling concert.

Science moved from one period a week, confined to the top form from 'the Esso kit' (a termly box of tricks that dealt with such subjects as 'the weather'), to a properly organized school subject with laboratories and equipment. IT moved from zero to a part of normal life. Latin moved from compulsory for all with six periods a week, to confined to A streams only.

As the school increased in size, streaming and setting became possible and hugely beneficial. We had a fairly wide range of ability in the school and were now able to group pupils so that almost all could work at a suitable pace. A scholarship form would be together for certainly two and often three years. There was a form called 'C.E. Non Latin', which I was sometimes referred to as 'Common Entrance Never Likely'!

Between 1960 and 1985 there was a huge change in the attitude towards parental involvement, visiting and access. Early on there was little communication: parents almost handed over their children at the start of term and picked them up at the end. But let it be clear that regulations that seem restrictive now were then generally accepted, and the atmosphere was a happy, robust one – tough might be the word but for almost all there was happiness and involvement. In 1962 or 1963 we introduced 'half-term', which ran from Saturday lunch to the evening of Sunday, the next day! Soon parents were welcomed to coffee after 'leave weekend', two a term on either side of half-term, and half-term lengthened. Parents watched matches and came to tea, and they began to know each other and the staff. One is bound to admit that there were disadvantages – over-talkative people at coffee and over-involved fathers at the touch line. As any change comes in it is accepted and becomes the norm. Did this new 'freedom' make pupils any happier? I don't know. They were happy before and happy afterwards, but it would be a tough task if anyone were to try and reverse the changes!

Corporal punishment was permissible until, I think, 1972. Right or wrong? Answers depend on the culture of the time. In the 1950s it was acceptable, but in the 1970s it was not. My view is that it was a good thing to have corporal punishment as long as it was not used. Its disappearance has meant it is far more difficult to think of suitable punishments, although rewards are better than punishments anyway.

The changes in facilities were quite amazing. My memories of my own prep school – in the 1930s – were that we had cricket bats and a Latin grammar and not much more. Fifty years later there are swimming pools, science labs, language labs, theatres, music schools, AstroTurf, sports halls and so on. What is important in schools are classrooms, and there are some who would say that schools have gone over the top with expenditure, overstaffing and overcharging. But it is the culture of the time, rather like the change in the look of cars in the school car park!

When the fees rose to £100 a term for boarders the school did not close. Inflation did not close it, nor did recessions. Let us hope that Foremarke continues, that the fine old house remains, and that many more generations of youngsters will enjoy and benefit from their days in the school. I expect that Sir Francis Burdett rests happily too.

Tom Davies

FOREMARKE HALL, 1985–2000

My first visit to Foremarke occurred years before I succeeded Tom Davies. I remember I was struck by an atmosphere of freedom and energy. It was a school that had grown at such a pace that the buildings seemed to be straining to keep pace with development. At the centre was the Hall with its impressive splendour and formality. All around it were ugly ex-army buildings and pre-fabs. The refinement of bygone days, when money had been no object, lay incongruously alongside school buildings that were cheap and rather tatty. That is not intended as a criticism. With the emergence of the school after the war, every penny mattered. Development was, by necessity, piecemeal, but few prep schools could compete with Foremarke's extensive grounds. It is much to the credit of Tom and his predecessor, Ken Jackson, that the balance between freedom and control was in favour of the child, whether organized on the games field or allowed free time activity exploring the woods.

My second visit was at Tom Davies's invitation. He was retiring and the post had just been advertised. I remember handing him a bottle of whisky and saying it was not to be seen as a bribe. It was October and the Hall, covered with deep red Virginia creeper, looked quite stunning. As this was an unofficial visit at a time of much speculation, meeting others was not possible. It was, therefore, the setting that made its mark. I remember Tom opening the door of St Saviour's, saying it was a gem of a church that meant much. With the evening sun falling across the simple box pews, I could see what he meant. Later I read a description of its restoration in a 1960s *Preptonian*:

> *This lovely building in the school grounds became the school chapel … But the fabric was decaying and there was no lighting or heating. Those who saw the church in those early days will hardly credit the miracle that has taken place. The gallery has been removed and the chocolate paint scraped off all the beams. The hatchments, altar rails and iron gates leading to the Hall were removed to London and restored by experts. Practically all the work was done by Mr & Mrs Tullo. They laboured unsparingly and had the knack of attracting willing helpers. Their name will always be remembered for having saved Foremarke Church from decay and turning it into a beautiful place of worship.*

I was appointed to the headship of Foremarke in 1985. I remember the newness of it all and rushing to answer the phone in my first week. A voice asked, 'May I speak with the Headmaster?' and I said without thinking, 'I'm so sorry, he left in August'. The Governors were good to me. They allowed £150,000 to spend on 'improvements' over my first two years. It was a tidy sum in those days and clever thinking on their part, for it gave me a much freer hand to formulate strategy with the staff. Lots of things were made possible: cosmetic improvements to the dining room, old block and bedders, landscaping Front Square, enlarging the tennis/netball courts, redecorating the principal rooms, and grudgingly spending money on replacing Westmorland slates on the five pitched roofs of the Hall with so little to show for it. Boarders were drier, of course!

During that first year I found that I had sole responsibility for 160 boarders after lights out. Bedders were situated on three floors – top, surgery and main – and keeping tabs on discipline when I didn't know Joe from Adam involved constant surveillance well after 11 p.m. Those causing disturbances were frogmarched with their duvets and separated, only to be released when all were sound asleep. On one occasion I forgot a boy planted in the Library. He had to be woken for breakfast. And on another, someone complained he could smell burning. Others in the bedder agreed. I sniffed the air but could detect nothing. Were they having me on? I told them I would search all rooms in the Hall and report back. I could detect nothing. However, as I opened the bedder door to give due reassurance, there was indeed a distinct whiff of burning. Action was called for. Sound the alarm! Evacuate the school! I dialled 999 full of self-importance. 'A boarding school did you say? What was the name again? How do you spell that? Where is it near?' It took nearly an hour for the ambulances, police and fire fighters to reach us, but long before they came I went outside to be ready for them. To my horror the air was thick with smoke but it was not coming from the Hall. It was from an adjacent field – the local farmer had been burning his stubble.

Then came the holidays, during which 26 boys rode bicycles from Land's End to John O'Groats accompanied in the saddle by an American ambassador whose son was in the party. He took more looking after than the rest of the group put together, especially when he forgot that we drive on the left.

Marketing the school during my first decade was the sole responsibility of the Headmaster. Maintaining numbers was, of course, the key to survival, and happily for me the late 1980s were buoyant times. There was a notable increase in girls, who eventually made up for more than one-third of our entry. Dissatisfaction with state education led many, especially ex-grammar school parents, to consider the independent sector. The government's Assisted Places Scheme helped the trend, too. However, in those days there was little concept of Repton and Foremarke providing continuity from 7 to 18, 'two schools offering one education'. Repton was well served by a number of prep schools, and housemasters were reluctant to have too many from one source.

At first, co-education at Repton was confined to the sixth form. Unlike the boys, there was no progression to Repton for

Lakeward bound.

the girls. They had to look for another school at 13 or even at 11, the age of entry for most girls' schools. By 1991 Repton adjusted to our needs, helped by a wind of change from an increasingly competitive market. Derby Grammar School for Boys was founded a little later and became a direct competitor for the Foremarke day market. Even so, within a decade our numbers had increased by over 100, with day pupils now outnumbering boarders by two to one.

With such growth came considerable restructuring. As a school we were more accountable to parents and to the Secretary of State for Education. No longer was the prep school head the first port of call for the parental query. Management committees, Directors of this and that, form tutors, bedder staff and Year Group Heads all came into play. Inspections were beefier, and the Social Services Department monitored boarding. Since my appointment the Headmaster's role had changed from being largely autocratic to being largely bureaucratic. By 1995 Foremarke was a big business with a

turnover of nearly £3 million, well managed by our own bursarial department. It is hard to believe that ten years earlier my predecessor, Tom Davies, managed the whole operation without even a bursar. How times had changed!

With strong growth came an expansion of facilities, necessary to accommodate a much bigger community and wider curriculum. Games and activities also benefited from a sports hall and indoor swimming pool, and there was a dedicated theatre for drama. But probably the most significant decision the Governing Body made since the starting of Foremarke in 1947 was giving the go-ahead for the development of a 'pre-prep', catering for children from as young as the age of three. All around us other independent schools were taking on younger and younger pupils, so when the decision was made in 1995 to start our own pre-prep within the grounds, we were the only prep school in the Midlands to be without one. I had mooted the possibility in 1989 when Home Farm, right on our doorstep, came up for

The lake at Foremarke.

sale, but the Governors felt then that we had a duty to protect St Wystan's, at the time a principal feeder for Foremarke and a school that had been founded at the turn of the century by the wife of the Headmaster of Repton. Such considerations were later to change when St Wystan's parents found Derby Grammar School more affordable.

Our expansion was made possible because we were able to buy land: the market garden, adjacent to Foremarke and part of the original estate, was up for sale and ideal for what we wanted. The pre-prep was purpose built and is now probably one of the best equipped in the country. The drive to get children very young is largely about loyalty. Once a child is in the system he or she is likely to stay the course and not be tempted by competitors, and that means a more stable base for Foremarke and, ultimately, Repton. Since 1996 it has been possible for a child to spend ten years at Foremarke.

So what about life at Foremarke and what it has meant to the vast majority of pupils? We are, of course, dealing with formative, biddable years and with compliant pupils who are easily engaged and much less likely to argue. But they found the

experiences of growing up in such an environment highly attractive with the lure of bomb pit and den building, midnight walks and, in my early days, acting as 'secret agents' in competitive groups let loose in the Peak District. The List of Events is littered with red letter days aimed to excite and to challenge. Inclusive plays involving huge casts, Shakespeare in the grounds, concerts, games fixtures, sports days, 'History mystery' excursions, the entrepreneurial zeal of school fetes, camps and 'wear-what-you-dare days' were an endless enterprise programme that complements all the hard work and serious business of academia and gives pupils the confidence to excel and to surprise themselves.

In making this happen we were blessed with a talented staff, teaching and non-teaching, who understood the prep school mindset and thrived on it. Most of us felt at home in the Peter Pan environment. Sir James Barrie once said, 'Nothing that happens after we are 12 matters very much.' Good teaching mattered. It is, quite simply, the essence of good schooling. And in our boarding community good matrons were the essence of good care. Of this we were reminded when we were celebrating

Ringing the changes at Foremarke.

50 years at Foremarke in 1997. We held three events for ex-pupils covering the eras of the three headmasters. It seemed universal that the prep school years were, without doubt, 'the happiest days …'.

One particular Speech Day is worthy of recall. It was in 1991 and our distinguished guest was none other than the Secretary of State for Northern Ireland, Peter Brooke, who had nephews at Foremarke. In those days Northern Ireland was a hot potato. There had been an IRA cell in Derby, and security was exacting. At 5.30 a.m. preparation began with scores of police, some with tracker dogs, checking drains, outbuildings and going through every room in the school, sealing doors once checked. Just before breakfast, as the dust was settling, I met a boarder coming down stairs.

> *'What's going on sir?'*
> *'Promise you won't tell?'*
> *'Yes.'*
> *'Well this is my last day at Foremarke and I'm rather afraid that the teachers might get their own back, so I have asked for police protection.'*
> *And I heard his voice trailing in Bottom Corridor, 'I know why all these police are here …'*

Happy selective memories! It was a privilege to have been entrusted with Foremarke for 15 years and to have worked amongst some inspiring people, young and old. There is something so special and unpretentious about the atmosphere at Foremarke, well established by Ken Jackson and developed by Tom Davies. Once absorbed, I recognized its importance.

Richard Theobald

FOREMARKE INTO THE 21ST CENTURY

'Standing on the shoulders of giants' – or at least following their well-crafted and entertaining prose – is a daunting task! I will limit myself to a simple situation report.

Debbie and I arrived at Foremarke in August 2000. We joined a school that faced challenges but did so with spirit. A full review of all aspects of school life was quickly followed by a number of important changes to the use of facilities and time in the day, but in all this we sought to preserve the important essence that is Foremarke: a happy blend of rigour and informality.

Boarding facilities were entirely upgraded in 2001–2, with Bottom Corridor becoming a boys' boarding house. In 2003 new AstroTurf was installed on top field, and in 2005 the pre-prep was finally completed with an impressive new nursery, a hall and a dedicated ICT suite. Tom Davies's 'New Block' was renamed the 'Tom Davies Building' and extended further to provide changing for seven- to nine-year-olds as well as three additional classrooms in 2006.

The school's five-year plan for 2007–12 encompasses even more ambitious plans, including a full extension and redevelopment of 'Chaggers' and the replacement of 'Old Block' with a brand-new, state-of-the-art classroom block.

Pupil numbers have moved to record levels, running counter to national trends, and the school presently accommodates almost 470 pupils aged from 2½ to 13. Sport goes from strength to strength in all areas – our boys have been national prep school soccer champions for two of the last three years.

Foremarke Hall may have changed its shape and size over the years, but I believe that it remains true to its roots and is a very special place to be, whether you are 12 or 52!

Paul Brewster

The Pre-Prep let off steam.

'Neither Tatty nor Tarty':
The Arrival of Girls at Repton

In retrospect, the most significant event of my headmastership was the admission of girls. But just as J.R. Seeley once wrote that the British Empire had been acquired in a 'fit of absence of mind', so the same might be said of Repton's admission of girls.

To understand how it came about one needs to go back to 1968, the year in which I was appointed to Repton, in which our daughter, Hilary, was completing her O levels at Sherborne School for Girls and in which John Dancey – a very old friend and then Master of Marlborough – admitted a clutch of 15 girls to his school. Hilary, who had a brother there already, was keen to be among the intrepid young women who entered Marlborough's Sixth Form, and this was a plan that my wife, Meg, and I strongly supported. Thus, although I didn't go to Repton with any missionary purpose in that direction, the idea of admitting girls to the sixth form of a boy's boarding school – an idea unthinkable only a short time before – was one with which I was familiar and comfortable.

I had been at Repton for about a year when a girl who lived in the village, entirely on her own initiative, came in and asked whether she could do her A levels in Repton's Sixth Form. I thought, 'Why not?', and was minded to accept her if the Chairman of Governors was agreeable. With a flash of inspiration he said, 'OK. As long as she can find another girl of the same age and inclination.' So the official response became, 'Yes, but you must find a like-minded friend to keep you company.' She did so, and that is how, in 1970, Carole Blackshaw and Sally Keenan became members of the Repton Sixth Form. In those days such a step was not exactly groundbreaking, but it was still quite unusual and hence attracted a certain amount of publicity in both the local and even the national press. (The question of fees was not difficult. As day girls they received only the teaching available to the sixth form, with none of the sporting or other facilities; they were charged a day boy's fees minus a substantial discount.)

Not very long afterwards the Chaplain offered me his resignation (for completely unrelated reasons). The man whom I wished to replace him had four children, of whom two were girls of Repton age. He wanted to take the job but he also wanted to send his daughters to Repton. The fortress had already been breached and I wanted him to take the job, so I agreed, and in 1971 Linda and Diana Soper joined the school, doubling the number of girls.

Other members of staff began to ask if their daughters could come to Repton, and were told, 'Yes, at sixth form level', Diana Soper being the sole and exceptional lower school girl. The general principle had thus been established that Repton

A future Lady Mayoress of the City of London in Andrew Rudolf's History Set.

Sixth Form was open to the daughters of members of staff and local day girls of the right age.

The next significant event was brought about by a visit from A. Steele-Bodger, the brother of England rugby international Micky Steele-Bodger and an equally commanding figure, with whom one would not wish to argue. Mr Steele-Bodger wished to send his daughters to the school. When I pointed out that he lived too far away for them to be day girls he suggested that they might find digs in the village. I said, 'Yes – if there were members of the Repton staff willing to act as their hosts,' as this would not only offer a welcome additional source of income to members of the common room but also provide the school with greater control over proceedings.

The Mitre.

Co-educational Repton today. Ian McClary teaching in the English Department in the refurbished Old Mitre.

Two Steele–Bodger girls duly arrived – Fiona in 1972 and Gillian a year later – and became the first non-local girls at Repton. During their time in the Sixth Form the neighbourhood became increasingly aware of this semi-boarding status, and the number of girls increased annually to a point where there were 16 girls in the school, at which stage the Bursar said that we could afford to build a girls' house without having to go to the bank.

As Headmaster I was always conscious – perhaps too conscious – of the balance sheet, and it seemed sensible at least to investigate the possibility of taking in more girls in the Sixth Form, especially as this was working so well at schools like Marlborough. I thought it important to consult Common Room and called a special staff meeting to decide whether we should stop dipping our toes in the water and take the plunge by creating a sixth form girls' house, girls having hitherto had their base in the Sanatorium. To my surprise and great pleasure, the proposal was passed nem. con., with only one abstention. This was not only because of the prospect of giving their own daughters a Repton sixth form education, but also because, having had experience of teaching girls in the school, the staff felt that it was a good idea in itself.

The Governing Body gave its approval, and planning permission was sought and gained, so that the construction of what became the Abbey had already started when I left Repton in July 1978. The house was so named on the grounds that Repton had once had a religious house for both men and women and ruled over by an abbess. In addition, the Abbey chimed with the ecclesiastical nomenclature of the Priory and the Mitre.

Jill and Gerry Pellow became the Abbey's first house-parents. About a year before the house was opened, they took over the responsibility for the girls already in the school from Heather Hawkins, who, assisted by her husband Dennis and with three daughters of her own, had been in charge of the first

> *The school instilled in me solid values from a young age and gave me the confidence to go out in the world to do things that I might not otherwise have done. For all this I am very grateful and I'm proud to be an Old Reptonian.*
>
> **Amanda Fallon (G 1996)**

'*Repton gave me a solid academic grounding that has opened many doors, but it was education in its broadest sense – camaraderie, good manners and thoughtfulness, which were instilled in me during my formative years there – that allowed me to seize those opportunities. I am indebted to my inspiring mentors, and have treasured the friendships formed.*'

Ji-Peng Olivia Li (F 1997)

'*House spirit is one of the things that makes Repton so special. When at school it shapes your identity and makes everyone feel part of the team. When you leave, you take that spirit with you ... once a Field House girl, always a Field House girl!*'

Sarah Taylor (F 1998)

girls. Heather had the enviable knack of keeping the girls on the right road with a light touch, and it was in these early days that certain ground rules were established for the girls. For example, whereas boys were addressed in those days by their surnames, it was decided that girls should be 'Miss X' or 'Miss Y' (though this did not last long). The question of dress had also raised its potentially troublesome head at quite an early stage, and the general rule of thumb – 'neither tatty nor tarty' – had been established.

The year 1979 not only saw the first woman occupant of 10 Downing Street but also the arrival of the first real girl boarders to Repton. The admission of girls to the school may have had much of the ad hoc about it in the very early days, but I am modestly proud of the way in which Repton had, by the end of my headmastership, consciously embraced the spirit of co-education and was well on the way to providing proper facilities for girls.

John Gammell

Left: Studious in Sykes Corridor.

Some Recollections of the Early Days of Girls at Repton

When Fiona Steele-Bodger became the first boarder, the Headmaster, John Gammell, asked me to act as housemistress to the girls, 'a mixture of academic organizer and moral guide'. This was the beginning of the corporate life of the girls. A room had already been set aside for them in the Hall where they could relax together and drink coffee. We met for lunch twice a week at Askew Cottage (the home I shared with Dennis Hawkins, the Director of Art), and we discussed current problems and ideas for their further unique contribution to the life of the school. Personal relationships were a vital and sometimes difficult topic! Guidance was backed up by rules about the hours in which girls might visit boys' studies and about public behaviour – no walking about holding hands and the like. As far as I can observe, this rule, which took a little initial enforcing, seems to be still alive and well!

Heather Hawkins and Sixth Form Girls, 1973.

Group feeling was now strong enough to demand a house photograph, which was taken outside Askew Cottage in the summer of 1973. The lack of any uniformity of dress, which so annoyed many boys, is very evident!

By Michaelmas 1973 there were eight or nine girls in the school, and the need for a space of their own became pressing. We were given our first 'day-centre' in a pre-fabricated building, called the Terrapin, behind the Art School. Furnished with easy chairs and a few tables, it served as common room, study and games room. It was also the changing room. Squash and tennis were now organized activities, and the girls were coached by Nim Wilkinson, herself a county tennis player. Any interviews with the Housemistress took place in her study, a large, but well-furnished, broom-cupboard! But, however small the nest, the girls were starting to soar! Jane Bossons was the first girl to take the lead in a school play, which she did twice, and was then joint-winner of the drama prize. Most girls entered the Duke of Edinburgh Award scheme, and one, Vivienne Sharpe (A 1973), became a member of the CCF Commandos. As a group they were confident enough to put on their own house play, *World of Women*. It was clear that the girls were here to stay!

1975 was the year of the most significant and exciting progress. Numbers had now risen to 11, and these girls moved into the east end of the old sanatorium (now the Music School). By the end of the year we had a common room, a quiet room, a proper study for the Housemistress and a dining room. Although the boarders were still lodging with staff in the village, the girls could eat lunch and an evening meal together five days a week thanks to the good offices of the School Matron, Catherine Hadwen, and her staff, who gave great support to this new development. We were able to entertain guests to lunch, both other members of staff and visitors, and we also had the space to invite a housemaster's wife, Pauline Bryant, to run a ballroom dancing class, which proved to be a well-attended out-of-school activity.

In this new setting the spirit of a community grew and flourished. We had long discussions on how we wished to be together as a group within a larger society. There was a general consensus that rules should be kept to a minimum and that common sense and courtesy should guide behaviour. From the beginning the girls had been sensible of the fact that they were pioneers – and highly visible ones – and that they were setting a pattern for the future. It was at this point that, as a mark of their developing importance within the school, that they acquired a name. Many suggestions – both serious and ribald – were made before the Headmaster in a letter to parents announced the final choice. He wrote:

> *We think it is time that the girls' house had a name. In Saxon times there was an abbey at Repton. Of this foundation, Alec Macdonald, who was a master here 50 years ago, wrote in his History of Repton 'like most Saxon monasteries, especially those of the northern church, it was open to men and women alike;' it therefore seems appropriate that the girls' house be known as the Abbey.*

Now that we were recognized by name we were able to appoint a Head of House, Sue Anderson (A 1974), who became the first girl to be a School Prefect. Her enthusiasm and unobtrusive leadership contributed greatly to the active and happy life of the new Abbey. The academic successes continued and increased, girls' names appearing in every type of award. Music and drama continued to be well supported by the girls, but now there was also an interesting fixture list for the hockey team. Perhaps one of my favourite recollections from this time is the first stall the new Abbey organized for the Sale of Work, selling homemade sweets. The initial chaos of sugary stickiness and wrapping paper was well rewarded by a handsome sum of money for charity and the satisfaction of a team effort.

This seems a good point at which to leave these recollections. The next few years saw an ever-increasing need for *Lebensraum*, temporarily answered by expansion into other parts of the San, but leading to the building of the present Abbey House.

I wonder whether boys – and present girls – can realize the courage that was needed to take part, as a minority group, in many activities for the first time. In those early days the girls came to join the sixth form because they were aware that this boys' school had many more opportunities to offer them in academic standards and cultural life than their single-sex schools. They, in turn, had something to give the school in their individual talent

and, often, in an alternative way of looking at things, in a different order of values. In 1979 the opening of the custom-built girls' house set the seal of recognition on the fact that boys and girls learn with and through each other and, hopefully, develop that respect and understanding of difference that makes a happy life possible.

Heather Hawkins

A moment of leisure in the Mitre.

The Hong Kong Connection

Hong Kong has a long and close association with Repton. The first Reptonian was Andrew K.N. Li (H), who entered the school in the Michaelmas Term of 1963. Repton was recommended to his parents by the Anglican Bishop of Hong Kong of that time, Bishop R.O. Hall. It was thus Repton's strong association with the Church of England that was instrumental in forging the Hong Kong connection.

Andrew was the only Chinese student at Repton until 1965 when his brother Michael (H) joined him. Andrew went on to Cambridge to read Law and after pupillage in London returned to practise in Hong Kong. He was appointed Queen's Counsel in 1988 and in 1997 was appointed Chief Justice of Hong Kong SAR.

I was at Repton myself (L 1966) before reading Electrical Engineering at Imperial College, London and then obtaining a Master of Science degree at Stanford. When I started at Repton the Hong Kong contingent had grown to around 10 pupils.

It was natural that the able and ambitious should look beyond Hong Kong for before 1963 it had only one accredited university. Places were obviously very limited and most higher professional qualifications needed to be obtained in the UK. Moreover, at that time the local primary and secondary schools had an average class size of over 40 pupils and there was very limited, if any, space for sporting activities. Thus many of those parents who possessed sufficient resources sent their children to UK boarding schools to give them the opportunity for a better education. Repton was a very popular choice, with parents hoping that their offspring would acquire some knowledge, a better command of English, the ability to interact with their peers and the strength of character to surmount problems later in life.

Today the Hong Kong contingent has grown to roughly 20 pupils split fairly evenly between the two sexes and there are now well over 100 Old Reptonians who originated from Hong Kong. Many have cherished memories of their time in Repton, although its food is rarely remembered fondly, particularly by the boys!

M. Tam, A. Kong and E. Niem in the Latham Dinning Room, 1968.

The Old Reptonians in Hong Kong are active in a variety of professions and some of the older ones are eminent in their fields. Mention has already been made of Andrew Li, the Chief Justice of Hong Kong.

Whenever the school has sought to raise funds the Hong Kong Old Reptonians have responded generously to the call. They were in the forefront, for example, of funding the building of the Studio Theatre in 2003. Dieter L.T.Yih (H 1982), Jean Paul Yih (H 1982), E.Y. F. Niem (L 1966), A. S. L. Chiu, A. C. T. Kong (L 1966), E. C. S. Kong (N 1967), I.C.M. Kong (N 1973), D.T.Y. Chui (P 1989), M. S. M. Chui (G 1992), M. K.W. Tam (L 1966), K. T. R. Tam (L 1970), K.Y. H. Wong (N 1977), D.Y. K. Wong (N 1977), R. J. R. Owen (P 1953) and The Hon Mr Justice A. K. N. Li (H 1963) were particularly generous in their donations.

Eddie Niem (L 1966)

Copies of 'The Reptonian' in the Audit Room.

THE
REPTONIAN
—
1897-98.

REPTONIAN
1897-8

THE
REPTONIAN

THE
REPTONIAN
—
1899-1900.

1898-1900

ART

There have been only four Directors of Art at Repton. Before Maurice Clarke in 1909, Art was taught by drawing masters who were teaching it as a second or third subject. Excellent though some of these well-meaning amateur artists were, with no permanent home and no curriculum, few boys made art.

From the time of its conversion from gymnasium to Art Room in 1915 the Tithe Barn was the centre of the visual creative impulses of the boys in the school until 1975, when Dennis Hawkins moved the department into the village primary school. In this period Art was taught by practitioners, and the Tithe Barn Art Room was a dark jumble of stools, benches, cupboards, drapes and still objects. The evidence of this is both in the paintings made in the period and from the contemporary photographic records of the building.

The years 1915 to 1930 were a golden age of art at Repton. The list of renowned artists cultivated under Clarke, Norris and his assistant, Harold Gresley, from that time included Anthony Gross (H 1919), Rupert Shepherd (H 1922), Brian Cook Batsford (N 1924), Anthony Devas (P 1924), Denton Welch (B 1929) and, for his contribution to photography, Roald Dahl (P 1930).

Anthony Gross is perhaps the most renowned of all Repton artists of the 20th century. He published his first etching while he was still at school and exhibited in the Paris Salon soon after leaving Repton in 1924. His reputation was based on his career as a printmaker but he was also recognized as an outstanding painter and for his two highly ingenious animated colour films, *La Joie de vivre* and *Around the World in Eighty Days*.

I was fortunate enough to meet two artists from that period. The first was Rupert Shepherd, an eminent painter and teacher whom I met in his studio in Chelsea when he was executing the portrait of the late David Jewell. As a result of that encounter, he offered to exhibit a selection of paintings he had made while a boy under the tutelage of Arty Norris and the expert visiting watercolour artist Harold Gresley. Norris was a

The Art School, Tithe Barn.

Masonry from the Priory Church, in the Undercroft.

Denton Welch self-portrait.

Anthony Gross painted by Alfred E. Orr, 1926.

good painter but not in the same mould as Gresley, who was an outstanding exponent of the watercolour tradition. It seems also that the more proficient you became, the further afield you went to paint with the tutors. The evidence for this is in the pictures of the scenes looking back at school made by Norris, Gresley and the boys in fields as far away as Willington and Newton Solney.

The second person from that period whom I got to know well was the Foundation Benefactor Robert Beldam (P 1927). My first encounter with him was when the school commissioned Patrick Gibbs (tutor and artist-in-residence 1987) to paint his portrait for the Beldam Concert Hall in the Music School. Robert was, in his day, a prize-winning artist and had ambitions to train at the Slade School of Art, which for Reptonians was the favoured graduate establishment. In fact, Clarke, Norris and Hawkins were all Slade trained, as, too, were

all the aforementioned famous pupil artists. However, Robert will be best remembered for his selfless generosity to the school and to the Art School from 1999 onwards, when he single-handedly paid for the complete rebuilding of the department in four phases of development. As a result of that generosity, thousands of Reptonians will benefit from his vision and beneficence in the decades to come.

In Dennis Hawkins, Norris's successor, the school had one of the greatest painters of his generation teaching and practising at Repton. In contrast to his predecessor, Dennis was a modernist, and it is hard to imagine the change that he would have brought to the school in 1952 with his youth and vitality. From the start he was an encourager of talent among the boys. Numerous ORs testify to his enthusiasm, drive, quiet manner, intellect and warmth. A Quaker and staunch supporter of Amnesty International, a glider pilot and sailor, Dennis brought a wealth of knowledge and experience to the department and school as well as an immense talent for fine and applied arts. He believed in the importance of drawing and practised everyday as an artist with the pupils. He was a man of boundless energy and ambition, executing big work with the boys in the Art School and on the stage of the 400 Hall. He was also responsible for moving the Art Department into its current premises. This put the department in a prominent and highly visual setting in the heart of the village and made it geographically independent of the rest of the school. The dislocation of the building from the other academic departments was very much in keeping with Dennis's notion of the distinctive nature of his teaching and the subject: as a cultural lifeboat in glorious isolation in a school of Philistines.

John Thorn speaks warmly of Dennis the teacher and the man in *The Road to Winchester*.

On half holidays, when the inescapable compulsory games were over, the Art School filled with boys. Dennis appeared to take no notice of them and was often to be found hard at his own work. But that was an illusion. He was teaching them all, for they approached him freely and fearlessly, called him over to tell them what to do next, engaged him in discussions on religion, literature, aesthetics, or motor cars.

Roald Dahl (with camera), c 1930.

'*Repton provided some of the best times of my life, mainly due to my time in Field House, Sarah Tennant and Bren being like an extended family. It was such a welcoming and friendly atmosphere in Field, and the friends I met from all years I'm sure I'll stay in touch with for life. One area of Repton that I took advantage of was the Art department: nowhere at Repton was there a better place to relax and to work. Only now do I realize how much fun I had at the school and want to thank everyone that made my time there so special.*'

Lydia Wilkinson (F 1999)

As beneficiaries of Robert Beldam's generosity, in September 1999, in the 14th year of my incumbency as Head of Art, the department moved into the first phase of the newly renovated Art School. Over the next four years the department was completely redesigned to suit the needs of the expanding numbers of pupils taking the subject at examination level and their ambitious schemes as artists. The department now has two painting studios, a large photographic darkroom, a pottery, a sculpture studio, library, computer suite and gallery space, all of which resonate late into the evening with the sound of the pupils hard at work. This buzz of hard work, striving for excellence and intelligent debate continues at every level of the work in the present day Art School.

The current Head of Art is a career teacher. However, the notion that Reptonians are taught by practitioners has been at the heart of the work in the Art School since 1985 and is still very much in evidence with the artists-in-residence/part-time teachers programme. 2007 sees the Artists-in-Residence move into new studios in the Old Squash Courts on the Burton Road, which will also provide the school with a Textiles Department and a large gallery space. The five artists who teach in the department provide the foundation for boys and girls to continue to find the creation of art an enjoyment, a simulating academic subject, a path to successful careers, an entry into further education, a skill learned for life and a refuge at the heart of the Repton school community.

Jeremy Bournon

Drama

THE 400 HALL: THE FIRST 40 YEARS

In 1957, to mark Repton's 400th Anniversary, Lynam Thomas proposed that a theatre should be built in the new precinct, across the road from the Arch.

Hitherto school plays had been presented in Pears School during Speech Day week (then in June). The proscenium arch, the curtaining to mask the stage, the lights with all their wiring and equipment, machinery to open and close the curtains and, of course, all the scenery and props had to be built and in place in time for the dress rehearsal, and then to be dismantled immediately after the final performance to leave the stage clear for speeches. It placed heavy burdens on the stage manager and his light, sound and stage staff.

Other productions, including the Pedants (every four years), staff plays (mostly once a year) and occasional house plays, were also put on in Pears School when possible, most house plays taking place in house dining halls after the end-of-term suppers.

For school plays the casts had to change and apply make-up in the Cloisters classrooms or up the narrow spiral staircase in the Tower, where the small green room housed the costumes. Masters who taught in the Cloisters (including the formidable Dick Sale) complained frequently about wads of cotton wool all over the floor, sticks of make-up left on desks and inappropriate messages scrawled on blackboards.

Audiences, especially if vertically challenged, found it difficult to see the stage and hear the actors unless they were sitting in the front few rows.

So a new hall, primarily intended for play productions, was an urgent need and eagerly awaited.

400 Hall Comedy.

400 Hall Tragedy.

'A Midsummer Night's Dream', 2004.

Michael Barnwell (O 1957) as Ophelia in the first play produced on the 400 Hall stage.

dress rehearsal. There were around 180 separate lighting cues in *Hamlet*, and the lighting crew had to operate blind as the lighting panel was behind the proscenium arch and level with the top of it. When the stage curtains were hung, it was virtually impossible to check which lights were on and where they were pointing. Michael Milford and his crew worked gallantly with the newly installed, totally unfamiliar switchboard but couldn't see the effects of their work, and it was a miracle they managed as competently as they did. (It was about 20 years before we were able to move them to the OR Room and have holes put in the wall there so the crew could actually see what they were doing.)

To make matters worse, on the first night someone came into the auditorium just as the first big scene-change was taking place (transforming the misty battlements into the brightly lit royal court) and said to me, 'Please stop the show and ask if Mr So-and-so [chief surgeon at the Derbyshire Royal Infirmary] is in the theatre, as he is urgently required in the hospital.' I had to dash round to the back of the stage, hastily brief the stage manager, sound and light people, and abruptly break into the big court scene to make the announcement. All the cast had then to quit the stage and repeat the grand entry of the court, so they could re-focus on the play and resynchronize the sound and light changes. Of course, Mr So-and-so was not present. I began to wonder if the theatre was jinxed.

We happened to have two outstanding young actors that year, Rodney Knight (O 1954) and Andrew Urquhart (O 1955). Unable to decide which to cast as Hamlet and which as the King, I asked them how they would feel about each playing both parts. Both thought that alternating was a great idea and eagerly settled down to learn both parts.

The original proposal was that it should seat 200–250 but under pressure from those who felt that a hall that could seat fewer than half the school could prove to be a white elephant, the number 400 was agreed on: hence the name, 400 Hall, a building to seat 400 and to celebrate Repton's 400th Anniversary. (I don't think its cost was £400,000.)

The year 1957 was my third in charge of school drama, but it wasn't until the summer term of 1959 that we were able to use the 400 Hall stage, and the building was not completed until the week before Speech Day. The opening production, *Hamlet*, was rehearsed in the last few weeks of building work, and the lighting board wasn't finally installed until the day of the first

Both their Housemaster and the Headmaster became anxious that they might be taking on more than they could fairly manage, so I gingerly approached the one who, at that time, seemed to be the marginally better Hamlet. However, he was adamant that it would be totally unfair to his rival (who happened to be a good friend) not to have his chance at both parts. The Headmaster, secretly rather pleased, I felt, by this reaction, allowed them to proceed and neither made any mistakes, though each placed different emphases on his

Mike Charlesworth directing the School play.

characterizations (both as Prince and King), and it was very hard to judge whose performance (in either part) was the better. Both sailed through their A levels.

However, it became clear during the run of *Hamlet* that our brave new theatre was by no means perfect. Among its most obvious drawbacks was that, as built, it could not achieve a complete blackout, a pre-requisite in any theatre. Thus 'dead' bodies could be seen walking off stage unaided, and stagehands in modern dress were visible changing the set.

It was some consolation when I went to the opening of *Macbeth* in the new Uppingham theatre. Boys there had soon found that they could fill their theatre with a swelling sound of mooing cows by simply massaging the expensive leather seats. At least our less luxurious seats were silent (unless knocked over).

We were too delighted just to have a new theatre of our own to look that gift horse in the mouth, but we soon became aware of other shortcomings. The stage, for instance, had a hard, shiny, wooden surface, which could be distractingly noisy when walked across in hard shoes. And it was alarmingly slippery for Laertes and Hamlet to duel on it. The stage and auditorium floors, assiduously polished by bursarial staff, were potentially perilous. One lady, arriving late for a performance, tripped and broke her leg. Fortunately, these were days of stoicism rather than litigation.

A further misfortune was that the 400 Hall had been built over a hidden spring. This, from time to time, flooded the dressing rooms under the stage, saturating the costumes stored there. The legendary patience of our indefatigable wardrobe mistresses, Jill Pellow and Patricia Wilmot, was sorely tested.

Nor was there (until a long shed was built at the back some years later) anywhere suitable to paint scenery, a notoriously

messy job. Luckless stage hands tried to do the painting outside, but that needed dry weather and risked a ticking off for spilling paint on the precinct's lawns and footpaths, which were among Repton's showpieces.

It was clear that the distinguished architect, Marshal Sissons, had given us a handsome hall for our quatercentenary, but a hall that had serious limitations as a theatre.

Nevertheless, it has proved surprisingly adaptable and has housed a wide range of productions. Plays of all kinds, from Brecht to Shakespeare, from Restoration comedy to Victorian farce, from monologues to musicals, have presented Reptonians with plenty of opportunities to experience live theatre, and for that we should all be grateful.

The arrival of girls greatly enhanced the school's drama, both in terms of the scope of plays we were able to mount and of the confidence with which we could present them.

There had been many outstanding performance by boys playing women's parts: Andrew Urquhart as Beatrice in *Much Ado About Nothing*, Paul Whitworth as Abigail and Neil Munro (both H 1963) as Elizabeth Proctor in *The Crucible*, James Francis (H 1951) as Mrs Posket in *The Magistrate* were all exceptional performances. But trebles were increasingly reluctant to be cast as sopranos, and the school's theatre has been greatly enriched by the presence of girls in ever larger numbers.

Having been associated with the 400 Hall since its opening and been in charge of drama at the school for most of the time between 1954 and my retirement in 1989 (and with two school productions by way of a postscript in 1998 and 1999, when I stood in for the then head of drama who was ill), I hope I may be forgiven a few reminiscences.

I found it helpful to audition a potential cast before choosing a play. That's not such a cock-eyed idea as it may sound. When we had few strong singers a musical would have been unwise. When talented comic actors preponderated, a Restoration comedy, French farce or witty modern play could be chosen. If we had a few really strong performers it was time to tackle *Macbeth* or *King Lear* or a modern tragedy, such as Arthur Miller's *The Crucible* or Brecht's *Galileo*.

In general it seemed to work out that in a three-year cycle one play would be Shakespeare, one a relatively modern play, and the third might be a musical. The most enjoyable – and most exhausting – of the latter were the three 'homemade' musicals we put on in the 1960s, when William Agnew (N 1945) was Director of Music. It happened that, before then, I'd adapted *The Beaux' Stratagem* as a musical, using (with permission) tunes from *Lock Up Your Daughters*. I asked William if he could teach the cast the (adapted) songs and accompany them in the show, which he successfully did.

Mike Charlesworth about to perform in the 1955 Pedants.

After it was over, William suggested that we write a musical of our own, an adaptation of the novel *Don't Mr Disraeli* by Caryl Brahms and S.J. Simon, which was a comic version of a Victorian *Romeo and Juliet*.

William was happily gifted with a rich vein of melody and composed a string of delightful songs. I enjoyed the challenge of playing with rhyme and rhythm and inventing lyrics. Over the next six or seven years we collaborated on three musicals: *Bite Your Thumb*, the Victorian *Romeo and Juliet*; *Curry Favours*, an original script about the shady goings-on in an officers' mess in India in the 1890s, the two most memorable songs in which were 'Other Men's Wives' and 'Don't Mention a Lady's Name in the Mess'; and *Phineas Finn*, an adaptation of Anthony Trollope's novel.

Hectic as it was for William and me to write, rehearse, organize and present 2½-hour musicals and run our respective Music and English departments (all in the course of some three months for each musical) it was hugely enjoyable, especially in the week of performance, by which time William's fingers were bleeding from the pressure of accompanying so many rehearsals and I was dizzy after choreographing something like 20 songs in each show.

There were some near disasters. Christopher Frayling (P 1960, now Rector of the Royal College of Art and Chairman of the Arts Council) was in his first year at Repton and, as the school's best treble, was playing the 'Juliet' part in *Bite Your Thumb*. He had many songs to sing and some vigorous fast waltzing to perform – and he broke his leg in the week before performance. Although he missed some key rehearsals, he gallantly returned in time for the dress rehearsal with one leg encased in heavy plaster. His dancing was understandably rather rigid. But he kept going and performed heroically.

In *Curry Favours* we needed a strong chorus of trebles, so employed about 20 B Block boys (as urchins in some scenes and mess waiters in others). They raced about, singing their hearts out and trying to drown the tenors and basses. And for the party after the final performance those turbaned trebles, still in mess waiter kit, carried round trays of curry, which we'd bought from a Derby Indian restaurant. (The curry arrived in a large dustbin-like, but very clean, container.)

Phineas Finn was, by common consent, the best of the three musically. The lead role was beautifully sung by Philip Dennis (H 1962, now a professional singer), and we had plenty of talent to back him up.

Soon after that, however, William went on to be Head of Music at Bedales, and I became Housemaster of the Hall. No more homemade musicals.

While I was at the Hall, Gareth Williams, my Assistant Housemaster, took over the school drama, which I had begun to find incompatible with full-time teaching and running a double-size house. He put on a brilliant *West Side Story* and *Oh What a Lovely War*, and I repeated *The Beaux' Stratagem* as a House play, so musicals were still in the school drama repertoire.

The staff production of 'The Italian Straw Hat', Repton, 1956.

Later, after I'd finished at the Hall and Gareth had gone to teach at Tonbridge, I again became Director of Drama. Together with Michael Salter (i/c music) we put on *Guys and Dolls*, which reminded me how much fun a musical could be.

We initially had problems over the audibility of one or two singers, because the score for *Guys and Dolls* is quite a noisy one, and the only place for the orchestra to play is in the orchestra pit, between the stage and the audience. I was against using microphones, which were very unreliable in those days and prone to feedback. The problem was solved by building a walkway round the orchestra pit, with a forestage in front of it. Once the orchestra was in place and Michael was ready to start the overture, a hinged section of the walkway was lowered and the orchestra were sealed in. Then, as soon as one of our softer voices was about to sing, they would set off and sing their way round the walkway to the forestage. From there the singer could be easily heard, with the orchestra now behind them.

I've said a lot about musicals, which generate an extra dimension of excitement, but there is a musical quality in Shakespearean language, and we put on a great many Shakespeare plays. This was partly because they have big casts and so give a greater number of students the chance of acting, but it was chiefly because it seemed important to give each generation the opportunity of experiencing, from the inside, the greatest plays this country has produced. Greatness of language, of thought and of characterization – all that in Shakespeare brings an extra dimension of its own. And in my 15 years as Housemaster of the Hall I could even include some Shakespeare among our house plays. At that time we had up to 110 boys in the House, and by combining with the Abbey we

were able to put on *The Taming of the Shrew* and musical versions of *The Comedy of Errors* (with two pairs of identical twins, one of the two wealthier twins being Guy Levesley, H 1975) and of *The Merry Wives of Windsor* (my final Hall production).

Soon after I completed my 15-year stint at the Hall, I was happy to resume the responsibility for Repton drama until my retirement in 1989.

Between 1954 and 1989, apart from the musicals and Shakespeare plays mentioned earlier, we put on *Much Ado About Nothing*, *Macbeth*, *King Lear*, *The Winter's Tale* and *Love's Labours Lost*. Other productions included Congreve's *The Way of the World* and *Love for Love*, Anouilh's *Antigone* and *Ring Round the Moon*, Fry's *The Lady's Not for Burning*, Brecht's *Galileo*, Hochwaelder's *The Strong are Lonely*, Priestley's *When We are Married*, Dylan Thomas's *Under Milk Wood* and two Feydeau farces.

Meanwhile Sir John Port's Pedants continued to flourish every four years, presenting the staff's view of Repton and much else besides. Few will forget the Bolshie Ballet and its version of Swan Lake, with first Peter Toynbee and then Roy French irresistible as the Dying Swan, Barry Downing with a long hunting horn as the dashing Prince Siegfried and Russell Muir as the Black Russell Fairy. Or *The Sound of Music*, with David Wilkinson as the Abbess. At the start he was seated, in nun's habit. But when he stood he was in mountaineer's kit from the waist down and passionately sang 'Climb Every Mountain' as he clambered furiously up and down over the set. There were staff plays and house plays, and (at the initial suggestion of John Thorn) a set of B Block plays was introduced, which did wonders for the confidence of many a shy new arrival.

My successor in 1989 was Martin Amherst Lock. He had already proved an invaluable assistant in my last few school plays, and once he was in charge himself he directed a number of impressively elegant, thoughtful and well-spoken productions. He was always a perfectionist, and I remember as particularly outstanding his productions of *A Man for All Seasons* and *Amadeus*. But his finest achievement was a gripping production of *Cabaret*.

A final glance at more of the 400 Hall's shortcomings. With its dominating proscenium arch, its relatively high stage, its limited wing space and its initial decor, the 400 Hall at first looked distinguished but rather inflexible. Over the years that look has markedly changed, losing the bright colours in favour of darker hues, which are better suited to a working stage.

For a long time the heating gave problems. The ground floor of the auditorium – especially toward the front, near the two sets of draughty and noisy doors by the orchestra pit – used

Shakespeare in the 400 Hall.

to be decidedly chilly. Meanwhile, the gallery (often something of a staff preserve) collected stuffy hot air. I believe that recent improvements have at last eased the air-circulation problem.

Much has been done to improve the lights, which are now (as they should be) mostly hung on secure bars from the auditorium roof. In the early days there were only six smallish lights to brighten the wide area in front of the tabs. We first added some stronger lights on vertical bars up the sides of the auditorium, but getting at them to adjust them could be perilous. One of the light crew had to climb up a long metal ladder, and because the floor was so slippery another of the crew had to stand at the foot of the ladder. I still have nightmares about the occasion when I entered the theatre and saw no one standing at the foot of the ladder, which was just slipping as a crew member was at the top peering at a light. The ladder crashed to the floor, and the boy followed it. Luckily, with great presence of mind, he clawed at the long window curtains as he fell, reducing the pace of his fall sufficiently for his injuries to be only superficial. But the memory stays with me to this day.

Another catastrophe was narrowly averted when a grand piano had been wheeled out into the open on a cold, wet winter evening. Arriving to find it in that woeful state is another of my recurring nightmares.

Perhaps my grimmest memory of the building was when we were rehearsing my first *Macbeth* in the 1960s. The Priory boy playing Macbeth was a strong actor but had a weak memory. Moreover, he seemed to have made little effort to learn his lines. In the penultimate week I repeatedly warned him that I couldn't let him go on stage with the important fifth act seemingly absent from his memory. 'If you don't know it by heart at the dress rehearsal,' I told him, 'I'll play it myself.'

The dress rehearsal came. He coped reasonably well with the first four acts. But as he was furiously attacking the 'Cream-

faced loon', I could see he was losing it, with several pages of script still to come. He took his copy from his pocket and started to read his part. I decided on shock tactics. 'GET OFF THE STAGE,' I bellowed and climbed on to it myself, while he disappeared. (Evidently he went to the bridge over the Old Trent and contemplated suicide, so he told me subsequently.) I didn't, of course, know every word – but I knew a good deal more of Act V than he did and didn't use a book. Risky as it was, the show of fury on my part worked.

'Can you learn it?' I asked him on his return to the theatre, knowing that we had under 48 hours to performance. Considerably shaken, he said he thought he could. And he was as good as his word. He stumbled now and again, but kept going. Sometimes only an explosion will bring about results, but I don't recommend it. That one shook me almost as much as it shook Macbeth!

The 400 Hall may sometimes have been jinxed, and it has had its frustrating moments, but it has enabled us to put on all those plays I've mentioned and a great many more. We couldn't have done anything like so many productions on the old Pears School stage. We owe a great debt to Lynam Thomas and everyone who contributed to the financing and building of the 400 Hall. It may not be perfect, but it has given great pleasure to many Reptonians for nearly half a century. Good luck to all who sail in her!

Mike Charlesworth

Open-air drama in the Garth.

'Revizor (The Government Inspector)', 2005.

REPTON DRAMA, 1999 TO THE PRESENT

When I arrived in 1999, fresh from Hampton School and the Edinburgh Festival Fringe, it was clear that the 400 Hall was indeed a space that had its limitations but also that it would be the envy of many schools. Beyond the proscenium arch was a good stage, complete with trapdoor, gallery, cyclorama and enough lighting bars for an ambitious rig. The wings were small but serviceable, and there was the machinery for flying in small pieces of scenery and furniture, even if not a full-size fly tower. However, there was much to be done to bring some of the auditorium up to scratch and, with the Governors' generous help, I was soon able to replace all of the black drapes on the stage and the navy front of house tabs. There was not quite enough money to replace the curtains throughout the auditorium, which, as Mike Charlesworth has said, let in

> *Having lived in Repton for 12 years before attending the school, I had always looked forward to the days of playing cricket on the square, buying sweets from "the Grubber" and wearing a suit like those grown-up-looking pupils! Little did I realize the quality of teaching or the extreme variety of challenges and opportunities ahead of me.*
>
> **Tom Auden (O 1999)**

annoying shafts of light during the summer, so they were cleaned and fire-proofed. It was only then that it was found that the original curtains had been hung upside down, their fabric thus catching even more dirt than normal. This may, of course, have added extra friction for the lad who slid down them!

With some keen volunteers the next task was painting as much as possible in matt black emulsion. Also in my first year came the purchase of a sophisticated new mixing desk for sound control and an overhaul of the entire sound system.

That said, the stage is high and, for a decent view, one has to sit at least 10 feet back from it. For this reason my first school play, Orton's *What the Butler Saw*, was performed at an angle in the corner, almost under the gallery, and hired seating was tiered in the shape of a rough amphitheatre. There was some discontent about there only being six in the cast, even if the six included George Rainsford (M 1996) and Ashley Williamson (N 1995), both of whom went on to drama school and careers in the theatre. I couldn't go wrong with them in the cast, but since then school plays have required large casts as was traditional – and right.

The plays have included *Twelfth Night* and *The Roses of Eyam*, both of which benefited from some excellent set building and painting by John Ward, Jeremy Bournon and James Matthews. In the Shakespeare Tom Hird (P 2000) was a memorable Sir Andrew, resplendent in leathers as he arrived on stage on his moped, and Sir Toby was played by Jasmine Walker (F 2001),

'The Ragged Child', 2005.

over from Chicago for a year and a very convincing man. In *The Roses of Eyam* a 13-year-old Edwin Hillier (S 2002) was eerily impressive as the Bedlam.

As the workload of all the aspects of Repton's drama increased, Guy Levesley's help with productions became indispensable, and he was soon able to take over the direction of school plays altogether. Some of his most inspired and memorable ideas included having the Mechanicals in *A Midsummer Night's Dream* as window cleaners, first seen on ladders outside the 400 Hall, looking in at the audience and, in his first Lower School play, *Teechers*, having two quad bikes drive at full pelt onto the stage.

By the end of 2000 the Governors and, in particular, Robert Beldam and his Drama Trust, were willing to consider building the Studio Theatre between the 400 Hall and the Design Block. This would be a modern 'black box' auditorium designed to hold up to 150 for smaller, more intimate productions and, perhaps more importantly, for the teaching of class drama. Mr Beldam was extremely generous and supportive, eventually paying for over half of the costs of this building, costs that included the purchase of about a 100 new theatre lanterns, a portable sound equipment and mixing desk, and a computerized 98-channel lighting desk. The Studio was finally opened in May 2003 by the charming Patricia Routledge, infamous as 'Mrs Bucket'.

The idea of such a space is to be completely adaptable. There is no fixed stage but portable staging, which can be used to tier an audience into any shape or to create a stage in any part of the space. Drapes hang around the entire perimeter, a metre from the walls, and can be arranged for entrances, exits and

backdrops. The Studio Theatre, with its attractive glass-fronted foyer, has become a popular venue for Socials. It is also virtually soundproof and has been used by film and music companies for recording videos and CDs. In all, it superbly complements the more traditional 400 Hall.

In 1999 the academic Drama department consisted of one teacher, one theatre and two GCSE sets totalling 19 pupils. In 2006 the department had two teachers, two theatres and seven sets, GCSE Drama through to A2 Theatre Studies, totalling nearly 90 pupils. In 2005 Repton welcomed its first Drama Scholar, Charlie Pass (L 2005), and Drama Exhibitioner, Blair Dunlop (S 2005). In 2006 there were five Drama Scholars and Exhibitioners, and it is certain that the scholarships will further enrich the school's drama. The building of the Studio Theatre meant that there was a regular space for the teaching of

> *The Repton staff, like teachers in general, are a peculiar bunch. Open fires and dogs in classrooms (not at the same time), interesting choices of fancy dress and tutu-wearers are the norm (at least when Wear What You Dare Day and Pedants give them licence). That said, I would challenge schools the world over to equal the immense dedication which the Repton staff display on a daily basis. It is the unique environment which Repton offers that allows these dedicated teachers to become friends and teach us a great deal more than that which is outlined on the syllabus.*
>
> **Sarah Fearns (F 2001)**

examination practical drama, and the employment of Guy Levesley as teacher, productions director and Theatres Manager meant that enough staff members were available for the teaching of more sets as the subject's popularity grew.

The OR Room above the front door of the 400 Hall was converted into a classroom for theory lessons, and the lighting and sound control was moved onto a raised dais at the back of the gallery so that it would be in closer contact with the 'action'. Examination specifications require the creation of 'devised' drama, and at A2 groups choose their own plays to perform. Few who saw it will forget *End of the Line*, a devised piece about the London bombings, which required the transformation of the storeroom into a tube station and train that had to hold the audience and performers, their 'rescue' into a cold, smoky and pitch-black Studio and the 40 or so blanket-covered 'bodies' ranged across the lawns in the Precinct, which were seen as the audience left the building.

The B Block Drama Festival has been replaced by a regular, large-cast Lower School play, and the main school play has moved to November to allow March's Charity Cabaret to be moved from Pears School to the 400 Hall, taking advantage of its better lighting and sound facilities. I should also mention *The Ragged Child*, written and directed by Jeremy James Taylor who spent 2005–6 at Foremarke. This ambitious project, the first joint production between Repton and Foremarke, was a stunningly professional show with a cast of 40, two orchestras, dozens of swift, complex scene changes and hundreds of lighting cues.

With the building of the Studio a fire door was closed off in the 400 Hall and the capacity was reduced to 330, thereby making the gallery almost redundant. Staff and dignitaries became used to having the raised seats at the back of the ground floor reserved for them, and filling the seats downstairs created a much more satisfying atmosphere for any show. Oh, and those brown seats were replaced with plush blue ones, courtesy again of the unending generosity of Robert Beldam. Below the main stage, in the wardrobe department, much work has gone into controlling the floods and Robert financed a new floor, decoration and storage areas throughout. The area has been named the David Wilkinson Rooms in memory of the long-serving teacher and Governor.

Much has changed and there will be even more change when the 400 Hall soon undergoes a radical refit. As the 21st century reaches its teens Repton will be able to boast an exceptional theatre complex to rival any of our competitor schools. And dramatic pursuits will surely remain a vital part of Repton's life, contributing in no small way to the all-round education that is so central to the school's ethos.

John Sentance

The 2007 Charity Cabaret.

The Pedants

The Sir John Port's Pedants was introduced in 1935 by Donald Lindsay, who was appointed to the Repton staff by John Christie. Before coming to Repton, Lindsay was an assistant master at Manchester Grammar School, where in 1933 he introduced a revue called The Pedagogues *('in evening togs') to cheer up a rather formal Common Room. The MGS staff continued its annual production of this revue after Lindsay's departure until the early 1960s.*

The first few productions of the Pedants were directed by Lindsay and involved eight or nine staff on the Pears School stage. In 1936 the introductory songs 'About Ourselves' (complimentary) and 'About Other People' (highly scurrilous) were given their first showings. This traditional start has been maintained in subsequent editions, with the staff sitting in formal attire in a semicircle on stage. Other sketches included a play based on *Macbeth*, an operetta on 'The Priory Ghost' and a finale, *I Battatori*, a very grand opera with cricket as its theme. At the end of 1942 Lindsay left Repton to become the headmaster of Portsmouth Grammar School, and the director's mantle fell to Graham Bain, one of the original 1935 cast.

In 1946 the Saturday performance of the fifth edition of the Pedants was part of a weekend reunion for Old Reptonians. The pupils in the school watched their performance on the Monday.

On Bain's retirement in 1953, Brian Kemball-Cook took over the reins for the 1955 production. He had first taken part in the 1939 and 1951 performances, but missed 1942 and 1946 because he was in the armed services. The 1955 production saw the introduction of one of the great Pedants, Michael Charlesworth (O 1941), to the cast list. Charlesworth had seen the wartime production in 1942 and the first post-war performance in 1946, and he wrote the critique of the latter show for the March 1947 edition of the *Reptonian*.

In 1956 Kemball-Cook was appointed Headmaster of Queen Elizabeth Grammar School, Blackburn, so Charlesworth and David Gribble, an Old Etonian just appointed to the staff, produced the 1959 performance. The 1959 edition could be viewed as a renaissance in the history of the Pedants. It had a much younger cast because Michael Milford and Bernard Thomas, who had both taken part in the first edition in 1935, did not perform on stage (although Milford did help with the lighting). New scripts were written, and old scripts were discarded. The idea of a ballet first took shape in 1959 as the Polovtsians in the 'Bally Bolshies' under the tutelage of Tim Fisher. After Gribble's departure, David Wilkinson (H 1946) altered the ballet in 1962 (the first time the Pedants took place in the 400 Hall) into 'The Dying Swan', as it is known today, with music by Tchaikovsky and Peter Toynbee as Swan-Princess Dronehilda. Since then Roy French and David Morris have danced as Swan-Princess Rosebodge and Swan-Princess Morris Minor, while Barry Downing, Pat Silvey and Adrian Mylward have danced, respectively, as Prince Siegfried of Baz, Prince Patrick of Pedigree and Prince Adrian of Algebra. It was also in the 1959 edition that the 'pop music' element came into the Pedants. 'B5 Special' (1959) gave way to 'The Pick of the Slops' (1962, 1967) and then to 'Our Music and Yours' (1971), followed by parodies of 'The Old Grey Whistle Test' (1975, 1979). Finally, 'Peaks of the Pops' (1983) was replaced by 'The Cornucopœia of Pop' (1987, 1990, 1994, 1998, 2002, 2006). The 1979 edition of the Pedants saw the first outing of 'YMCA', although, at the time, it was known as 'OMCA', the Old Mitre Charlies' Association. Such was

The Pedants 1952.

Swan-Princess Rosebodge, Prince Siegfried of Baz and the Corpse de Ballet, 1990.

the success of that dance routine that it spawned a new idea for a sketch, the 'Jazz Ballet', which was first performed in its own right in 1983, 'The Kids of Shame' based on the film/hit single/TV programme *Fame*.

'The History of Humour' was introduced by Andrew Cox in 1979, and it has not lost its ability to amuse. The supremely deadpan faces of the helpers, the inane cackle of the Professor of Humour and Tim Scott's 'nose-pick' will long be remembered. 2006 saw two new recruits, John Plowright as the Professor and Frank Watson as Wilfred.

It was in 1987, whilst taking part as Le Clair, a disguised French Resistance worker, in Paul Jenkins's loose adaptation of the TV programme *'Allo 'Allo*, that James McLaren performed his famous stunt routine of riding a bicycle off the front of the stage. In 1990, much to the disappointment of both pupils and staff, he managed to stay on the stage!

It was also in 1990 (Charlesworth's and Wilkinson's last show, having been co-directors of every edition of the Pedants since 1962) that there was a successful parody of 'Nessun dorma', followed by Adrian Mylward's stunning imitation of Tina Turner in 'Simply the Best'.

Martin Amherst Lock and Peter Bradburn, who took over the directors' chairs in 1994, introduced an emphasis on performing fewer sketches of more substance in a slicker manner. Some old sketches had necessarily to go, such as DBW's 'Pianist' and RMC's 'Notices', while new sketches, 'The House Plays Pastiche' and 'The Pantomime', took their places. Some old ideas saw a resurrection: a sung version of the 'School Rules' and that old chestnut 'YMCA'. It is interesting to note that three of the 1979 Village People took part in 1998. Unfortunately, Russell Muir has made his Pedants' swansong. Members of staff have since filled his cowboy boots and have managed to sign YMCA correctly!

Amherst Lock departed to Harrow to become Head of English in 2001, but he did return to see the 2002 Pedants, and he and Mike Charlesworth gave valedictory speeches at a party to Patricia Wilmot, another Pedants' stalwart, who had sorted out costumes since 1971. Mike Keep (O 1969) became a co-producer in 2002, so there are now two Old Reptonians producing the Pedants as there were in the Charlesworth–Wilkinson era.

The Sir John Port's Pedants have been an integral part of the school's history for over 70 years. Let us hope that this unique tradition will continue for many years to come.

Peter Bradburn (P 1967)

The Corpse, 2006.

MUSIC

A BRIEF ACCOUNT OF REPTON'S MUSIC, 1967–94
I came to Repton as Director of Music in September 1967, appointed by John Thorn. Much to my disappointment, he left for Winchester a year later, but the disappointment was soon tempered by his replacement, John Gammell, who proved equally supportive.

The music staff, teaching in what is now the geography department on Boot Hill, consisted of six full-time members of staff. T.H. Kent (Tom) taught all the stringed instruments, Robert E. Blackburn taught the piano, as did David E. Kettlewell, who also taught the flute. David Haines, who had encouraged me to apply for the post, was a fine trumpet player and a charismatic teacher of all the brass instruments. Finally, there was John Pryer, one of the finest organists in the country. He made the Chapel organ, a fine Harrison and Harrison of 1929, sound different from anyone else. I well remember him playing the Liszt *Prelude and Fugue on the Name of Bach*, one of the great virtuoso pieces, on the first day of the Michaelmas term without having touched the organ for eight weeks.

It was clear to me that there were weaknesses, and over the next few years changes were gradually made. David Hadwen came to teach the upper strings and remained for all my time and beyond. He improved this area immeasurably and produced many fine players, not least his own children, Nick (B 1985) and Richard (B 1986), who went into the profession. Lawrence Cooper came to teach the piano and clarinet. One remembers him playing Beethoven's Fourth Piano Concerto with great sensitivity and authority. When he left for Roedean (an improbable move) we appointed Neil Millensted, who remained as head of piano teaching until he retired in 2007.

Mervyn Williams, Director of Music, 1940-1964.

At about the same time Tony Garton joined the staff from Christ's Hospital. It was a vital appointment, and one of the best we ever made. Tony revolutionized the teaching of the woodwind, as David had for the strings and Neil for the piano. In spite of all known advice, he taught all the woodwind instruments spectacularly well, not only his own instrument, the clarinet, but also the others, perhaps especially the bassoon.

Michael Salter directing Mussoc and the School Orchestra.

Jonathan Harvey (N 1953). A 1959 portrait of the composer as cellist.

Players like Jean Owen (A 1979), a bassoonist who went into the profession, always pay tribute to the excellence of his teaching.

Over these years the brass changed hands several times, from David Haines, whose business grew too much for him to regard teaching as the main emphasis in his life, to Mike Hutton, who never settled in Repton. Nigel Mainard was a great success and produced many fine players, eventually trying the business world before returning to education. He was followed by Nic Firth, another highly talented horn player and composer.

The Chapel and academic sides were well served by Fiona Lumb (now Brown), the first woman on the full-time music staff, and, when she left to get married, the highly energized John Le Grove. Peter Williams took over after John, and he achieved exceptionally fine results on the academic side. Over these years we were indebted to his wife, Margaret, who acted as a seventh full-time member of the teaching staff. She was also a fine accompanist and singer.

In this description of the music staff one must not forget the considerable contribution of the visiting teachers. They are too many to mention individually, but perhaps Christine

Palmer, who spent a year at the then Leningrad Conservatoire, and Peter Lacey come to mind as teachers of the highest quality.

The Chapel Choir, numbering about 70 pupils, was close to the Director's heart. There were real struggles in the early days getting enough trebles of the right quality, but this problem eased over the years as more girls came into the school. The carol service was always a special occasion, as were the visits to sing Evensong in cathedrals such as Lichfield, Lincoln, Worcester and Derby and at Southwell Minster.

Still on the choral side, Mus.Soc. was immensely important. There was the link with the School of St Mary & St Anne, Abbots Bromley, with its director of choir, Llywela Harris, one of the best choir trainers in the country. Anyone could join Mus.Soc. without a voice test, and many boys and girls did. Works performed included Haydn's *Nelson Mass* and *Theresienmesse*, Bach's *St Matthew Passion*, Prokofiev's *Alexander Nevsky* and, perhaps the greatest achievements, Elgar's *The Dream of Gerontius* and *The Kingdom*. Perhaps this is the moment to pay tribute to the inspiration of David Jewell, who persuaded the Director that Gerontius was possible. These works were performed with the school orchestra, assisted by a handful of musicians from outside the school.

One would like to mention how indebted Repton music has been to those from beyond the school and within it who took part in its music. It is dangerous to single out individuals, but people like James Foulds (O 1968) who acted like an adviser, John Crane (B 1967), Arthur French, the Cowdery family, with Ilse a wonderful cellist, all come to mind. There were many staff members and their wives who formed a great core of support: Martin Amherst Lock, David Wilkinson (H 1946), Richard Grew (O 1946), Andrew Cox, Richard Hiller and others too numerous to list. Finally, one must pay tribute to the help that Joseph Clark, conductor of the Chesterfield Choral Society and later the Derbyshire Singers, has given: a true friend of Repton music.

Drawing drama and music together were the musicals and it was a privilege to work with two fine directors of drama. *Guys and Dolls* was directed by Mike Charlesworth, and Bernstein's *West Side Story*, directed by Gareth Williams and accompanied by a small orchestra playing in the pit. Musically, this was fantastically demanding, but it was one of the most exciting experiences.

The musical year was punctuated by an orchestral concert in the Michaelmas term, followed by the carol service and two vastly popular band concerts, conducted by Tony Garton and accompanied by a fund of dreadful stories, all adding to the entertainment of the festive season. The first three weeks of the Lent term were always dominated by the preliminary rounds of the music competitions, followed by the finals. These began after lunch on the Friday and ended with the house unisons on Saturday evening. Many fine adjudicators came, among them Ivy Dickson of the National Youth Orchestra of Great Britain and Noël Cox, second-in-command at the Royal Academy. Many would argue that this assessment of the whole music department was the most important musical event of the year, but it was also a great festival. It was usually followed a week later by a charity concert organized by Nic Firth.

The Jazz Band, 2007.

It is impossible to give details of all the concerts that took place during the year. There were string orchestra concerts conducted by David Hadwen, and brass concerts conducted by Nic Firth. Summer witnessed the eve of Speech Day orchestral concert, followed by the Commemoration Service and Band concert the following day. Most years witnessed a final concert, drawing together many strands of the music department and held in Lichfield Cathedral towards the end of the summer term.

Beyond the summer term were ambitious trips to Italy, two to Venice and one to Florence. These were, in spite of the difficulties involved, fantastic experiences. Which other schools have held concerts in St Mark's, Venice, and in the Duomo in Florence? There were concerts in Vivaldi's Pietà, in the great Frari church and in San Stephano.

At a different level throughout this period there were subscription concerts given by some of the finest musicians in the world. One remembers the visits of the great cellist Paul Tortelier with his daughter, Maria de la Pau, whose 21st birthday fell on the day of the concert, and John Lill, who had just won the Tchaikovsky competition in Moscow and came for £25. The Allegri Quartet brought three Stradivarius instruments with them.

In later years the one thing that made these occasions so wonderful was the quality of the Beldam Hall. Again, it was a tribute to David Jewell and his enthusiasm for music that he pushed through plans for the conversion of the old Victorian sanatorium into what I would consider to be the finest music school building in the country. The project was put into the hands of Derek Latham Associates, and the plans were drawn up by a fine young architect, John Goom. The result was a building of immense quality, officially opened by the Duchess of Kent in 1985. This couldn't have been achieved without the generosity of Robert Beldam, a marvellous man and benefactor, who gave so much to the school.

The excellence of the music depends on recruiting enough pupils of the highest quality. This has always been a battle, first in attracting them from schools such as Durham, Lichfield and Ripon, and, second, in persuading Headmasters to give enough money by way of scholarships. Here one can mention the excellence of the music at Foremarke without which Repton would have been much the poorer. Although it is invidious to mention names, Paul Heslop (C 1989), James Arnold (C 1989) and Gavin Richards (C 1989) come to mind, as well as CJMS (C 1972). It is obvious, too, that the vastly increased number of girls transformed the quality of Repton's music.

In summary, what were the outstanding achievements? The new music school, with its wonderful Steinway, Verdi's *Requiem*, *The Dream of Gerontius*, music competitions, band

The 2007 Abbey-Priory House production of Jesus Christ Superstar.

concerts, Italian tours and the Chapel Choir all come to mind, but none of them would have come about without an outstanding music staff and talented pupils and Headmasters who were willing to back up their aspirations.

E.M. Salter

MUSIC TODAY AND TOMORROW

I arrived as Repton's Director of Music in the Michaelmas term 2006 with the mission of building on the department's long tradition of excellence. I was assisted by a dedicated full-time staff of six and excellent performance spaces in the Beldam Hall, Pears School and Chapel. Succeeding Richard Dacey, who had taken up the reins from Michael Salter in 1994, I am fortunate to arrive as a significant redevelopment of the music department is planned.

Equally important is the legacy of enthusiasm for the extra-curricular programme of music, with ensembles including a symphony orchestra, string orchestra, jazz band, concert band, Chapel choir, chamber choir, close harmony group, chamber groups, rock bands, string quartets and wind groups. In my first two terms alone I witnessed the superb Abbey–Priory *Jesus Christ Superstar*, fiercely competed house unisons and harmonies and the highly polished Charity Cabaret.

Plans include continuing the tradition of international tours for our musicians, alongside performances at local cathedrals for the Chapel Choir, visits to top concert venues to hear the world's great performers and the participation of gifted pupils in the National Youth Orchestra and Choir. We are proud to continue to send pupils to take up choral scholarships at Oxbridge.

The Chapel Choir tradition continues strongly, maintaining numbers at about 70, and we are still fortunate to be able to enjoy the sound of the Harrison and Harrison organ, one of the few left in its original condition. It is one of the school's great strengths that all pupils and staff join together each week in Chapel.

As part of the 450th anniversary celebrations we have commissioned a choral work from Britain's leading choral composer, Bob Chilcott, planned a visit from the King's Singers and will play an integral role in the *Son et Lumière*. The professional subscription concert series continues to attract some excellent performers – including my wife!

I hope to preside over a period of intense musical activity and to revive Mus.Soc. to give the pupils the chance to discover the joys of participating in some of the great choral works. There is great support for music in the school and a feeling among common room and pupils alike that music has a central part to play in Repton life. Long may this continue.

John Bowley

> *Whether it be through playing in Orchestra or in a junior rock band, every one of us has the opportunity to get involved in music-making. Perhaps the most integral ensemble in the school is the Chapel Choir as Chapel plays a unique role in the life of a Reptonian, allowing us to reflect on the week gone by, and to prepare for the week ahead.*

Edwin Hillier (S 2002)

The Music School.

FILM

R *epton's connections with film add up to a great deal more than the MGM and BBC versions of Goodbye Mr Chips, although these are probably where one's thoughts first turn in this context.*

Both Christopher Isherwood (H 1919), whose passion for cinema-going once led to his wanting 'to learn to direct films', and Roald Dahl had books of theirs filmed. Both *I Am a Camera* (1955) and *Cabaret* (1972) were based on Isherwood's Berlin stories, while *Charlie and the Chocolate Factory* (2005), in which Blair Dunlop (S 2005) plays the young Willy Wonka, is just the latest in the long line of films based on Dahl's children's books, which began with *Willy Wonka and the Chocolate Factory* (1971).

Jeremy Bournon's piece has already referred to the animated films of Anthony Gross and, as Appendix 2 shows, Dahl's first book, *Gremlin Lore* (1943), nearly became a Disney animated feature. Although the film was never made one can't help feeling that George Miller's gremlin in *Twilight Zone: The Movie* (1983) and Joe Dante's *Gremlins* (1984) and *Gremlins 2: The New Batch* (1990) were probably closer to Dahl's conception of the creature than Disney's would have been.

Isherwood and Dahl both also wrote or contributed to numerous screenplays, the former's credits including Tony Richardson's adaptation of Evelyn Waugh's *The Loved One* (1965), whilst Dahl's credits include Ian Fleming's *Chitty Chitty Bang Bang* (1968) and *You Only Live Twice* (1967).

Less well known is the fact that the 1957 film *The Enemy Below*, starring Robert Mitchum and Curt

Above: 'Cabaret' film poster.

Left: Disney's vision of Dahl's Gremlins.

Right: St Wystan's from the Precinct.

becoming typecast but who successfully branched out into radio and television and was never out of work, although making several forgettable films before his death in 1967.

The career of Maurice Colbourne (H 1909) somewhat resembles Rathbone's. He, too, had a long career which ended on TV but his film career peaked with his first foray, as Sergius in the 1932 version of Shaw's 'Arms and the Man'.

Three years before Colbourne, Rathbone had insisted on going to Repton because, 'Repton School in 1906 was possibly the most renowned public school in England for its accomplishment in … sports'. Indeed, 'Repton was not a school that prided itself in the arts, and any boy so interested would definitely be suspect of being a "queer one"', as Rathbone confided in his autobiography. Thus Repton indirectly fostered Rathbone's acting talents by forcing him to dissimulate, keeping his love of theatre to himself, so that 'Little did the Reverend Arthur Cattley and my friends realize that, during homework in the dining room after supper, I was working on my first play, *King Arthur.*'

At least Repton positively encouraged the talents of its next pupil to make a significant mark in the film world. Nelson John Keys (L 1924) was supported by Fisher when, in 1927, he formed a school cinema club, with its own magazine and tie. Such was the boy's enthusiasm and precocity that he completed his first film, *The Hero of St Jim's* (a melodrama of public-school

A three-pipe problem for Basil Rathbone as Sherlock Holmes.

Jurgens, was based on the novel of the same name published a year earlier by Denys Rayner (M 1921).

Repton's links with the screen actually go back to silent days, as Basil Rathbone, more properly Philip St John Basil Rathbone, (M 1906), made his film debut in *The Fruitful Vine* (1921). Rathbone already had a distinguished career on stage and in the Great War, having been awarded the MC. In 1922 he made his US stage debut, and the rest of his career was spent almost exclusively in the States, at first alternating between the theatre (for which he received a Tony award) and films (for which he was twice Oscar-nominated).

Rathbone survived the introduction of the 'talkies', but it was not until the mid-1930s that his film career really took off, as one of the first Britons to fill Hollywood's need for smooth-talking and, on occasion, swashbuckling villains, most notably crossing swords with Errol Flynn (in *Captain Blood* and *The Adventures of Robin Hood*) and with Tyrone Power (in *The Mark of Zorro*). However, he is best remembered as a great – some would say definitive – screen Sherlock Holmes, portraying the Baker Street sleuth, alongside Nigel Bruce's Watson, no fewer than 14 times between 1939 and 1946.

Derided by Dorothy Parker as little more than two profiles pasted together, Rathbone was a fine actor who suffered from

A book which tells the story of the filming of 'The Hero of St Jim's' at Repton.

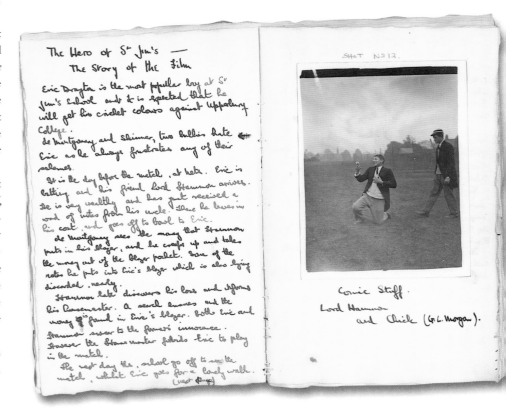

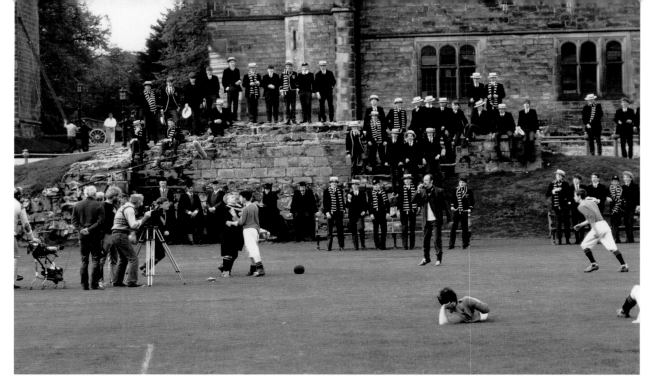

Roy Marsden as Mr Chips blows the whistle on some unsportsmanlike behaviour.

life), in 1927 whilst still at school. The national press picked up the story, and it helped the young Nelson go directly from school into an apprenticeship with a family friend, film producer and director Herbert Wilcox. However, Nelson was keen to avoid the charge that he was cashing in on his father's name – Nelson Keys was a noted actor and comedian – so he changed his name by deed poll to John Paddy Carstairs (the latter being his mother's maiden name).

Carstairs made his directorial debut with the thriller *Paris Plane* in 1933. In all he was to direct 45 feature films, as well as directing for stage and television, writing more than 30 books and having his paintings exhibited. Before 1948 most of his films were thrillers. After that date they were mostly comedies, including five films with Norman Wisdom, which established Wisdom as the top British post-war film comedian (as well as enjoying an enormous following in much of the communist world). No one would ever describe films like *Trouble in Store* (1953) or *The Square Peg* (1958) as works of art, but like most of Carstairs's films they were well crafted and successful.

The reason *Goodbye Mr Chips* (1939) was partly filmed in Repton when James Hilton's inspiration for Brookfields came from the Leys School, Cambridge, is wholly due to the good offices of Eric Maschwitz (H 1915), who was then working for MGM and who is credited on the film as one of the writers of the screenplay. Watching the film is a puzzling experience because it's so difficult to relate what one sees on screen to what one knows of Repton. The school is clearly used for several of the exterior shots, but thereafter life is made very difficult by virtue of the fact that 23 Brookfield School sets were clearly based upon Repton but were constructed on sound stages at Denham. These sets, which took 400 workmen

three weeks to build, were the largest ever built in Britain at that time and included an Arch, chapel, classrooms and houses for the masters.

Two hundred boys returned to school a week before the end of the 1938 summer holidays to help with the filming. They were not paid for their services as extras but apparently a deputation successfully approached associate producer Stanley Haynes with the request that MGM provide a sum to enable an OR (destined to join the Civil Service) to take his Oxford examinations.

The boys were housed in a camp on Lower Tower, and the Headmaster, Michael Clarke, allowed ordinary school rules to be relaxed, stating:

> *I, personally, think boys ill advised to smoke but they may do so if they are allowed to smoke at home. They must not smoke within the Arch except in the upstairs tearoom at the Grubber. It must be a point of honour that no boy persuades another to smoke who is not accustomed to do so.*
>
> *Boys who have cars of their own or are allowed the use of their parents' may come by road and park cars on the parade ground or in garages if they prefer to do so, but they may not use them during their stay in Repton. Boys may bring and use bicycles. They must not enter public houses, otherwise there are no bounds. That affords everyone reasonable freedom …*

Both a cricket and a rugby football match as played in the year 1870 were filmed, with supporters of both sides looking on and with Clarke himself taking the role of a linesman. Rugby was not then played at Repton, so the boys were coached in the game by Geoffrey Russel, a Lancashire county player.

Harold Abrahams takes the tape.

a 1912 Olympian. As his nephew Anthony put it, the film 'got only three things right. Harold was Jewish, he went to Cambridge, and he won the 100 metres'.

Every year on 7 July at 7 p.m. – the precise time of the Olympic final – Abrahams and his friend, the New Zealander and bronze medallist, Arthur Porritt, dined together until Abrahams's death 54 years later.

In 1983 Repton reprised its role as the setting for *Goodbye Mr Chips* when the BBC filmed a series with Roy Marsden in the title role. Mike Charlesworth writes:

David Jewell, assuming (rightly) that I'd be interested to be the staff liaison officer & assuming also (wrongly) that the BBC would pay me for the immense amount of work involved … put me in charge of seeing the BBC had everything they wanted … I was given carte blanche (by David Jewell himself) to take boys out of lessons at any time (which made me immensely unpopular with the staff for a time!), and the BBC would give me orders the previous evening like 'We want 70 sixth formers 9.30–11.00; 150 boys of varying ages from 11.00–12.00, & 45 thirteen year olds from 12.00–1.00' etc., etc.
That was difficult enough. My brief was to use volunteers only. The previous week I had identified all the volunteers (about half the school wanted to be in it), and listed them by forms and by houses.
That was the raw material. I then had to list, late at night, the boys required for each particular scene (who had to be there over half an hour early for costumes, which were hanging on rails all over Pears School …
These lists and times had to be photocopied for Housemasters and for all staff due to lose boys from their classes that day.
… Then the fun started. Flurries of rain delayed the filming, and vast numbers of boys stood around, missing lots of lessons they weren't supposed to be missing – or missing meals, or games, or music, etc., etc. … My lists were usually completely out of date and misleading within half an hour of the start …
It was probably the most chaotic and exhausting week of my life … but in a masochistic sort of way it was extraordinarily enjoyable. I was put into the show myself as the Chaplain … in the War Memorial Service in the Garth (… half the Staff got in on that one …) and eventually I was called in by a despairing director (who found it difficult to get hordes of excited Reptonians to pay any attention to him), to direct the boy 'crowd' scenes round the Arch myself, as they were all going wrong … I've never worked harder for less reward!

The 1939 Oscars were dominated by *Gone with the Wind* (which won eight awards), but Robert Donat deservedly defeated Clark Gable (and Laurence Olivier, Jimmy Stewart and Mickey Rooney) to win the Best Actor Award for Mr Chips.

Another Oscar-winning picture associated with Repton is *Chariots of Fire* (1981), which was nominated for seven Academy Awards and won four, including Best Picture. The film is (loosely) based on the true story of two British runners who competed in the 1924 Paris Olympics: Eric Liddell, who was played by Ian Charleson, and Repton's own Harold Abrahams (M 1914), played by Ben Cross.

In the film Liddell refuses to run the 100-metre dash, his specialty, because the heats are held on a Sunday. The Sabbatarian Scots missionary refuses to budge, despite direct pressure from British officials and the Prince of Wales. In his absence, Abrahams wins the 100 metres, but Liddell then goes on to win the 400 metres.

The film depicts Abrahams as driven by a desire to combat anti-Semitism and the cult of the amateur, aided by his personal trainer, Sam Mussabini (Ian Holm), but in fact he was motivated by the desire to outdo his two older brothers, one of whom was

Nor does Repton's connection with film end there. The eagle-eyed Reptonian watching Ken Russell's *Tommy* (1975) or

Charles Sturridge's made-for-TV movie *Shackleton* (2002) can spot Adrian Mylward and Barry Downing, respectively, among the extras.

As well as Blair Dunlop, Repton's contemporary cinematic acting credits include Tom Chambers (*Rep Radio*, 2001; *Fakers*, 2004; *Collapsed*, 2006), about whom one should hear a great deal more if talent is justly rewarded.

Last but not least, to list Professor Sir Christopher Frayling's scholarly contributions to the world of cinema would require an article in itself but, as he has admitted elsewhere, his own film studies were stimulated by bunking off school. For many years Sir Osbert Sitwell's entry in *Who's Who* contained the phrase 'Educated during the holidays from Eton', and Sir Christopher might similarly say that this branch of his career at least owed as much to his time outside as inside the Arch. Given our school motto we could hardly take the credit, even if it were otherwise.

John Plowright

An hirsute and harassed Mike Charlesworth prepares for his cameo appearance.

The 1980s double for the 1900s.

SPORTS

CRICKET

How good it was that Chris Adams (P 1987) should lift the county championship trophy at the end of the 2006 season to reward Sussex for their second triumph in four years. After an eternity without winning the championship – in 2003 Sussex was the last of the established counties, besides Gloucestershire, Northamptonshire and Somerset, to prove themselves the best – they won it again in fine fashion, with much the same side, to prove how right they were to recruit Adams, who had begun his career at Derbyshire, by offering the bait of captaincy.

Adams, from Whatstandwell, between Derby and Matlock, has therefore accomplished what Charles Burgess Fry and a host of others could not do for Sussex-by-the-Sea. Fry was a Reptonian (C 1885) and enjoyed one of the most celebrated lives – sporting or otherwise – of the 20th century, but his leadership couldn't quite bring Sussex what they craved. Adams, a Reptonian in the sense that he attended the school for a year in the sixth form (which makes him a Reptonian of sorts, if not a fully fledged one), brought home the bacon, and how the seaside choristers sang!

There isn't much else to link Adams with Fry. One is the creature of the modern age, a good, forceful county batsman a shade under Test class, though he did play for England in South Africa in 1999 and might have found his feet in a more settled side. The other was one of the most lustrous figures of a game that is not short of strong characters. Fry, a champion of 'the golden age', really deserves a chapter of his own in any history of English sport for his achievements on the cricket field and elsewhere. He made more than 30,000 runs in his gilded career, with 94 centuries and an average of 50, and was good enough to captain England at the age of 40.

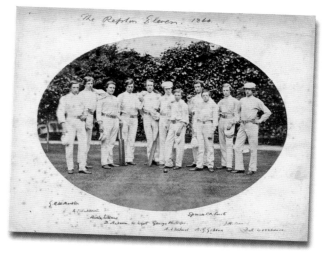

The Repton Eleven, 1860.

Fry, who also played for Hampshire, excelled at other games. He was the only amateur member of the Southampton team that reached the FA Cup Final in 1902 and represented England at full back. He would have been an Oxford Rugby Blue had injury not intervened, he played for Blackheath, and he equalled the world long jump record at Oxford, 23 feet 6½ inches (7.17 metres), between puffs on a cigar! Later he was the director of the training ship *Mercury* on the Hamble River, turning out a succession of fine sailors for the Royal Navy and the Merchant Navy, despite being hen-pecked by his wife. He wrote for the popular press and commentated on cricket for the BBC, when he once upbraided a man who had called him 'Charles' with the lordly response: 'Captain Fry to you, sir!'

Most famously, he was offered – and refused – the throne of Albania. The Albanians had been impressed by his speech-writing talents for Ranji, his Sussex team-mate, who was a

The Cricket Pavilion.

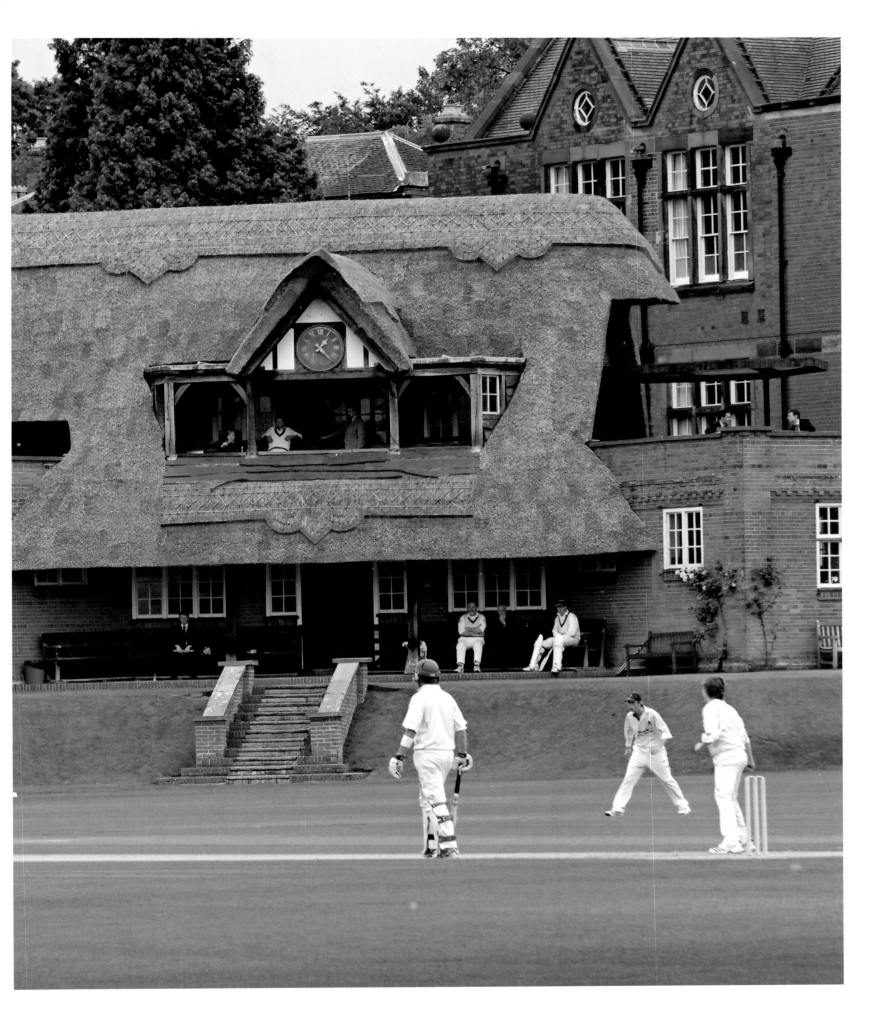

C.B. Fry at the crease.   F.S.G. Calthorpe, Sussex, Warwickshire and England Cricketer.   Donald Carr, Derbyshire and England Cricketer.

delegate at the League of Nations, and thought he was just the chap to sit on the throne. 'And damn it', he said some years later, reflecting on the royal offer, 'if I'd accepted it, the Italian invasion would never have happened. It would have been ideal in the spring, in that clement weather, to have had counties out there playing cricket, and if the Italians had barged in with county cricket going on, the Royal Navy would have been absolutely obliged to step in and stop it! It might have stopped Mussolini but, at the time, it seemed a damn bore!' Fry stayed in England. The Albanians got King Zog instead.

In later years, when his mental health was not so good, Fry met Hitler, whom he admired, and he tried to persuade von Ribbentrop that cricket was just the game to reinforce the spirit of German youth! He failed in that venture, which was just as well, given German domination of Association Football down the years. But Fry didn't fail often. He called his autobiography *Life Worth Living*, and he wasn't fibbing. Yet, for all his renown, for all his feats and the brilliance of Ranji, he didn't lift the County Championship for Sussex, and 'Grizzly' Adams did.

Charles Burgess Fry to Christopher John Adams – and so many in between: 128 Reptonians have played first-class cricket, most recently Chris Paget (P 2001) for Derbyshire while he was at school. The school has supplied every county, except the most recent arrivals, Durham, with players, and has given – if that is the verb – nine captains to the counties, including Jon Batty (L 1991) to Surrey, where he remains the wicketkeeper. There have been 10 England players, including

three captains – Fry, F.S.G. Calthorpe (C 1907) and D.B. Carr (L & M 1940) – and two presidents of Marylebone Cricket Club, Harry Altham (O 1902) and Charles (C.A.) Fry (H 1953). That is a record to celebrate.

Of course, the first thing to admire about Repton cricket is the Square itself. Housed between the Boot Inn, that unremarkable pub that boys rarely entered (some did, one gathered later) and the Trent water meadows, half a mile away (though the river seems as remote as the Mississippi), with the paddock sloping down to the outfield and 'Pears Crack' watching over proceedings, Repton boasts as fine a ground as any school. Derbyshire play Second XI cricket there, but, sadly, when the first team went there in 1990 to play a Sunday League fixture against Middlesex, rain spoiled the day. Furthermore, to the great regret of the Reptonians who attended, it was clear that the ground was not equipped for such a match and that failing had little to do with the school. Of school grounds the superbly equipped – and handily situated – Cheltenham College is a place apart, but if Oakham and Whitgift can stage county cricket, and they have done, with notable success, Repton should be flying the flag.

How many schoolboy cricketers have sat in that fine pavilion, under the thatched roof – the newly rethatched roof – and dreamed of the runs they will make or the wickets they will take? It is the most beautiful of school grounds and makes a picture that will never be forgotten by any of the boys who played there or by those, who, lacking the talent, have returned there in the years since to imagine what might have been. Even those boys who didn't play cricket, who emerged from the Grubber licking ice creams, munching cheese cobs or simply skiving prep, knew that their school had the most glorious cricket ground. And that, one hopes, will never change.

Repton will never be as posh a school as some of the others that have provided England with players – Tonbridge, Eton and Harrow to the fore – but it is rooted in native soil and has its own distinct history. Whether or not the boys came from Derbyshire (most didn't, though one senses that is changing), it offered a sense of place. The parish church of St Wystan, after all, provided the Christian name of one of the greatest of all 20th-century poets, W.H. Auden, who spent much of his life living in Manhattan, Ischia and Austria, yet who claimed the only place he could find a decent martini in England was in Ashby de la Zouch!

Repton making runs (2006 Twenty 20 competition).

England batsman Chris Adams hits a four.

Fry may be the most celebrated Repton cricketer, but there are others, from J.N. Crawford (B 1901) to Jonathan Batty, Surrey men both. There is also the not insignificant figure of Lionel Palairet (H 1884), by all accounts one of the most handsome batsmen of the golden age, and the Carrs, father and son, Donald and John (H 1976), and Richard Hutton (H 1956), who followed his famous father into the Yorkshire side, then briefly the Test team, and also picked up something of his father's wit.

Years after he left Repton and was making his way at Yorkshire, R.A. Hutton was at the crease, batting against Peter Lever and Ken Shuttleworth in a Roses match on a capricious Headingley pitch (they were uncovered in those days) when a rather sheepish Chris Old made his way to the middle. Having fended off three balls from Lever, who was making the ball take a divot, Hutton greeted the new batsman in mid-wicket between overs with the words: 'Welcome to Dunkirk, Chilly!' Donald Carr, of course, became one of the great fixers of cricket, rising to the post of chief executive of the Test and County Cricket Board, as it used to be known, after leading Derbyshire and England, and managing MCC (as the touring team used to be known) on three overseas tours. Now his son, John, who enjoyed a fine career with Middlesex, is also an administrator, as the director of cricket manager at the England and Wales Cricket Board.

It was Carr senior who led the Pilgrims when they won the inaugural Cricketer Cup, the competition for the old boys of public schools, in 1967. The Pilgrims won it again in 1983 and reached the finals in both 1985 and 1992. In recent years the competition has been dominated by Tonbridge and Bradfield Waifs, so it is high time the name of Repton appeared once more!

Michael Henderson (N 1972)

The 1903 1st XI.

FOOTBALL

Amongst early references to football at Repton was a contribution to the *Reptonian* of May 1895 in which Mr Justice Denman (H 1833) describes a rough-and-tumble game being played in the school yard in the space bounded by the Arch and the Pillars of Hercules, and between the Priory and the churchyard wall. This game involved long kicking, hacking and dribbling, while handling was allowed in certain circumstances and 'falls upon the gravel caused many an abrasion'. Sides varied. Those housed inside the Arch against those outside, or Married vs Single, where the 'Married' were boys with brothers or namesakes in the school. Another version was Tops vs Bottoms, where the boys ranked in the top half of the class opposed the academically challenged.

A set of rules dated 1862 (revised 1872) codified the school's game and was the background against which Frederick Smith, first president of Notts County, invited some public school men, including three Reptonians, in 1864 to codify the rules for the Football Association. It was also the formative experience for H.H. Stewart (L 1861) and A.J. Stanley (H 1866), who earned FA Cup Winners' medals with, respectively,

the Wanderers in 1873 and Clapham Rovers in 1880, as well as for D.R. Hunter (P 1867), captain of the Cambridge University Association Football team in the second university football match in 1875 and his team-mate, S. Roberts (O 1866).

The Association game was gathering momentum, particularly around London, with men from the public schools and universities influential in the discussion of the emerging rules of what was to remain an amateur game until 1884. Advice from ORs at Cambridge persuaded the school to accept this form of football, leading in 1878 to the first match against outside opposition. These matches were known as 'foreign' matches, and the first was against Nottingham Lambs. The school suffered a 5–0 defeat to a team containing four members of the Cursham family, generations of which have attended Repton. Henry Cursham (H 1875), eight times an England international, played for Notts County and scored 48 goals in the FA Cup in ten years from 1877–8 when Notts County first entered the competition – a total unmatched since.

The high standard of football in the school was soon reflected in numerous Oxbridge blues. Cambridge recipients included F.E. Saunders (M 1879) and three-time England

Dribbling practice.

international B.W. Spilsbury (H 1876). C.B. Fry (C 1885) was the most notable Oxford footballing blue. He played for England against Canada in an amateur side in 1891, his first year at Oxford, but his only other international was not until 1901 against Ireland, after which he represented Southampton in the FA Cup Final of 1902. G.P. Dewhurst (M 1883) and R.R. Barker (B 1883) played together for England in the last all-amateur team against Wales at Queen's Club in 1895.

Inter-school matches started in 1893, first against Shrewsbury, and then, the next year, Malvern. *Terminal Letters* took pride in enumerating Reptonian achievements. A total of 36 Reptonians were awarded Association Football blues at Oxford and Cambridge in the period up to 1914, a total exceeded only by Charterhouse, Eton and Winchester, and many appeared for those distinguished amateur clubs, the Corinthians and the Casuals. Indeed, R.R. Barker was a defeated finalist for the Casuals in the first FA Amateur Cup Final in 1894. Moreover, by 1895 as many as 17 OR fixtures had been arranged in the London area.

Reptonians were in good shape when the Arthur Dunn Cup competition started in the 1902–3 season, and the ORs appeared in six of the twelve finals before 1914, winning in 1907, 1911 and 1914. The 1914 side included five of the six Reptonian blues who had earlier that year contested the varsity match, together with two former blues. One of the latter, R.A. Young (H 1899), who briefly taught at Repton (1908–10) contested all six finals as well as finding time to play two Test matches on the MCC tour to Australia in 1907–8. Young also played an amateur international in 1907, while N.V.C. Turner (H 1901), R.F. Popham (B 1906) and M. Howell (P 1907) won amateur caps either side of the war.

Salopians were to play a significant role in Repton football, with M.M. Morgan-Owen, a Welsh international, running school football for almost a quarter of a century (the war years excluded) from 1909. He was responsible for restricting matches to 40 minutes each way in his first season in charge, and L.B. 'Bill' Blaxland, who joined the staff in 1922, was a vital influence behind the scenes until he became responsible for the school side in 1937. Their reputations were built on Corinthian principles, with Blaxland's feat in captaining four Salopian Dunn Cup winning teams in the 1930s having a telling impact. Repton's 13 Oxbridge blues between 1919 and 1939, a total exceeded only by Charterhouse, Winchester and (marginally) by Shrewsbury, should have brought some Dunn reward, yet the ORs managed only two unsuccessful finals.

Blaxland assumed responsibilities for school cricket and football and in the war even took on the groundsman's role, so he would have been relieved when Dick Sale took over school

The 1911 1st XI.

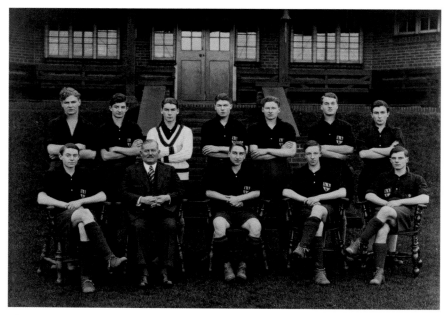

The 1936 1st XI, with Lt.Col.M.M.Morgan-Owen.

football in 1947. Colourful touchline comments from Dick ensured that no member of his squad dreamed of shirking a tackle. Good sides emerged in the 1950s and formed the basis of subsequently successful Dunn campaigns. Dick had been at the heart of the Dunn side too, and he and Donald Carr (L & M 1940), a member of the Pegasus FA Amateur Cup winning sides of 1951 and 1953, were the only enduring members of the OR teams to contest Dunn finals in 1947, 1957 and 1958. Also playing in the 1957 and 1958 finals was Gerry Citron (P 1948), who had been in the Corinthian Casuals side that took Bishop Auckland to a replay in the 1956 final of the Amateur Cup.

Professional input was provided through occasional sessions with Derby County staff. 'Scottie' Cheshire, who took on the school side in 1959, was as keen a student of the beautiful game as one could meet, and he continued to emphasize the tactical and technical aspects of the game. Matches against the youth teams of both Coventry City and Derby County gave the squad further insights and enabled 'Scottie' to create a club atmosphere.

Success in the Dunn finally came with six appearances in the finals 1960–70, with three victories and one draw against Malvern, and a fourth over the Foresters. A team was also entered for the Arthurian League in 1967–8. Additional teams have entered in subsequent years, but it was not until 2001–2 that Repton finally took the honours in winning the Arthurian League's premier division under the captaincy of Des Anderson (P 1982).

The school fixture list had featured the traditional six opponents for several decades, and it was under James McLaren from 1972 that new opponents were introduced to replace some of the local grammar schools, whose switch to comprehensive education had weakened their strength on the pitch. His successor from 1986, Noel Bennett, added further to the strong northern independent content of a much extended school fixture list.

Many of the long-standing fixtures against adult club teams have been gradually discouraged on health and safety grounds, but fixture congestion could still occur if the school XI had a good run in the Boodle & Dunthorne Cup. This knock-out competition has proved extremely popular since its introduction in 1992–3, and after a lack of success in its first five years, Repton reached four semi-finals in the next eight, losing two of them on penalties and another after extra time. This achievement is all the more creditable given that the later stages of the competition are held in the Lent term, when the call of other sports take precedence.

The school team had an outstanding run of success over the three seasons from 1978, losing only two school matches of the 40 played, while the 1997 side's achievement of winning all 18 school matches stands comparison with that of any independent school. The 42 goals scored in 1979 by John Wood (L 1978) remains a record, although Matthew Gooderick (C 1992) came close in 1995 with 37.

Innovation continues, and it is interesting to note the recent appointment of Tom Statham, one of Manchester United's youth coaches, as Director of Football Coaching. His role, working with the younger boys, is to create a better understanding of skill needs and tactics at an earlier stage of their footballing experience.

The ORs, meanwhile, had a rather fallow spell, reaching only one semi-final in the ten years after winning the Dunn in 1970. However, the cup was won in 1981, and ORs reached four finals under the captaincy of Mark Stretton (H 1975) in the seven years from 1987, winning in that year and in 1991 and being losing finalists in 1989 and 1993. Mark Stretton also appeared in a losing final in 2001 under Des Anderson. The present captain, Neal Rushton (P 1994), faces the age-old problem of assembling talented footballers from around the country to play together often enough to establish the teamwork necessary to match Reptonian ambitions.

Repton's school sides remain as committed and competitive as ever.

Ian Payne (L 1955)

Harry Cursham stills holds the record for the number of goals scored in the F.A. Cup.

HOCKEY

Stick and ball games have been played for thousands of years. The earliest record of man playing a form of hockey can be found in the Ancient Egyptian tomb of Beni-Hasen, while mob hockey games could be found all over medieval Europe. The game's name appears to be derived either from hok, the Anglo-Saxon word for a hook, or from hocquet, the French word for a shepherd's crook.

The modern game evolved in England's public schools, with boys adapting the game to their surroundings. Thus Repton's early games date from the mid-18th century, with the boys using inverted walking sticks and the Arch and the Pillars of Hercules as the goals. It is unknown whether the boys used an old cricket ball or a solid rubber cube, as was then fashionable.

An offbeat insight into the existence of mid-Victorian hockey at Repton is provided by an anonymous correspondent to the *Reptonian* of July 1917 who wrote:

> *My experiences of Repton began in Michaelmas Term 1858 … The first head of my study was a really religious young man but his religion savoured much of Old Testament ideals. On our introduction he told me that every day after breakfast I was to read a chapter of the Bible and that then he would thrash me with a hockey stick until I could bear pain like a Trojan or a Spartan. This process was literally carried out, and it was not long before I was as proud of the toughness of my hide as he was of showing me off …*

The game spread among schools and clubs, not least as a winter alternative to cricket, and in an attempt to agree some common rules the Hockey Association was founded by ex-public schoolboys in 1886. Early rules included the introduction of a 'striking circle' and a limit of 11 players per team.

Former public schoolboys also spread hockey nationally (as assistant masters) and globally (as army officers), and the game spread throughout the Empire, enabling India, Pakistan and Australia to become dominant forces in the international game.

The first organized game of hockey played at Repton appears to have taken place in 1900. There was a house league competition, which lasted a week, in which anyone not in their house football team could play. Six houses raised teams. Shortly afterwards, in the *Reptonian* for 1901, there is a mention of the first match for the school XI:

> *For the first time on record a foreign hockey match has been played, and our team showed its mettle by defeating its opponents [A.S. Barnwell's XI] by 4–0. During the last few years hockey*

Ben Sharpe, Great Britain and England Hockey player.

has been making long strides forward in the favour of the school, and this is distinctly satisfactory so long as football does not thereby suffer. But at Repton football must always come first.

The following year the school team played two matches, drawing 1–1 with Burton HC and defeating Derby HC 2–1. By 1929 the school had a fairly extensive fixture card, although the only inter-school match appears to have been against Uppingham. The other teams played that year included local clubs and Notts Casuals and Bacchanalians, both of which still provide opposition for public schools today.

As with the game of hockey at large, women's hockey lagged some way behind men's hockey at the school. As girls entered the sixth form in 1970 there was still no women's hockey in the Olympic Games (it wasn't introduced until 1980). The first record of a girls' hockey match was one played in the summer of 1975, against a Brook House XI, which the girls won 2–1. The earliest inter-school matches were against Derby High School, Abbot Beyne, Ratcliffe, Rugby and Uppingham, with the Repton girls experiencing mixed fortunes.

In the early 1970s synthetic grass pitches began to be used for hockey, and this had a considerable influence on the game's evolution. Rule changes have afflicted hockey more than most

Right: The 1st XI boys' hockey team after having won the county and regional titles in the National Schools Championships.

Below: The U18 girls' hockey squad after winning the National Schools Championship for Girls for the third year in succession.

sports, and this has occurred largely in response to changes in skills and strategies brought about by technological advances in the game. Repton didn't build an AstroTurf pitch until 1992, but this didn't prevent Reptonians from making progress in the modern game. Andrew Griffiths (O 1982) was one of the first to play international hockey in the modern era; first for England at youth level in 1984 and then appearing for Canada at the 2000 Olympic Games in Sydney.

Soon after this Repton started to gain something of a national reputation for hockey. In 1990 the boys won their first Midlands title, beating Uppingham in the final 1–0. This team was largely influenced by two boys: Luke Allen (O 1987), who was considered to be one of the best young players in England at that time, and Ben Sharpe (B 1989), who went on to represent Britain at the Sydney Olympics. Despite acquitting themselves well in their first appearance in national finals, they eventually lost in the semi-final.

However, Repton did not have to wait long for national success, and in 1995 the Under 16 team beat Eastbourne College in the national final. Over the next five years, Repton was one of the most successful school teams in the country, appearing in four national finals in various age groups. The Under 18 teams of 1998 and 1999 might legitimately consider themselves to have been unlucky to have finished as national runners-up, as both finals were lost on penalties. These teams included M.L. Jones (C 1997) and M. Taylor (C 1997), both of whom went on to represent England at senior level. Still only 26, Jones has already appeared in two world cups and amassed over 100 caps.

Whilst the boys have narrowly missed out on national triumphs since (losing by the only goal in the semi-final of the 2007 competition), they have been crowned Midlands champions on three occasions in recent years, and during this period it has been the girls' turn to fly the Repton flag at national level, keeping the school's name at the forefront of GB hockey. Indeed the girls appeared in the last six Under 18 national finals, winning gold in 2005, 2006 and 2007. Not satisfied with dominating the outdoor game, the Under 16 team also captured the national indoor title in 2006.

Moreover, Reptonian girls have also made their mark at the international level with S. Gilbert (F 2002), G. Twigg (F 2003) and C. Craddock (A 2005) all key members of the squad when the Under 18 Girls won the European Youth Nations Championship for the first time ever in 2007. Craddock's two goals against Ireland were a key part of the campaign which propelled England, the only unbeaten side in the competition, to a deserved gold medal success.

Simon Clague

TENNIS

A most surprising omission from Repton 1557–1957 is the fact that there is no mention of an OR Wimbledon Men's Singles champion. 'Bunny' Austin (O 1920), who reached the men's final twice in the 1930s, remains the school's most celebrated tennis player and rightly so, yet Herbert Fortescue Lawford (L 1865) was Wimbledon Champion in 1887 and also reached the final on five other occasions. In terms of appearances in the Singles Final he was the equal of Laver, Connors and Borg. Had it not been for the Renshaw brothers, it is likely that Lawford would have won the title more than once and thus perhaps have been somewhat better remembered. He was also Men's Doubles champion in 1879. In *Wimbledon 1877–1977* (1977) Max Robertson describes him as:

> *one of the great characters of Victorian tennis, a broad-shouldered, upstanding man of firm countenance who, in his shirt with wide horizontal stripes, cavalry style trousers tucked into socks just below the knee and the whole rig topped with a cap resembling a pith helmet, looked as though he was about to set off to discover the source of the Nile, rather than play tennis. His main asset was his strength and power, which he unleashed in full measure in his forehand drive, like a shell from a cannon.*

Unfortunately, there is no record of tennis in Lawford's years at Repton, nor, indeed, whether he played the game at school. There is, however, a reference to a 'Lawn Tennis Ground' started in 1879 by Thomas Price (Staff 1875–1912), and the *Reptonian* of the 1880s contain numerous letters, both opposed to, and in favour of, tennis: sentiments that were echoed in the 1980s, when the attempt to pursue tennis throughout the school year met initially with considerable resistance.

Austin was at Repton during the first half of the 1920s, and it can hardly be a coincidence that the first hard courts, seven in all, were built during this period, one of them under the direction of the Orchard Housemaster using mainly boy labour and thereafter known as 'Carter's Court'. Whilst at school Austin won the Under 16 Public Schools' Championship at Queen's Club in 1921 and the Under 18 event from 1923 to 1925. He also won the National Junior Championship (Junior Wimbledon) in 1922, yet it was clear when speaking to him in later years that his fondest sporting memory of Repton was his century for the First XI cricket side in his final match against Malvern. He maintained that one of his contemporaries, the Repton Test cricketer Bryan Valentine (O 1921), would have been a better tennis player than Austin himself had he pursued the game. Austin first played in the Wimbledon Championships

in 1926, and over a ten-year period from 1929 to 1938 reached at least the quarter finals of the singles in every year – a remarkable record. He was also part of the successful British Davis Cup team when there were four consecutive triumphs, 1933–6. Before this the last victory had been in 1912, and there have been none since. Although Fred Perry was the star of the team, Austin's Davis Cup record was outstanding, with 36 wins from 48 matches played. He reached the Wimbledon Singles Final twice, first in 1932 and again in 1938, and his defeat by the American Donald Budge in 1938 was (at the time of writing) the last appearance in the men's final by a British player. He reached the final of the mixed doubles in 1934. He

Herbert Lawford, Wimbledon Singles Champion.

'Bunny' Austin. Wimbledon, 1938.

was twice ranked World Number Two and was the top seed at the 1939 Wimbledon championships.

The 1920s and 1930s were a golden age for Repton tennis. In addition to the exploits of Austin, J.W. Nuthall (O 1926) won the Under 16 event at Queen's in 1926, and in 1929 he won the Under 18 event at Queen's and at Junior Wimbledon. Further successes in the Queen's Under 16 event were achieved by J.S. Nuthall (O 1929) in 1931 and D.D. Warwick (M 1937) in 1939. In 1932 four Old Reptonians played in the Wimbledon Championships: Austin, M.V. Callendar (B 1921), J.W. Nuthall and R.K. Tinkler (B 1923), and Nuthall and Tinkler represented both England and Britain in senior internationals, though not in the Davis Cup. An exhibition match featuring the 1920 Wimbledon Champion

'Big Bill' Tilden was watched by the whole school. Much of this success was based on the efforts of J.F. Carter, Housemaster of the Orchard, who himself was a fine player and an excellent coach. There were many successes in doubles events at national level and other fine players too numerous to mention.

Three more hard courts were laid down in 1946. Although the various sets of courts were all slightly different in texture, the school then had ten courts that could essentially be called 'red shale'. The 1950s, 1960s, and 1970s were not particularly distinguished ones from the tennis standpoint, although there were several players of quality in the school during these years. A public schools' championship for teams of four players, the Youll Cup, was introduced in 1947, and an Under 15 event for pairs, the Thomas Bowl, soon followed. Repton entered the Youll Cup for the first time in 1950, and with a strong side succeeded in being runners–up. In 1961 Repton won the Thomas Bowl. Apart from these achievements, however, success was scant. A major change came in the early 1970s when all the courts were replaced with an 'Instaplay' (all–weather) surface.

At the end of the tennis section in Repton 1557–1957, R. Hodson states: 'We can only hope that the great victories of the 1920s and 1930s may at some time be repeated.' There

> *What sets Repton apart from other schools is its strong sense of community, both within the house, within a year group and throughout the whole school. This is manifested in the friendships made and in the continued success of the OR Society.*
>
> **Anna Perham (A 2002)**

Left: Roger Thompson (Master i/c Tennis), Andrew Jarrett (right, then Coach, now Wimbledon referee) and the 1987 squad. All nine players were of national championship standard and were winners of the Glanvill and Clark Cups.

has been no one to match the achievements of Austin after he left Repton, but at school level the years since 1980 have seen the school become a dominant force again. In the 25 years between 1981 and 2005 Repton won the Youll Cup 15 times and the Glanvill Cup (the national schools' championship, which it entered for the first time in 1980) 11 times. The British Schools Under 19 Championship, the Clark Cup, was won in 1981 and from 1983 to 1988 (when it was discontinued), and the Inter-regional Championship was won from 1981 to 1984 (when it, too, ended). In addition, the Thomas Bowl was won twice and the Aberdare Cup (the National Schools Girls Championship) was won for four consecutive years in the mid–1980s. During this period several pupils won national singles titles: A. Grant (A 1983), N. Pashley (N 1985), P. Robinson (N 1986), A. Livermore (N 1987), S. Silvester (M 1989) and P. Cooper (C 1989). Several others (in addition to those named above) represented England or Wales at senior or junior international level: N. Beedham (O 1980), D. Ison (H 1983), S. Heron (H 1983), A. Fleming (A 1985), D. Bishop (N 1985), M. Loosemore (N 1986), S. Bonham (M 1990), D. Loosemore (N 1990), A. Barnes (H 1995), M. Powell (H 1995) and M. Llewellyn (N 1996). Two others represented their countries in the Davis Cup: D. Sweeney (H 1984) (Zambia) and M. Choy (H 1990) (Singapore).

Three ex-Wimbledon players who served as Head Coach at Repton for part of these successful years were Nick Fulwood, Leighton Alfred and Andrew Jarrett, the last named having taken over as Wimbledon referee in 2006. The school's success at tennis persuaded the authorities to agree to the construction of two indoor courts, and these were opened in 1989 by Tony Pickard (then coach to Wimbledon champion Stefan Edberg). Throughout this period our main rivals have been Millfield

School, and in addition to clashes at national events, there have been regular weekend fixtures with them, home and away, on an annual basis. At the time of writing there are plans to develop an academy attached to the school together with a proposal to provide either clay court facilities or further indoor courts. From 1980 to the present, tennis at the school has been strongly supported by Wilson Sporting Goods Company Ltd.

To maintain the school's high standards the players involved had to train and practise throughout the year, usually at the expense of participating in other sports, and this degree of concentration was not universally welcomed at first. Interestingly, in a conversation with Austin in the late 1980s, he himself said that he would not have wanted to concentrate on tennis to that degree at school as he loved all sports. Certainly several of the players named above found their way into the First XI football teams of their respective eras, and it does not seem to have harmed their tennis. Today most of Repton's sports either overlap over two or three terms or are played throughout the year, as competition has become stronger. The future of Repton tennis looks secure in the hands of Head Coach Richard Physick, who spent several years coaching in Germany and who has plans to continue and improve the Repton heritage.

Perhaps it would be fitting to return to Henry Wilfred Austin. 'Bunny' (believed to be a school nickname, from a cartoon rabbit named Wilfred) died on 26 August 2000. A month beforehand the school sent him a framed photograph of the Repton cricket field (believed to be his favourite memory of Repton), which he hung on his wall. The picture is now in the home of his daughter, Jenny, in Canada. Below it is a short inscription: 'To Bunny – a fine cricketer and Repton's greatest tennis player.'

Roger Thompson

RUGBY

*'With a fine disregard for the rules, Richard Morris picked
up the ball and ran with it.'*

So started the rebirth of rugby at Repton in the Michaelmas
Term of 1972. Richard Morris, a New Zealander who had been
recently appointed master at Repton, was a man of unbounded
enthusiasm for any cause he espoused, and he responded with
gusto to a request from Jeremy McArthur (M 1968) and myself.
Having tested the water with a couple of highly unofficial games
played on the remote wastes of Sale Flats, Jeremy and I knew
the demand was there. But how were we to crack the years of
tradition that Repton was a soccer school and to overcome the
understandable reluctance of the soccer hierarchy not to lose
any talent to the 'thugs' game played by gentlemen'?

The answer lay in Richard Morris. Jeremy and I visited
him one evening in the Old Mitre, and asked him to consider
championing the cause of rugby at Repton. His reply, as befits a
man from the nation of the All Blacks, was unequivocally
positive. He went straight to the top, and John Gammell gave his
strong backing. In doing so, perhaps unwittingly, he was
maintaining a tradition established by Fisher, who is recorded as
having organized and captained in 1920 the first ever rugby

match played at Repton: it was against Trent College on the
Steinyard, and we lost 17–6.

Chapel Hall was designated as the school's rugby pitch
for use in the Lent term, which was a great fillip for the two XVs
that were rapidly established. Richard chose the team jersey –
red to hide the blood – and I rather suspect he was influenced by
Wales's great endeavours of that period. Sunday, 11 February
1973 saw the first home game played by the First XV, fittingly
against a Rugby School XV. The Reptonian records
diplomatically that: 'With tremendous support … Repton,
although on the defensive for most of the game, were able to
entertain the crowd with some good attacking moves.'

The game continued at Repton, never threatening other
sports but providing the opportunity for those boys who
wanted to try their hand at it. For some it provided great
exercise and fun, for others the unmissable chance to do
honourable battle in the boys vs staff match. For me it was a
wonderful springboard to a continuing passion for the game,
involving a Blue for Cambridge in 1976 and subsequently some
eight years at Nottingham. I still treasure John Gammell's
telegram of support, delivered to the Twickenham changing
room, and at every Varsity match reunion I raise my glass in
thanks to Repton.

Peter Nixon (O 1969)

Scrum down, 2006.

C.B. Fry: Repton's Greatest All-rounder

Many people today have never heard of Charles Burgess Fry (1872–1956), but in the early years of the 20th century he was the most famous man in the country. John Arlott, BBC cricket broadcaster, described C.B., as he was often known, as 'perhaps the most variously gifted Englishman of any age'.

C.B. Fry's achievements were many, great and in a variety of sporting disciplines. They included playing soccer for England and appearing in an FA Cup Final for Southampton. As a student he equalled the world long jump record. He played rugby for Oxford University, Blackheath and the Barbarians. Outstanding performances as a cricketer are also among his achievements: he captained the England cricket team without losing a Test Match and scored six centuries in successive innings.

His school career, six years of which were spent at Repton, proved that his academic abilities were as impressive and varied as his sporting skills. It should be no surprise that the school continues to describe him as our 'greatest all-rounder'.

Born in West Croydon, Surrey, it was by accident that C.B. came to Repton, as he explained in his autobiography, *Life Worth Living*: 'I was intended for Aldenham School, but found myself at Repton, because I was sent there for practice, and got a scholarship by mistake.' He arrived in Repton in 1885 and boarded in what was then known as Forman's, now the Cross, with studies then the size of hen-coops and just the one hot bath a week, according to schedule.

Whether he intended a Derbyshire education or not, Fry clearly loved the village, and in spite of travels that took him around the world he always remembered Repton with pride and affection.

Many visiting the village today would agree with him that 'the view of the Old Priory through the school Arch as one walks towards it along the ancient wall which bounds the playing fields from the village is one of the fairest instances I know of historic England exhibited in shapely grey stone'. He expressed no surprise that when film-makers sought a school with the most typical English

Vanity Fair sketch of Fry.

C.B. Fry.

surroundings for the filming of *Goodbye Mr Chips* they chose Repton. He was invited to help produce the old-time cricket and football scenes, but a Test Match commitment prevented him from doing so.

While scenes such as that of the Arch and the Old Priory have changed little since Fry's time, other aspects of the village and surrounding area have seen alterations. When he was at Repton the bridge that crosses the Trent between Repton and Willington was gated, and he ran paperchases on Donington Park, long before it hosted motorcycle or car races.

There is no shortage of information about Fry's sporting achievements during his school career. These were, as the *Reptonian* reported, many and varied. In *Life Worth Living* Fry refers, as one would expect, to many of them. He specifically refers to the football team, of which he was a member, being capable of putting up a good show against Derby County and drawing against Cambridge.

When it came to cricket, he won a place in the First XI at the age of 16 and played alongside other great cricketers, including Lionel Palairet. Fry recalls Pat Exham, a coach of the time, who was greatly admired by Repton pupils of the day for his ability to break the tiles on the pavilion roof with his on-drive.

Fry compared playing in house matches at Repton with competing against international opposition: 'These matches were played under the kind of high pressure one encountered later in Test Matches.'

It would appear that a number of Repton experiences played a significant role in Fry's sporting career. Probably one of the most frequently recounted of his stories concerns the man who, he said, was his only ever coach in athletics, his Repton housemaster, Mr Forman. Fry recalled that Forman passed by one day as he was practising the long jump on rough turf into an elementary pit on the paddock. 'He stopped for a few minutes, told me I did not jump high enough, took off his black mackintosh and made a heap of it between the take-off and the pit. The mackintosh frightened me into jumping much higher.' Fry goes on to say: 'It is rather interesting that up at Oxford … when I did a world's record in the long jump … I saw a ghostly mackintosh and remembered Mr Forman's vibrant voice.'

Although it is Fry's outstanding sporting achievements for which he will always be remembered, he was equally impressive as an academic while at Repton, carrying off prizes for German, Latin prose and verse, Greek verse and French. The school archives record that he was an excellent debater and actor and an accomplished singer too: truly an all-rounder.

With so many achievements, one might expect smaller details to escape the memory, but in his autobiography Fry mentions many of the more minor events, such as being taught drawing out of doors in the summer: 'We sat on camp stools and drew our versions of trees and birds and anything in sight'.

Fry left Repton in 1891. He died in 1956 after a distinguished career. On 28 September his ashes were interred at Repton parish church, next to the school and near the grave of Arthur Forman.

Today, his memory and inspiration live on in the school. Each year Repton offers up to five entrance awards, the C.B. Fry Awards. As one would expect, these awards recognize all-round achievement and potential – in short, they are offered to boys and girls naturally gifted in a variety of fields, like the great man himself.

Sue Grief

INTER-HOUSE RIVALRY

Why are Reptonians so fiercely proud of their respective houses? After all, house members are no more than a group of people thrust together not by choice but by the whims of their parents. The people we have breakfast, lunch and dinner with each day are often not our best friends but a random hotchpotch of folk who have happened to descend on the same building at the same time as ourselves. Why then is house rivalry such a key part of Repton life? Is it the sense of belonging? The chance for an individual, no matter how talented or socially skilled, to belong? Is it the chance to play for a team or sing a song under the banner of one's particular house? Or is it the chance for us to be ourselves within the walls of these private houses, with no teachers telling us to straighten our ties or rearrange our shirts? Exactly why the house system is so unique at Repton is not easy to fathom, but it is an unquestionable truth that inter-house rivalry is one of the key factors that make the Repton experience such an enjoyable one.

Schools up and down the country will talk of the 'healthy competition' brought about by house system. In this, Repton is set part. An Old Reptonian will introduce him or herself not by which years they attended the school, but which house they were in. Indeed, the current prospectus states: 'Every Reptonian staunchly believes his or her house is the very best at the school.'

It may be said that inter-house competition at Repton is less about 'healthy opposition', as at some schools, and more about intense rivalry. This is not to say that there was animosity between pupils from different houses – far from it. What it meant was that for the 90 minutes of a league match or for the recital of house unison, these friendships were put aside in the common goal of making one's respective house the best. A sausage roll at break would taste that much sweeter in the knowledge that your house had defeated your friend's from up the High Street in a league match. And it wasn't just the pupils. Housemasters and house tutors were just as bad! Many masters were known to give inspirational (or so they thought) pep talks before a league match or cross-country run. So obviously those bragging rights extended to the Common Room.

The easiest way to see how house rivalry manifests itself within Repton is at a house sports event. Be it football, hockey, swimming, water polo or athletics, whether the stakes were high (a senior cup final) or inconsequential, the hope was always to win and enjoy the boasting that followed. Inter-house sports matches were always defined at Repton by the impressive support that followed a match, be it Fourth House or a cup final. Many will remember their housemaster or mistress announcing after lunch that every member of the house would be expected to support the team during the coming afternoon

The contemporary face of House spirit. Garden in the May 2005 Tug-o-war.

Latham taking — and feeling — the strain.

and not slope off to the Grubber. Indeed, one housemaster (who will remain nameless) was known to take roll-call on the sidelines to check which members of his house had turned up. Songs were prepared during lunch for members of a team. Pitch invasions were even known from time to time (not officially encouraged, I might add). It's these times of togetherness, when sloping up to Sale Flats on a wet and windy Tuesday afternoon, that define the house experience. And if you were playing, the sight of a gathering of your housemates on the touchline was worth a goal in itself.

The annual steeplechase was a particular example of house-rivalry taking a grip of the school. The sea of different coloured shirts sprinting from one side of the square to the other, jostling for position, is a sight to behold and without doubt a great Repton image. As the last dregs of runners finally crept through the Hole in the Wall and out towards the fields of Milton, the anxious wait began to see which coloured shirt would re-emerge first through the door that led back to the square. The wait could be excruciating. Housemasters and mistresses, stopwatches and clipboards to hand, nervously waited to see if the colours of their house would appear first. The roar — or sigh — that accompanied the 'first back' could be one of surprise or expectancy, but by the look on the faces of the crowds gathered by the pavilion it was, without doubt, something that mattered.

It's not just on the sports field where inter-house rivalry is rife. The school quiz competition was a particularly boisterous affair, and one left the contest feeling rather sorry for the quizmaster trying to quell the hearty crowd.

The pinnacle of inter-house rivalry at Repton undoubtedly came during the time of the annual music competition, not the most likely source of high passion, one would think. The highlight of the music competitions was the House Unison competition, a time when every member of the house came together to recite a song to the (more often than not) derision of the rest of the school. There was no hiding this time! This very event highlights what is so good about Repton's house system and the school as a whole. This is when the Head of House, the B-Blocker, the sportsman, the intellectual join together with one common goal — to win for the house. All right, the talent on show may not be the best, but the event was not about musical excellence but about a sense of belonging and togetherness. This is the reason the house system works so well at the Repton, and why, years after leaving, we're still very proud of the houses we attended.

Matthew Gooderick (C 1992)

WIDER STILL & WIDER

*T*his section looks at four bodies to which Repton gave life: the Repton Club, which originated in an address to the school in 1894, the OR Society, which was one of the many fruits of Ford's first Speech Day in 1901, the Old Reptonian Lodge, which dates from 1914, and the Repton Foundation which was created in 1997.

THE REPTON CLUB

Oxford House was the first university 'settlement', established in the East End of London in 1884 (the year in which the Marquis of Queensbury's rules for boxing were agreed) by men of Keble College as a home to graduates, tutors and those intending to enter the Church to enable them to experience at first hand the plight of the city poor and provide a centre from which they might take practical steps to address social deprivation.

On 16 May 1894 the Rev. Arthur Winnington-Ingram, then head of Oxford House (and a future Bishop of London), was invited to address the school (probably by fellow Old Marlburian Vassall). He invited Repton to produce 'a rough boys' club' – that is, a club in London's East End for boys who had been barred from other clubs. So positive was the response that it was decided to rename what had hitherto been called the Blackguards' Club as the Repton Club.

Winnington-Ingram's protégé, Hugh Legge, secured a three-storey house in a suitably disreputable area and within a year built up a membership of nearly 60 evil-smelling 'tough, wiry fellows, with tons of pluck ... with first-rate fighting qualities' and with 'a rooted objection to most forms of discipline, and a kind of pious horror for any man or thing that they call "religious".' Thereafter Legge was 'very

The wall of the Repton Club.

discriminating in choosing boys ... keeping the club down to the proper standard' so that it served those who most needed it.

Legge believed that 'the great secret ... of keeping the club in the right direction' was to encourage boxing, and the boxing saloon on the top floor became the institution's heart. Indeed, it ultimately developed into the most famous amateur boxing club in Britain, which at the last count had produced 10 Olympic boxers (including Audley Harrison), 97 international representatives, 21 national champions and two world champions, Maurice Hope and John H. Stracey.

The current entrance to the Repton Club.

REPTON BOXING CLUB
Est: 1884
ENTRANCE

THE GARY. BARKER. GYMNASIUM.

Two Boxers at Repton Club, which was also the location for the card game at the start of Lock, Stock and Two Smoking Barrels.

In the words of Dave Robinson, Repton's long-serving chairman:

> *Boxing helps keep the kids off the street. If it weren't for the club, many of them would be out mugging one another, doing gear or nicking cars ... once people come here they become more self-disciplined and start to make something of themselves.*

This philosophy echoes that of the club's foundation: offering underprivileged boys the chance to improve their muscles and their moral fibre in order to divert them from a life of crime. Legge summarized it in the following six points:

> *(1) If a lad knows well how to use his fists, he, as an almost universal rule, does not use his boots or a knife. (2) The discipline of the ring is almost the only discipline these lads get ... (3) A man gets a high sense of fairness and honour from being accustomed to rules which disqualify him for a foul, forbid him to strike another fellow when down, and abhor such a thing as knuckle-dusters. (4) ... The best men with their fists will often put up with a deal more provocation than ordinary persons, as if, being conscious of their power, they have also been taught how to control it ... (5) The effect on the physique of the lads is great. If they did not box they would do nothing, and the result of doing nothing in Bethnal Green generally is oakum-picking. (6) Boxing is good for the morals.*

Repton appears to have severed its formal connection with the club not long after itself dropping boxing.

John Plowright

THE OLD REPTONIAN SOCIETY

Since becoming Secretary of the Old Reptonian Society my duties have taken me from Edinburgh to Paris, via Leeds, Torquay and Knutsford, with numerous visits to London in between. Venues such as the Mansion House and Houses of Parliament do not occur everyday, but they do come round every now and again. Many people have been met, and many new friends made.

One of the earliest requests I received was an urgent plea from the OR golfers to borrow a school flag. So important was this that a courier was dispatched to carry the flag from the Arch to the Valderama Golf Club in Spain, where it was to grace the clubhouse during a match between the Old Reptonians and the Old Malvernians. The latter won the match, but Repton enjoyed the moral victory as we alone flew the flag!

Another early experience was one that may indicate my lack of IT skills but also illustrates how busy the Old Reptonian office can be. The computer there was supposedly modified to allow me to receive e-mails for both my own personal address and the OR address, but while personal messages came in, the OR account was suspiciously quiet. When I called on the IT department for help it transpired that OR e-mails had

It used to be customary on Speech Day for boys to adorn their rooms with flowers and to design signs for their study doors. This example from Latham dates from 1914.

Although nominally a minor School sport, OR golfers have twice (in 1963 and 1986) won the Halford Hewitt (the golfing equivalent of the Arthur Dunn or the Cricketer Cup). Here are the 1963 winners.

inadvertently been frozen and on being 'unlocked' a backlog of 182 messages appeared. If you were one of those affected and had to wait some time for a reply, please accept my apologies for the delay!

One great pleasure of being Secretary is that you get to meet many Old Reptonians, male and female, old and young, on the various social occasions that we stage. The OR year always begins these days with Drinks in the City, a gathering in London, often at a club or wine bar. This convivial event attracts many younger members of the Society. Staff, too, are among the event's regular supporters, and a meal often follows. However, this has sometimes resulted in our staff group missing their train, despite a rapid dash across town.

Gaudies are also popular social occasions, offering the opportunity to certain age groups to revisit the school and see some of their old friends. When I was a housemaster we always looked forward to the gaudies because they involved meeting people who loved Repton. Reminiscences flowed freely, and there was a smile on every face. All that was needed was a fine, sunny day, and everything else looked after itself – or so it seemed! Now that I am in charge of organizing the event, I appreciate how much work goes into them. Current pupils are, however, unfailingly generous in giving their time to show OR visitors around. Even during the recent World Cup, when the Gaudy clashed with an England game, there was still no shortage

of volunteers – something for which I remain most grateful.

I have also been incredibly fortunate to have a tremendous team at the helm of the society with whom to work. Successive presidents, each serving one year, have been very supportive. The Chairman for the last five years has been Robert Bond, who has kept the ship sailing in the right direction and fully deserves the Presidency in our 450th anniversary year. Chris Charter, the Foundation Director, has also worked enormously hard, so much so that he was appointed assistant secretary and an honorary OR. He does a large part of the editorial and compositional work on *The Arch*, the new-look OR magazine, which was his idea. Neither must the role of Edward Wilkinson, Governor with special responsibility for the Society, be overlooked. His commitment to safeguarding OR interests is unflagging. Treasurer John Wallis completes the management team and has conferred unprecedented clarity on the OR accounts.

The Arch attracts so many compliments that we are all convinced of the wisdom of the decision to depart from the traditions of the *Terminal Letter*, making the publication more pictorial and lively, while maintaining the focus on keeping readers informed about developments at Repton and in the OR world. Once again, I could tell you that the work involved is not insignificant, but it is enjoyable. In fact, the same could be said of all the tasks involving the Society. An association that exists according to its constitution to promote the interests of Old Reptonians is as relevant and as lively as any time in its history. Long may it thrive.

Mike Stones

THE OLD REPTONIAN LODGE

Freemasonry has been established for well over 300 years, with the first Grand Lodge founded in 1717. Although there have been many changes since then, the organization still focuses on the three key principles of Brotherly Love, Relief and Truth or Fellowship, Charity and Integrity. The fellowship extends beyond Britain to many other countries and provides an opportunity for those who move to establish firm friends and contacts in a short time. In the last 25 years alone the total funds distributed by the charity amount to nearly £77 million, much to non-masonic charities, including nearly £6 million to various hospices in recent years. Integrity may be best described as the maintenance of a code that espouses the highest personal and business ethics. Freemasonry is not attached to any religious order, and in many lodges there are members of most of the leading faiths.

The Old Reptonian Lodge was formed on 4 June 1914 at the Café Monico in London. The ceremony was conducted by the then Grand Secretary, Sir Edward Letchworth FSA, who installed Colonel C.W. Napier-Clavering (M 1871) as the first Worshipful Master. This senior mason was then the Provincial Grand Master of Northumberland. There were 25 founder members of the lodge, two of whom, H.C. Hayward and J.L. Crommelin Brown, were later to become housemasters. At the Lodge's first regular meeting in July 1914 there were three new initiates, Henry Vassall, the Rev. Henry Napier-Clavering (M 1874) and Reginald Popham (B 1906). It was Vassall who proposed that the Headmaster should be initiated, and the Rev. Geoffrey Fisher was duly made a mason on 11 January 1916. The lodge continued to meet at the Café Monico and other establishments in London until it moved to its present home at Freemasons Hall, Great Queen Street, in 1948.

The minutes of the Lodge's early years make many references to Brethren being unable to attend as a result of military service. On one occasion the Brother due to take part in the ceremony was absent as a result of blood poisoning resulting from wounds received at the Front. In 1926 the Lodge acted as sponsor in the formation of the Old Salopian Lodge, proving that rivalry on the sports field does not extend to matters masonic.

There appears to have been no celebration of the 25th anniversary of the Lodge, probably because this coincided with the outbreak of the Second World War, and again the minutes reflect the impact of war on proceedings. One of the more interesting entries refers to a request from Grand Lodge to surrender masonic jewels to be melted down and the proceeds presented to the Treasury as a masonic gift.

Lord Fisher, Archbishop of Canterbury.

In 1944 the lodge welcomed the Headmaster, T.L. Thomas, as a joining member, and in 1948 the former Headmaster, Michael Clarke, was installed as Worshipful Master. By this time Geoffrey Fisher had taken up the reins as Archbishop of Canterbury, and he wrote to the lodge that: 'I would have gone to all lengths to come to the lodge meeting to complete the trio of Headmasters – but this is impossible owing to other engagements.' Of these three Headmasters, Geoffrey Fisher became Grand Chaplain, and Michael Clarke eventually rose to the office of Assistant Grand Chaplain and Provincial Grand Master of Warwickshire.

On the school's 400th anniversary in 1957 the Lodge presented an engraved trowel, which was used by Geoffrey Fisher when laying the foundation stone of the 400 Hall. This same trowel was used for laying the foundation stone of the Abbey and was suitably engraved by subscription from the Lodge. The 50th anniversary was celebrated on 19 May 1964 at Drapers' Hall with the initiation of L.P. Thompson McCausland, the Chairman of the Governors. In September of the same year the last surviving founder member, H.G. Redman (L 1898), resigned because of ill-health.

In May 1974 R.F. Popham retired as Treasurer of the Lodge, a post he had held for 35 years. As a mark of esteem he was presented with a silver rose bowl, which he immediately donated to the lodge as a permanent memento of his term of office. In May 1986 John Bradburn (P 1928), who had already served as Grand Registrar, was promoted to the office of Junior Grand Warden, the sixth most senior mason in the country; he thus became the most senior mason in the history of the Lodge. The 75th anniversary in 1989 was marked by a visit from the then Assistant Grand Master, the Rt. Hon. Lord Farnham. The following year Robert Latham (N 1942) (No. 2) and Nigel

Tablets commemorating three Archbishops. Fisher's alludes to his freemasonry.

> *The CCF has played a prominent part in the education of everyone who has been to the school. Its fostering of camaraderie, promotion of excellence and development of personal skills are intrinsic to the ethos of Repton. The cold afternoons spent perfecting drill may remain in the minds of many, but for me involvement in the CCF allowed me not only to develop as an individual but also participate in the development of others.*
>
> **Victoria Pym (F 2002)**

Grindrod (L 1936) (No. 5) were both Grand Stewards: a rare event for any lodge. One of the recent Worshipful Masters of the Lodge was Bill Lane (L 1937), who was recently President of the OR Society.

Because the Lodge is based in London it is entitled to be a member of the Public Schools Lodges Council. Every year there is an annual festival, which representatives from all the schools are invited to attend. The first time that Repton hosted the festival was in 1928, when the Worshipful Master was the Headmaster, Geoffrey Fisher. At the meeting he delivered what was considered to be a thoughtful account of the school's history, which has been read on subsequent meetings of the Lodge.

In 1995 the Lodge again hosted the Public Schools Lodges Council Festival at Repton, in the presence of the Deputy Grand Master, Iain Ross Bryce. On this occasion the Lodge made a donation to the New Masonic Samaritan Fund of £4,000. It also presented to the school the steps leading down from the Paddock to the Cloisters, which had been subscribed for by members of the Lodge. The Worshipful Master was John Bradburn, whose son, Richard (P 1964), will be in the chair for 2007. The next time that this festival will be in Repton is in 2014, when the Lodge will celebrate its centenary.

As with nearly all fellowship organizations there was a decline in membership during the 1980s and 1990s, but the Lodge is now experiencing an upturn in both membership and interest and can be said to be in very good heart.

Bill Summ (N 1958)

THE REPTON FOUNDATION
Repton is not a well-endowed school, and when the government announced that it was to abolish the Assisted Places Scheme the Governors, under the chairmanship of Nicholas Wilson (L 1949), took the visionary step of establishing the Repton Foundation in December 1997. It was set up as a separate charity with the aim of providing both

Repton and Foremarke with an enduring endowment that will secure their future and allow the schools to concentrate on the principal task of delivering educational excellence.

At their first meeting the trustees declared that the Foundation should fund the nine pupils who were at Foremarke under the Assisted Places Scheme as it was phased out so that they could continue their education at Repton up to their sixth form years. This commitment was seen in terms of renewing the legacy of Sir John Port. To recognize and thank those who have kindly indicated they are leaving a bequest to the schools, the Sir John Port Society was formed. The Foundation also assists with funding to develop the educational, sporting, art, drama and music facilities at both schools.

An equally important aim of the Foundation is to renew friendships among all those who are, or have been, connected with the schools and, where appropriate, to renew associations with both schools. The Repton Foundation is more than just a means of raising funds. It is a commitment to the very ethos of the schools and the acceptance of a responsibility to the community for education. There is little doubt that the Foundation is benefiting both current and future generations of Reptonians and will be seen as one of the most far-reaching decisions taken during Repton's long and proud history.

Chris Charter

Robert Beldam, CBE., Foundation Benefactor.

MATTERS ACADEMIC

THE MEDIOCRE IS THE ENEMY OF EXCELLENT: THIRTY YEARS OF CHANGE

I had been warned by David Gibbs (Staff 1955–64) when I returned from India in 1965 that I might find Repton old fashioned. Considering that education in India was then in a time-warp akin to Britain in the 1940s and 1950s it may surprise some that I found it to be true.

The boys still wore heavy, grey, woollen herring-bone suits that I remembered from my own school more than a decade earlier. Moreover, fagging was widespread, bullying was not

The tribulations of Saint Guthlac, as depicted in the School Library.

unfashionable, and a rigid hierarchy existed among both boys and staff over such trivia as hands in pockets and how many buttons could be left undone. Worse than this was the hierarchy that placed excellence in sports meteorically higher than academic or cultural excellence. Later I was to read a damning HMI report on Repton that endorsed the impression that Repton was – at least in matters academic – unimpressive.

John Thorn had been appointed to change this, and I - along with Barry Downing (Modern Languages), John Fishley (Physics) and Dick Morgan (Geography) – was among the staff appointed to try to introduce academic excellence. It was not always easy. In the rigid staff hierarchy Housemasters were demi-gods, and new members of staff existed to be snubbed – especially if they did not think cricket important. Teachers under the age of 35 were still referred to as 'junior staff'. The Old Mitre (for DBSMs, Dedicated Bachelor School Masters) was run like an officers' mess, with silence at breakfast and staff fags to ferry in food from the kitchen. This ludicrous left-over from *Tom Brown's Schooldays* continued until the Rev. H.A.P. (Peter) Wills, who had come to us from a post in industry, dropped a tray of food outside the door of the Old Mitre dining room after those within had refused the courtesy of opening it for him. Arriving in Repton after seven years teaching in India I found it all rather juvenile.

The attitude to work was studiously blasé. I had seen this at Oxford and noted that it characterized a proportion of those who had been to major public schools and who had jobs to go to within the family business or who had contacts that ensured employment without undue effort. The cult of effortless superiority has a long lineage, and Castiglione's *The Book of the Courtier*, which was translated from Italian into English only

The view in the School Library towards the Vassall Room.

The Yard Set (Mid-50s).

four years after Repton's foundation, was no doubt a handbook for early Reptonians. C.B. Fry remains Repton's great exemplar of the cult, and it was an attitude – a refusal to be seen to be trying too hard – that lost the First XI matches even in recent times.

The staff that John Thorn appointed in the early 1960s came from grammar or minor public schools where the work ethic prevailed, and intentionally or otherwise they revolutionized the academic life of Repton. Quite simply they professionalized it.

Until the late 1960s departmental meetings scarcely existed. All staff were Oxbridge graduates and could be relied on to teach well without more ado. In theory. In practice, watching First XI cricket on the Square from the upper windows of the main teaching block might be a priority for some. For others, running a team or a house might take precedence over preparing lessons. It was, in matters academic, frankly lightheartedly amateurish. One did not begrudge the fun nor the fact that a housemaster might understandably give priority to running his house, but the job of a head of department is to make sure that his subject is taught well, is taken seriously and enables the pupil to maximize his potential. This does not preclude enjoyment – far from it. Any subject will be taught best if taught by enthusiasts, and enthusiasts make the learning process fun. One of the aims of a Repton head of department in the 1960s and 1970s was to establish that academic work could be as much fun as games and that it should be taken at least as seriously. In the late 1960s the supremacy of Brook House or the Priory in the senior house matches was the only area of school life to be taken seriously. Distinguished scholars, such as James Fenton, who

later became Professor of Poetry at Oxford, or exponents of art or music had a low status among their peers.

There was a legitimate sense of grievance among boys who were keen to do well academically or culturally that their contribution counted little with many of their housemasters. I remember attending a meeting of the Literary Society in 1966 at which James Fenton gave a talk of stunning brilliance on Malory's *Le Morte D'Arthur*, a book it is doubtful that many of the staff (I include myself) had read in its entirety or at all. He received no credit for it. Later that year I took a party of A level and Oxbridge students to hear W.H. Auden talk at Horninglow church in Burton upon Trent. Auden was the most famous poet writing in English at the time – I had attended his lectures when he was Professor of Poetry at Oxford in the 1950s – and the fact that he was speaking in Burton upon Trent was remarkable. It was on this occasion that James Fenton introduced himself to Auden and established what later became an important friendship. Fenton wrote Byronesque poetry with enviable fluidity, and I admired both his literary skill and his confidence in his art. My point is that – with the honourable exception of Heather Hawkins, a part-time teacher of English – he received virtually no encouragement or praise in the Repton of that time.

Drama under Mike Charlesworth and Music under William Agnew were the school's great cultural strengths, despite limited facilities. John Thorn himself tried hard to encourage intellectual debate and cultural activity – a new music centre was first planned in his time – but Repton, described by Lynam Thomas (Thorn's predecessor) as 'a place for the beta-query-plus boy', was not ready for serious change, and he moved on to more sympathetic climes in Winchester.

John Gammell (1968–78) was a great reconciler, and part of his role was to heal the conflicts. Paternal in style, magnanimous by nature and a good listener, Gammell looked after both staff and pupils as if they were an extension of the house he had run at Winchester. Under his benign patronage some important forward movement was made.

Shortly before he left, John Thorn from the top of Jacob's Ladder had dismissed one mass demonstration after Sunday chapel with cool aplomb, and it said much for the respect in which he was held that the demonstration melted away peacefully. John Gammell inherited the maelstrom and was the right man to handle it. In the face of student rebellion – 'Down with Chapel/Corps/cross-country/rules on dress, etc.' – student councils and discussion groups were set up. Chaired by senior housemasters and containing a cross-section of staff and elected pupils, they discussed and reported back on the key grievances. I was on an early one (chaired by Bill Blackshaw) that unanimously – and uniquely among the eight groups discussing the same topic – agreed that Repton should take girls. They duly arrived and proved good value, even though some staff and parents remained opposed to them.

With the girls came a renewal of drive in the Art School, music and drama. In subjects like my own (English) they brought valuable alternative viewpoints and insights. The Abbey opened in 1979, but before that the first full-time female teacher – Alison Webb – was appointed (to teach Physics). She was still expected to 'make the tea', and lazy boys could take the easy way of blaming their own failures on the fact that they had a woman teacher. Fortunately, John Gammell supported his appointees.

Academically progress was made. In the late 1960s form teachers in B Block were expected to teach English and History, whatever their degree. I found myself teaching American history, about which I knew little. And a classicist with spare periods might be teaching English but with no relish for the copious marking it involved. One of my early campaigns was to get away from this amateurish approach and

James Fenton (H 1963).

insist that English be taught by staff with English degrees who were committed to the subject. Another was to increase the number of periods of English. It was normal then for some lower school forms to have six periods of Maths, French and Latin, but only four of English. Fortunately, the Rugby Group had recently been set up (consisting then of 17 public schools), and I was able to amass statistics showing that English at Repton had a share of teaching time significantly below the average for our competitors. John Gammell – who, like John Thorn, was a trained historian but taught English by preference – was sympathetic, and change came about. Dedicated English teachers appointed in his time included Angus Graham-Campbell (who moved on to Eton), and Tim Scott.

It is easy – and facile – to depict English as an easy subject because it is the language we speak. As far as I was concerned, it was a rigorous – albeit hugely enjoyable – discipline, and perhaps in this I was influenced by the Oxford approach, where the introduction of English as a degree course had met with opposition for this very reason. I always believed in the importance of grammar and word derivation in the interests of precise and clear expression, and I faced scowls of disapproval at a meeting of prep school Heads of English when I publicly maintained this view at a time (1969) when 'creative writing' and non-interference with a child's self-expression were all the

With so many exciting opportunities available at Repton, it is difficult to select just one specific memory. However, directing the Fashion Show was undoubtedly the highlight of our last year at Repton, allowing us to unite so many students together in such a colourful and creative production.

Kjersti Scotton (A 2002) and Alec Farmer (P 2005)

Gymnastics display.

rage. A good English teacher needs some background in the Classics and some knowledge of history to start with. You cannot teach any early text – up until the time of the Romantics – without some classical background, and a knowledge of political and social history enriches the study of any text. In that sense, History and English are symbiotic. The Himalayas of English literature – Chaucer, Shakespeare, Milton, for example – require good teaching if they are to be accessible to modern readers. They were always central to our courses, and I doubt if many English departments could boast such enthusiasm to teach Milton as Repton's.

The dumbing down of English language started with the demise of the précis (the only exercise in English that could reduce a pupil to tears of frustration) in the late 1960s, and it was soon followed by the elimination of grammar and word derivation and the need for correct spelling and punctuation. Few lamented the loss of the précis, but the emphasis on a child's creativity to the exclusion of any concern for accuracy or precision in communication is reflected in a decline in the quality of writing in much of our 'quality' press. In Literature coursework favoured the diligent but less incisive; simple though worthy texts, like *To Kill a Mockingbird* and *Of Mice and Men*, did away with the need for a teacher; and argument and analysis were replaced by the use of the text as a trigger for the candidate's own creative writing.

Weekly departmental meetings became the norm in the 1970s. They gave unity and purpose and encouraged what is now called 'best practice' by the sharing of ideas and enthusiasms.

With David Jewell's appointment in 1978 a further and sometimes painful prod was given to the academic slowcoaches. David made it clear in so many words that he saw the heads of department as the driving engine of the school, not the housemasters as hitherto. Heads of departments whose academic results were faltering soon found themselves looking for other jobs. David was more than averagely ruthless in eliminating opposition to his reforms, and though I personally found it stimulating, many members of staff learned to live with anxiety during his time. In this he was the opposite of John Gammell. Oxbridge places became one of the criteria by which a department head was judged, and David himself was not over-scrupulous in leaning on heads of colleges to secure entry for a Reptonian.

The problems faced by girls in a still-predominantly boys' school is illustrated by an early incident in David's career and gives the flavour of the times. It had been reported that during PWs (periods for private work in the Library) the sixth form girls had been distracting boys from their study. It was decided that girls should therefore be banned from the Library. During my lunch hour I wrote a stiff note to the Headmaster pointing out, first, that the girls were new to the school and had a greater need to familiarize themselves with the library than the boys who had three years start on them; second, that the girls' parents paid the same fees as the boys and would be incensed that their daughters were denied one of the school's major facilities; and third, that if the *Daily Mirror* got hold of this story, as was more than probable, Repton would be the laughing-stock of the country. The decision was reversed by teatime. I should add that, in general, David Jewell was a great supporter of the girls and that this hasty decision was untypical. But that I was outspoken in opposing what seemed to me a dangerously knee-jerk reaction stood me in good stead later, for in 1985 David appointed me the school's first Director of Studies.

My role as Director of Studies was primarily to oversee the implementation of the new reforms that government was then introducing – the new GCSE exams, the National Curriculum, which involved the merging and simplifying of the many examining boards, and SATs. It was a time of educational ferment, and the conservative public schools were not always enthusiastic about implementing changes that they sometimes saw as a threat to their status or as a levelling down of academic excellence. The job also involved running weekly meetings of the academic heads of department, an extension of the meetings that individual departments now mostly held. As I had been running the English department for some 16 years and was out of the running for a house, because of a newly introduced (and mildly controversial) '40-year rule' that prevented staff aged 40 or more from taking over a house, this was a welcome challenge and one that I greatly enjoyed.

Dragging the feet over reforms that government was determined to introduce seemed pointless. If we had to change – whether or not we agreed with the changes and no matter how mind-numbing the 'cascading' meetings and the new terminology – the important thing was to handle the change professionally and to emerge competitive. In this David Jewell and myself saw eye to eye. David also initiated the practice of inviting groups of prep school headmasters to visit Repton, to hear talks by selected academic heads of department on current changes and to attend some musical or other cultural event, a practice that impressed prep schools and recruited good entrants.

Such a forceful headmaster could not expect to be popular with staff, and though I did not always agree with his sometimes brusque handling of problems there is no doubt that David effected reforms that other headmasters would have blenched at. I have mentioned the 40-year rule, which ended the practice of bestowing houses for long-term loyalty. Dick Morgan, myself and Mike Salter were the three immediate victims, and although it was painful at the time I approved in principle of the decision. Belatedly it has even occurred to me that since the three staff concerned were heads of departments with outstandingly good results he may even have decided that they would be wasted in houses. For David effected a monumental and overdue shift in the balance between departmental heads and housemasters, whom he saw as essentially 'child-minders', and I believe he enjoyed the lively debate of meetings of heads of department much more than the social and domestic problems of housemasters' meetings.

His great strength was in appointing high-flying staff from outside Repton, and though there were exceptions he was generally a shrewd judge of character. David Exham was brought in as Second Master, and John Driver, Adrian Mylward, Graham Parry and Rodney Atwood were appointed as heads of department. Excellent additions to the English department were Polly Mander, Martin Amherst Lock and Heather Morland.

With Graham Jones (1986–2003) a new and more managerial style came. Posts in the 'top team' proliferated, and outsiders, who would be unquestioningly loyal, were again brought in to top positions. As it happens, I value loyalty highly, but loyalty to an institution should not be unthinking. If you care for an institution you must be prepared to argue if you think it is making a mistake or taking a wrong direction, and open discussion – even when difficult for a headmaster to handle – is ultimately more successful and less divisive than having meetings behind closed doors where a few decide for the many. But as one gets older, headmasters get younger and can see well-meaning reservations as a threat. Although as Director of Studies I had achieved all that I had been asked to do and was briefly part of what was called the 'Kitchen Cabinet' (consisting of the Headmaster, the Second Master [David Exham], the Under Master [Roy French], a retired housemaster [David Wilkinson], and myself as Director of Studies), it was clear to me that Graham would be happier with his own appointee in this role, and since I was in the unusual position of having throughout retained my own department and was not interested in doing the staff timetable, I was quite happy to revert to simply running the English department – the job that always gave me most satisfaction. I think I was offered some other title – Senior Head of Department, perhaps – by way of compensation but never used it as it had no job and therefore no meaning. In Graham's time James Carpenter and John Golding were excellent additions to the English department.

Graham increased the senior management team by appointing Pat Silvey in the dual role of Under Master and Director of Studies, and later created a new post of Senior Mistress, taken by Rosemary Harris, to look after the girls. Under his successor, Rob Holroyd, the process has continued with the appointment from outside of a Deputy (Academic) Head.

There are advantages and disadvantages in proliferating managerial posts to outsiders. They may bring fresh ideas and they will be loyal to the person who appointed them. But they may also create friction among those who have given long and loyal service, and since they do not know what makes Repton unique they may exert a homogenizing influence and accelerate the loss of the school's special characteristics and harmless eccentricities.

I feel privileged to have been able to work for so long in a school that encouraged excellence and discouraged mediocrity in all spheres.

John Billington

'*Repton has accommodated our family for over ten years now as my two sisters, myself and my brother have passed through the Arch. Starting off as timid, apprehensive B Blockers, the school has helped each of us to achieve our potential whilst finding a group of both friends and tutors who have helped shape the people that we have become, and will continue to play an influential part in our lives. I hope that many other families will benefit from the outstanding qualities that Repton has to offer.*'

Annie Smith (F 2002)

MATTERS SPIRITUAL

It is reported that when Eric Blair (the future George Orwell) was collecting the names of the religions of the new boys at Eton, he would inquire 'Are you Cyrenaic, Sceptic, Epicurean, Cynic, Neo-platonist, Confucian or Zoroastrian?' Matters spiritual at Repton have always been much simpler, tending to centre upon the individual asking him- or latterly herself, 'Will I make it to Chapel on time?' and 'How long will the sermon last?'

In our increasingly hedonistic, materialistic, multidenominational but largely post-Christian society, compulsory Chapel, despite changes to the number and nature of its services, is in danger of appearing as much a vestige of a bygone age as ink-wells, learning by rote or corporal punishment. The vitality of Chapel is due to the fact that it continues to be served by those who provide the best possible advertisement for their faith by the way in which they live their lives, whilst it has arguably never been more relevant to Reptonians in providing an opportunity for quiet contemplation on the eternal verities amidst the rising tide of competing pressures and pleasures.

In an age when many on Facebook proudly cite their religious views as 'agnostic', 'atheist' or (with presumably unintended irony) 'Richard Dawkins', it is gratifying to note that Reptonians of a certain vintage subscribe cryptically but not heretically to 'Sarah's Dad', the Sarah in question being Sarah Perham, and her father being the Bishop of Gloucester, the Right Revd Michael Perham. In short, ORs may not always like to parade their religious convictions but whatever faith they may ultimately profess, Chapel continues to exert a quiet and civilizing influence.

John Plowright

THE CHAPLAINCY

Being a chaplain at Repton always involved walking a tightrope! Whether it was the way a visiting preacher was being listened to or ignored or what the reaction to a particular service was going to be, one had to take into account both the reactions of the Headmaster, senior administration and staff and also the boys and girls. Sometimes if the Head and staff liked something, the pupils would not, and vice versa. If everybody was happy, it was a great victory!

One occasion in particular comes to mind. We had a service that was taken by an Afro-Caribbean choir from Nottingham. The boys and girls were enjoying it, joining in

The Choir stalls.

Interior of Chapel, 1896.

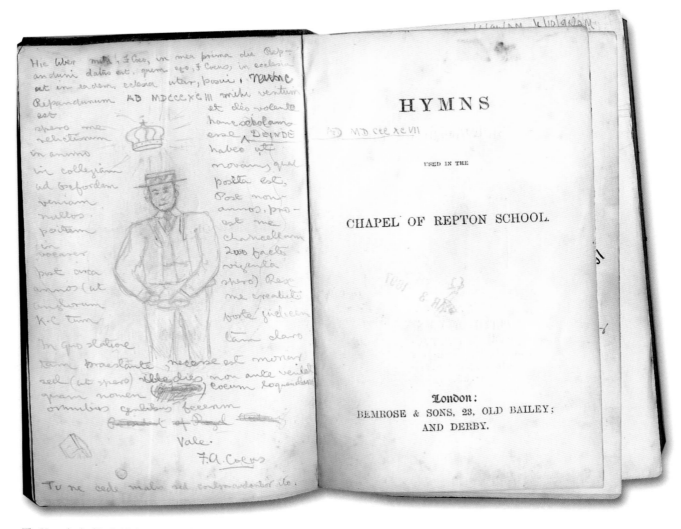

The Hymn book of Frederick Augustus Coe (P 1893), who was eventually called to the bar (Middle Temple) after attending Magdalen College, Oxford.

when asked, clapping and even waving their arms. However, the reaction from the 'other side' was less enthusiastic. I never had so much feedback as from that service: pupils talked about it for years afterwards, asking when the choir would be coming back to take the service. It was a slightly different tale from the staff.

On important occasions, like Remembrance Sunday, the pupils were tremendous – better than some ORs, in fact. They would walk over from Chapel to the Undercroft respectfully keeping silent as we lined up around the Memorial with the Head Prefect laying the wreath and the Headmaster saying, 'We will remember them'.

A major event was the funeral service and burial of Robert Beldam. After the service in Chapel, the boys and girls lined the Precinct on either side of the walk, while the hearse, followed by the choir, solemnly processed in silence to the Arch and finally to the spot where Robert was to be laid to rest. That

really underlined how the school is a community and how important Chapel has been to the life of the school.

A and B Block Chapels were different from the Friday and Sunday services when the whole school got together. They were more informal and relaxed, and I hope that they created an atmosphere that, even though they were compulsory activities at unpopular times, enabled the boys and girls to be open-minded about what they were hearing about the Christian faith. But it was never easy finding a balance between getting the pupils to think and maintaining the right atmosphere for Chapel.

In the classroom and on the sports field, it was a challenging opportunity to wear slightly different hats, although I always remembered that I was also 'on duty' as chaplain. On one afternoon I probably let the side down when I had a real stand-off with the Captain of the Under 16B cricket in the middle of the Square. Fortunately, there weren't too many people around to hear.

Coaching sport was great fun, but always a challenge. One team was memorable in that they came to me en masse one Friday afternoon saying that they didn't think they would be able to play against Cheltenham the next day – it was the FA Cup Final! They were quite serious, but I'm afraid I just laughed at them and said I'd see them in the coach. Needless to say they were all there.

The classroom could also be a challenge. There are occasions I would prefer to forget, but an event in my first year is engraved in my memory. I was having trouble with an A Block set that didn't want to work or think in their one compulsory lesson a week – they would rather chat to each other. One day two boys at the back were whispering away and I told them to be quiet. I had a sudden inspiration and said 'Look, if you were at a board meeting in the company where you worked, and while the managing director was speaking you started to whisper and laugh to the person sitting next to you, what would happen?' Quick as a flash, the reply came back, 'Nothing sir, because I would be the MD!'

The next year this lad was a member of my Under 16 cricket team. He had only ever played in the Bs up to that point, but he had potential. He was the most right-hand player I've ever coached, but he had an incredible eye, even though he was totally orthodox. We went to Oundle at the beginning of the season, and one of their players was strutting around in a Derbyshire Under Something sweater. He was fielding at mid-off, and after the first over of seeing 'Bill' batting, he said to his captain, 'This lad can't bat. I'll get him out!' He came on to bowl, all puffed up, and the first ball was hit through the covers harder than I have ever seen a ball hit at that age! The next ball sailed over the trees at mid-wicket! 'Bill' went on to make 70 and later played for the First XI. He never did become an MD because he became a missionary to students!

My years at Repton were wonderful. Our own children benefited from the excellent education they were given, and I hope that they gave as good as they got. It was an unforgettable time for the whole family. There were tragedies and disappointments, but God brought us through them all, and I have many happy memories of the privilege we had of being part of Repton for 11 years and of the many friendships that we made there.

The Rev. Bob Short

SOME REPTON MISSIONARIES

On 4 February 1885 a large crowd from all parts of London and all levels of society converged on Exeter Hall in the Strand. Their imagination had been caught by the Cambridge Seven, young men of wealth and sporting talent who were leaving their lives of privilege and sailing to China as missionaries. Three of the seven were Old Reptonians: William Cassels (Clucas 1873), Montague Beauchamp (L 1874) and Stanley Smith (L 1876).

Their enthusiasm to follow Jesus' command to 'go into all the world and preach the Gospel' had started at Repton, where the three had met regularly to read the Bible and pray in a little room over the Grubber, and their friendship and commitment had deepened in their years at Cambridge.

They joined the China Inland Mission (now the Overseas Missionary Fellowship), which was committed to working in the vast interior of China while most Protestant missions confined themselves to the costal provinces. And they ate, lived and dressed as did the Chinese, with shaven heads, skullcaps, long queues, baggy breeches, loose gowns and satin shoes. Cassels became Bishop of Western China. Stanley Smith was a fine linguist preaching fluently in Chinese. Sir Montagu Beauchamp was still there in 1939, where he died at his son's mission station.

Chapel Choir.

It is impossible to measure the harvest from the seed sown by such men, but by 1949 there were an estimated one million Chinese Christians. Today, despite over half a century of repressive communism, there are now around 50 million.

In a short and inevitably selective account it is impossible to name all Repton's missionaries, but one may conclude by referring to two Reptonians of the Edwardian era.

Captain Godfrey Buxton (M 1908) came from an influential family. His great-grandfather, after the death of William Wilberforce, led the crucial debate in Parliament in 1833 for the abolition of slavery, which was carried by a handful of votes. His father helped start the Japan Evangelistic Band. He himself, wounded in the First World War and awarded an MC,

travelled the world as a founder member of the Officers' Christian Union.

Dr Charles McLean (N 1909) was an equally colourful character. After Cambridge, Thomas's, the Navy and India, he was asked by 25 Jordanian tribal leaders, who signed the document with their thumbprints, to build a hospital in the primitive hill country around Ajlun. This he did, and travelling on horseback or camel he acted as doctor, surgeon, dentist and administrator, spreading the Gospel in Arabic. It is good to read in these fiercely divided times the tribute paid to him by the Muslim King Abdullah: 'God has many works in many places, and this is one, and we honour it.'

The Rev. Richard Grew   *Chapel Bell.*

 # If Old Hymns You Like

'Dear Lord and Father of Mankind' to the tune 'Repton' is one of the most popular of all hymns but it has a very chequered history.

The words comprise the last six verses of 'The Brewing of Soma', a poem composed of 17 five-line stanzas, by the New England Quaker and abolitionist John Greenleaf Whittier, which was first published in the *Atlantic Monthly* in April 1872.

The verses we all know are really a counterpoint to the first 11 verses, which speak of the perverse forms by which men seek to know God, through drug-induced ecstasies (the Soma of the title being a Hindu hallucinogen), flagellation, the whirling of dervishes, 'The cloister madness of the monk' and the like.

In 1884 W. Garrett Horder included 'Dear Lord and Father of Mankind' in his *Congregational Hymns*, and Whittier's truncated poem became a staple of Protestant hymnals by the turn of the century.

It was not until 1924 that Repton's Director of Music, Gilbert Stocks, fitted the words to the song of Meshollemeth, an aria entitled 'Long Since in Egypt's Pleasant Land', written by Sir Hubert Parry for his oratorio *Judith*, and the hymn became more popular still as a result of its 'Repton' melody. This is the melody adapted by Charles Ives in 'Serenity', which induces an hypnotic effect of gentle waves lapping at the Syrian sea's shoreline.

In view of the hymn's origins in 'The Brewing of Soma' and the fact that Aldous Huxley taught briefly at the school, it's interesting to note that 'soma' was the name he gave to the feel-good drug in *Brave New World*.

John Plowright

Chapel angel.

MY REPTON

In which some distinguished ORs look back at their time at Repton and its place in their lives.

SIR CHARLES PRINGLE KBE, FREng, Hon. FRAeS (P 1933)

I came to the Priory in September 1933 from my Irish prep school, Castle Park, which later came under the ownership of my elder brother, D.S. Pringle (P 1922). My mother had visited a number of public schools before deciding on Repton for two of her sons.

I started life at Repton playing cricket and soccer for the Priory First XI – in goal for soccer – but slowly went downhill to the Second and ultimately to the Third XIs. I ran long distance and led the Priory runners in the 1936 Steeplechase. However, my great interest while at Repton was motor racing.

Roald Dahl at 17.

I walked, cycled or begged a lift to Donington Park whenever I could. During one term I helped in the pit of F.R. Gerard, who picked me up at Repton and who, after the Second World War, became one of England's outstanding drivers, helped for many years by J.D. Furse (P 1932), whose interest in motoring I had initiated.

In my last year – thanks to Michael Milford (Staff 1935–66) who helped in developing a good workshop under the Corps room – H. Wills (B 1935), who sadly was a casualty of the Second World War, and I renovated and rebuilt a Gordon England Sports Austin 7, and on the last day of my last term we drove it proudly around the village.

I left Repton to go to St John's College, Cambridge, to study for the Mechanical Sciences Tripos, but I got an ordinary degree because I spent too much time with motor cars, which ultimately led to my career as an aeronautical engineer.

I always remember with gratitude a number of masters who helped me on my way. S.S. Jenkyns (Staff 1906–46), 'Binks', was my housemaster. His daughter, Nancy, who married John Deuchar (H 1937), now lives not far from me in Fordingbridge. To Noel Strickland (who was always very accurate with his chalk missiles) and to Michael Milford I owe what I learned of mathematics.

I was Roald Dahl's fag for my first term. He was always considerate and was an outstanding fives player. I remember him being selected for a public schools expedition to the Arctic, but he gave no hint – certainly in my mind – of his talent as a writer. I found his attack on Geoffrey Fisher in his autobiography completely out of character with the Dahl I thought I knew. I was fortunate enough to do only four, rather than the norm of six, terms of fagging, having been head fag to

Old Priory Pillars of Hercules and the Hall.

The Old Gym.

John Bradburn who was then Head of the Priory. He did beat me once, but, as I told him when I saw him frequently at various OR gatherings in the 1980s and 1990s, I did not hold this against him: I probably deserved it.

I visited Repton quite a lot between 1962 and 1967, whilst our son, Andrew, was in the Mitre. He had a much more distinguished Repton career than I did, becoming Head of School and doing well as a long-distance runner. He grew to love music, being strongly encouraged by John Thorn to become an opera addict. I was posted to Aden halfway through his time at Repton but managed a quick visit back for his confirmation.

My brother Donald and I attended the 400th anniversary celebrations in 1957, but otherwise I was an infrequent visitor to Repton after Andrew left. I first went to an OR dinner in the early 1970s and subsequently did my stint as President of the OR Society.

Then in 1985 David Jewell asked me (possibly for no other reason than I knew his father well in the aerospace industry!) to join the Governing Body, which was under the chairmanship of Geoffrey Dawes (P 1931) who had been a contemporary of mine at Repton but very much more scholarly. I greatly enjoyed working with him (he taught me a lot) and was invited to succeed him when he retired as Chairman.

I had a very enjoyable, but demanding, time as Chairman, despite having to undertake the long drive from the New Forest to Repton at least twice a term (at the Governors' Dinner to say farewell to me it was asserted that we had driven the equivalent of going round the world at the equator!). My wife, who came thoroughly to enjoy visiting Repton, invariably came with me. We normally stayed in the Hall (although occasionally in one of the Houses, which we also enjoyed). I am afraid that late nights,

over a glass or two of Scottish wine, were the norm with both David Jewell and Graham Jones as we sorted out current Repton issues, problems and plans.

When I became Chairman, Repton was taking girls only in the sixth form, and one of the major decisions we took was to admit girls at Common Entrance age. One factor was that it made good sense to take girls straight from Foremarke, rather than letting them escape elsewhere. We decided to build two new houses, adjacent to each other to allow some pooling of facilities, but to build only one, the Garden, initially. The Garden House was opened by the Duchess of Kent, whose second visit it was to Repton while I was a Governor (she had previously opened the new Music School, converted from the Old San).

During my time as Chairman the Governing Body agreed to very considerable development and improvement programmes, which were partly, but in no way wholly, funded by an appeal for £1 million – 'Into the Nineties' – which was successful through the generosity of ORs (yet again!) and parents, despite the pessimism of pundits who said we would never make the target. As well as the girls' houses, major new buildings completed or planned included sports halls at both schools, the indoor pool at Repton, two indoor tennis courts and the initial phase of the information technology centre. Much after my own heart and thanks to the generosity of Sir Reginald Verdon-Smith (O 1926), a past Governor and a friend of mine in the aircraft world, we extended the Design and Technology centre.

In addition to new buildings, we instituted a programme of improvement and refurbishing of, for example, the Chapel, Pears School, the Old Priory (thanks to the generosity of Robert Beldam and his Foundation), the Hall, the Old Mitre and the boarding houses. One project that we did not approve was the suggestion that we should build a new Headmaster's house to give more privacy to the Headmaster's family than in the Hall. Clearly, our appeal did not cover anything like this programme, so the majority had to be paid for out of current income because Repton was not a generously endowed school. However, we did manage to keep to reasonable and short-term overdrafts!

We also set up Repton Enterprises so that our superb facilities did not all lie idle during the holidays and we could generate income from them. We appointed Roy French to take charge of this.

I was indeed fortunate to have two excellent Bursars (and Clerks to the Governing Body) in Nigel Spurgeon and Pat Hargrave, the latter bringing greatly to bear his military staff training.

The open-air pool diving board (before the depth of water beneath it was declared unsafe for such dives).

from Germany to the Governing Body. He always attended our meetings and contributed much during my time.

Indeed, I was extremely fortunate in all my colleagues. I have mentioned some of them, but all 'pulled their weight'. We had many lively discussions at our meetings, with views often strongly held and expressed but always in a good-humoured way. Pat Lancaster, who had been Headmistress of Wycombe Abbey and who might well have been opposed to our policy of taking more girls, was a tremendous help in her advice to Governors and staff in how best to manage girls. John Tooley (N 1938), then the boss of Convent Garden, helped greatly on the performing arts side. Indeed, we had a great variety of backgrounds and experience including David Bellamy, nominated by the masters and having children in the school; Sydney Giffard (P 1940), ex-Ambassador in Japan; Dick Morris, an old friend of mine in the engineering world (and the best appointment I made to the Governors, later becoming an outstanding Chairman, although previously having had little contact with Repton); and Alan Bemrose (M & C 1945), a long-serving Governor, who ably ran the finance committee and kept us on the straight and narrow money-wise. We did have some problems in trying to make sure that we got the right Derbyshire MP, but that is another story! It was all fun as well as serious.

On Speech Days I aimed to have some distinguished engineers as speakers, including one whom I believe was our first lady speaker at a Speech Day, hoping, not all that successfully, to encourage more Reptonians to take up a career in engineering.

In summary, Repton has been a major influence throughout my life – as a boy, as a parent and finally as a Governor – as well as an enjoyable one. My successors as Chairman of Governors have made significant and welcome strides in further enhancing the reputation and standing of the school.

Probably the most demanding and decisive decision governors have to take is appointments. During my time as a Governor, we appointed Richard Theobald (one of a very high quality field of choice) to Foremarke and Graham Jones to Repton. In making these appointments, we were greatly helped in this (as well as in many other ways) by the wisdom and experience of Frank Fisher and Stuart Andrews as past public school headmasters. The appointment of Pat Hargrave was a straightforward one as he was well known to Guy Willatt through the latter's contacts at Sandhurst.

Soon after appointing Graham Jones, he kindly asked my wife and myself to visit his boarding house at Charterhouse. I apologized to the Charterhouse Headmaster for stealing Graham, and he replied (jokingly) 'I don't give a damn about losing him, but I do care about losing Vanessa!'

Richard Theobald was a great success at Foremarke. We always had problems restraining him from filling Foremarke beyond its capacity, but his thoughtful initiative led us to approve the taking of Russian children for a year. He was always meticulous in following up their progress after they had returned to Russia.

Talking of other countries reminds me that, wishing to encourage more European students and he already having children in the school, we appointed Dr Professor Pulverer

Two 'butterflies' about to land in the open-air pool.

SIR RICHARD EVANS KCMG, KCVO (B 1941)

Four of the five years I spent at Repton were war years, and during this time almost every aspect of school life was governed by wartime conditions. Teaching and management were in the hands of middle-aged men and women; there were no sporting fixtures against some traditional opponents, such as Charterhouse; and there were times when the boys felt very hungry. In conscious contravention of school rules, I used to steal into a baker's shop nearly opposite the Priory and buy a plain white loaf for twopence or so.

I went to Repton because I had won an exhibition at the school and to Brook House because the Housemaster, J.L. Crommelin Brown, was an old cricketing friend of my father's. My arrival at the school was an anxious time. I had never visited the school or the village; I had never met my housemaster-to-be nor any other member of the staff; and I had never come across any existing Reptonian. On leaving the Burton bus at the village cross I had to ask a boy who was standing there how to find Brook House. I shall never forget his face or name, which was Pete Morgan (P 1940).

In contrast to conditions at my prep school, the Dragon School in Oxford, there existed at Repton a strict hierarchy among the boys and a culture in which smart turn-out mattered

The Undercroft, showing Crommelin Brown's model of the Priory.

Outer Parlour and Slype to Cloister.

a lot. There were five grades or ranks in each of the seven houses, from prefect at the top to junior – bim fag – at the bottom. Elaborate rules and conventions governed who could or could not wear speckled straw hats, house ties and braiding on blazers. And there was a school argot. One of its more colourful phrases was 'Long James's braces' for the fire extinguishing hosepipes that hung down from the rampart of the southeast corner of Pears School, Long James being James Grundy, the Housemaster of Latham. The boys 'ticked' – greeted by raising their right hands – all ladies and all masters they passed in the street.

At the same time, there was a liberal side to the school ethos. Eccentricity was not punished. And I myself was not reproved when, as head of Brook House, I said that I would beat no member of the house and looked to the other house prefects to follow my lead. Nor was I discouraged when I told Crommelin, as we all referred to him in the house, that I wanted to go to a meeting in the village hall at which George Brown, the Labour candidate for Belper, would be speaking. Little did I know that I would one day work for George Brown, although at several removes!

Repton was also a catholic school. There was a strong tradition of cultivating and admiring excellence at games, with a long record of achievement behind it. Everyone at Repton knew of C.B. Fry, who was the speaker at one of the Speech Days during my time, but there were others whose cricketing records were almost as good. My own favourite among these was, and is, J.N. Crawford (B 1901), who made 144 not out for Surrey against the Australians in 1919, in an innings described by Neville Cardus as 'beautiful and dauntless and not to be forgotten'.

Alongside this tradition was a tradition of encouraging talent in music and the arts. Music, in my day, was under the control of Mervyn Williams, an exuberant Welshman who could manipulate 400 boys in the Chapel by charisma. I particularly remember one episode in a vivid career. One morning, when the whole school was rehearsing an anthem, Mervyn heard the laughter of lack of interest in one or two pews. 'Stop!' he exclaimed to the organist, and then said, 'Listen to me, you fans of jazz and syncopation: let me tell you that syncopation was invented by Palestrina, who lived four hundred years ago.'

Nor was there any neglect of formal education. Quite a few of those who taught forms or sets were enthusiasts for their subjects and talented at arousing interest in them among the boys. Crommelin was one. His subject was English and his knowledge of English literature was broad, and although he never taught me, he used to lend me books from his private collection. He liked fine style, and one of the books he chose for me was a collection of essays by C.E. Montague, a luminary of the old *Manchester Guardian*, which was distinctly precious. He liked wit as well as wisdom and chose *The Importance of Being Earnest* when asked to produce the school play in 1945. (I was Lady Bracknell, in which role I enjoyed myself hugely.)

Another talented tutor was Denis Wheadon, my form master for my two years in the History Sixth. He was known as 'Weary Wheadon', and it is true that there was a touch of gloom about him. But his knowledge of modern English history was profound, and he took infinite pains with his pupils. He once spent quite a long time explaining to me why there was an important ideological difference between Walpole's 'let sleeping dogs lie' and the economic laissez-faire of the 19th century. I owe him a lot.

I made quite a few friends at Repton. Perhaps my best friend was Michael Bishop (B 1941), who was a star turn at school and at Cambridge and whose family lived at Etwall. Alas, however, he died in his twenties. I lost touch with others because I did my National Service in the Duke of Cornwall's Light Infantry, whose catchment area was far from Repton, and because I lived abroad for many years, with few at home, after becoming a diplomat. In retirement in Wiltshire I often

'Dozing in one of the arm-chairs, with Lord Acton's lectures open and the right way up upon your lap, you might pass a very agreeable hour, and only once in a while a sudden well-placed kick, probably from the Headmaster, would remind you painfully that you were not already a grown-up member of a London club.' – Christopher Isherwood, 'Lions and Shadows'.

come across Old Reptonians, although usually of a younger generation. My solicitor in London is one; a newly elected member of the Court of the Ironmongers' Company is another.

I learned three particular lessons at Repton that have served me in later life. The first was that it takes all kinds to make a world, and that every man has his story. I learned to disdain closed groups of any kind. The second lesson was that persuasion is a better way of getting people to act in the ways one would like than is command. The third lesson was that it pays to take great pains in planning any important event. This lesson stood me in particularly good stead when, to my great surprise, the Chinese leader of the day, Deng Xiaoping, invited the Queen to pay a State Visit to China. There were no precedents for such an occasion, either for the Queen or for the Chinese. The consequence was that I had to spend several hours a day for several months in plotting every detail of a visit that was to last for six days and to extend to five cities in different parts of the country.

May Repton continue to flourish – even if, to the best of my recollections, the Trent is neither staid nor silver.

> 'Although I only joined Repton for the sixth form … I can easily say that they were the happiest two years of my entire school life … I have so many happy memories that I will never forget and I know that my Repton friends will be friends for life.'
>
> **Rachael Parker (F 2003)**

139

The Hole in the Wall.

SIR NICHOLAS BARRINGTON KCMG, CVO (H 1947)

There is something about the name Repton. It makes a good sound. I was attracted to the idea of going there when I saw it as a destination on my prep school honours board. It helped that my father had met the Lynam Thomases when he was doing war work at Rugby. My dynamic prep school headmaster, Max Burr, drove me and another boy up to Derbyshire from Sussex to take the scholarship exam, which we passed.

It was quite far from my parents' house in Essex, but few boys had any special desire to see their parents during term time – there was potential embarrassment over mothers' hats. At the school all differences of class and money evaporated. We had to make our mark and earn respect on our own. Almost all my friends were in my own house, and we never went inside other houses. Only in my final years did I make some friends outside the Hall.

Life was quiet tough for a small boy; one learned to survive. Some lessons were salutary. When I started to consume by myself a cake that I had been given I was told in no uncertain terms by my study holder that such things should be shared. If some senior boys were out to victimize juniors in the dormitories it was no use saying 'Don't attack me' to divert their aggression to someone else. Disgraceful, but that was survival!

On the whole, I appreciated the study system where we lived together in a sort of family of five different ages. The younger fag did the basic work. The study holder was often someone to look up to and learn from, and he had the boys in the middle, the 'seconds', keep an eye on the younger members and see they were not too homesick. We all voted to keep the fagging system, incredible as it may seem today, because we knew we would benefit from it (beds made, boots cleaned) in our final year when we would be under pressure to work and have responsibilities for organizing games and so on.

I did quite well in the classroom, achieving mostly Distinctions and a few Credits, in the School Certificate (I think this was that exam's last gasp). Then I decided to do French and German for A and S levels. I had a vague idea that I might try for the Foreign Office. Ted Burroughs was a great teacher, who would sometimes weep with emotion as he conveyed the beauties of French literature. But the stronger influence on me was Mr Bain. He taught German, but really much more. He told me to learn about world history and general literature – to have a zest for a wide range of knowledge. One could believe he had been a judge in India (I wonder if he really was) by the way he sat high up behind his desk, looking like a bald egg, dispensing witticisms and wisecracks. When a boy couldn't answer one of his questions, he complained 'always the same – I dunnow – ARRB!' That stood for the Average Reaction of the Repton Boy. He gave us useful quotations to insert into our examination papers. The story of his death is like that of an ancient Roman senator. When his wife was released back home in pain from an incurable brain tumour, he poisoned her and then committed suicide. Or so I was told. I could believe it of the man.

The ethos of Repton was predominantly on the games side. The natural heroes were those who were good at team games. Despite the wise leadership of Lynam Thomas, one had the impression that the housemasters, several of whom played cricket or football for their counties (Sale, Eggar), were a dominant force. At the Hall I was mostly under Frank Fisher. Though a sportsman too, he understood me very well and gave me the right mixture of encouragement and control. I owe him a lot. I was only average at team games but rescued my reputation a bit with athletics and cross-country running, of which I became School Captain. Running took me out into the countryside and to competition with other schools. In the summer I preferred tennis. One of the bravest things I did as a small boy was to refuse to box for the House when I had been told to do so by a prefect. I said I didn't agree with hurting other boys for sport. They never bothered me after that.

One of the things that kept me sane was to go to the Art School in the evenings to work with the master who was the antithesis

The coming of the train in Victoria's reign did much to make Repton a truly national school. Engine 926, Repton (built 1934), one of the Southern Railway Schools Class, still runs on the North Yorkshire Moors Railway.

of the sporting hero: Arthur Norris, with his bow-tie, trilby and grey curls. Compared with the more recent drive of the Art School to stimulate creativity in a wide range of media and subjects, 'Arty' Norris kept me on basic portrait and architectural drawings. But I loved the calm and the discipline. I did some pen and ink illustrations for the *Reptonian*, and I have framed some of the portraits I did then.

I also enjoyed taking part in school plays, particularly a memorable production of *Twelfth Night*. I was Viola and must have made an impact, because years later, at a reunion, when I tried to remind the Rev. Proctor of who I was and that I had been in his form, he peered at me and said 'Viola'! I was also rather proud of my performance (with an artificial Roman nose) as Caesar in Shaw's *Caesar and Cleopatra*. Kim Taylor got a good play-reading group together in the Hall. Later in life I played Malvolio in Brussels, Bottom in Cairo and Prospero in Islamabad!

Chapel at Repton was important, with a straightforward Anglicanism that made me treasure the prayers of the traditional Communion service. Confirmation was an emotional experience, and we enjoyed belting out hymns under the guidance of Mervyn Williams. We were privileged to meet Geoffrey Fisher, the Archbishop, who was so full of warmth and vitality that the room would light up when he entered. Michael Ramsey, too, was like an Old Testament prophet. Other distinguished people I remember talking to us were Harold Abrahams, the Olympic athlete who featured in *Chariots of Fire*, and William Beveridge, to whom I wish I had paid more attention. I shall never forget when the school was addressed by a Home Office pathologist in Pears School. I don't know who he thought his audience were, but he talked about recent murders and showed slides of corpses and victims of gruesome

attacks. Boys started to pale; some walked out with shaky step; others fainted. Finally Lynam Thomas got up on the stage and said in his familiar way: 'Err – I think we had better stop now!'

On reflection, I probably learned most from being a prefect in my last year. I was fortunate enough to be Head of House, Head Prefect and Head of School, and I took my responsibilities seriously. There was a prefects' common room at the end of the Cloisters that enabled the different Heads of Houses to meet and discuss issues. When the prefect system is properly deployed senior boys keep an eye on the younger ones, not only to enforce discipline but to stop bullying. I'm afraid that I must have been rather arrogant as Head Prefect, because I remember on one or two occasions going to the Headmaster, over the heads of housemasters and games masters, to say that some decision should be changed. Lynam Thomas agreed with me, which must have infuriated the masters concerned.

But I was brought down with a bump when I became a National Service gunner. Then after a commission as a very junior officer in the mess, I was a new boy again at university and a new recruit in the Diplomatic Service. It took many years before I achieved, as ambassador, the status that I had enjoyed as Head Prefect! It was only later that I discovered that several other diplomatic heads of mission had been to Repton. Sir Richard Beaumont (B 1927) (Cairo) was the doyen. Richard Evans (B 1941) (Beijing) and Sydney Giffard (P 1940) (Tokyo) were a little older; John Chick (P 1948) (Geneva) and Jimmy Glaze (H 1948) (Addis Ababa) a little younger. Thorold Masefield (H 1953) (Bermuda) and those still serving, like Edward Oakden (L 1973), have happily carried on the tradition.

Repton is unique amongst the public schools in having not only a steam locomotive named after it but also a locomotive named after its preparatory school. Foremarke Hall 7903 is a Great Western Railway 'Modified Hall' class steam locomotive, which still runs on the Gloucestershire Warwickshire Railway.

The Rt. Hon. Lord Justice Rose, Vice-President Court of Appeal, Criminal Division.

THE RT. HON. LORD JUSTICE ROSE (L 1950)

My paternal grandfather was a cooper who, after a seven-year apprenticeship, worked for Ind Coope in Burton upon Trent. My father was born in Burton in 1897 and, when still a schoolboy, used to cycle to Repton on Sundays. It was then that he decided that, if he had a son and could afford the fees, he would send him to Repton. He left school at 14 with few academic qualifications. He learned shorthand and typing and worked as a secretary for the Vicar of Rolleston. When he was 17 he lied about his age and joined the army. He became a morse-code signaller, missed the Battle of the Somme because he was posted to Ireland during the Easter Uprising, but fought in the third Battle of Ypres (Passchendaele), being mentioned in despatches.

After the war he became a keen oarsman (for Burton Leander) and rugby player, as a wing three-quarter of county standard. While he was playing rugby, he broke, at different times, his nose, ankle and wrist, and he concluded that, as sport was supposed to be physically beneficial, no son of his would go near the oval ball. Later, he qualified as a solicitor, entered local government, became Town Clerk of, successively, Glossop,

The Repton Fire Squad.

Hyde and Morecambe and was able (just about) to afford the Repton fees.

This was the background against which I came to Repton in 1950 and spent four years at Latham.

The abiding initial impressions were of the handsome buildings viewed through the Arch and the tranquil, green beauty of the cricket pitch and playing fields beyond.

The two masters who made a lasting impression on me were Bernard Thomas and Michael Charlesworth. Bernard Thomas was Housemaster at Latham and taught me A level history. He was a man of probity, authority, compassion and wit, who inspired great affection, as well as respect, in almost all his charges. Michael Charlesworth taught me O level English and directed brilliantly at least two school plays in which I appeared with questionable skill. He was wonderfully enthusiastic. He taught me a love of language and also that some kinds of work can be fun.

A more immediate cause of my going to the Bar was probably Michael Dennison as Boyd QC on television, but the teachers I have named displayed qualities that have had a much more enduring effect on me as barrister and judge.

The discipline of compulsory games (at which I was undistinguished), of piano and choir practice and of the classroom, and the necessity of prompt time-keeping for all appointments have remained with me throughout my life and were an invaluable training for meeting deadlines, well-prepared, in my legal career. There was a smidgen of corporal punishment, received and administered, but I was unaware of it playing any significant role in my schooldays and, looking back, I regard its impact as neutral.

My overall remembrance of the school is fond, and the family connection has continued. My son Daniel was at Latham from 1980 to 1985 and, in the sixth form, he met Victoria Sinclair, then in the Abbey and now his wife. Her father Michael and brother Adam were also at Latham (1955 and 1978, respectively).

TONY WILKINSON (L 1951)

I left Repton in the summer of 1955 and was soon one of a small number of young men doing my National Service in the Royal Navy. Twenty months at sea saw a rapid translation from adolescence to young adulthood. We did not have to grow up as soon in our day as now.

The world today is more crowded, busy, complicated and dangerous than it was for us. There was also less money around. I have a school fee receipt for £100 a term. I was involved in the movement of Repton preparatory school (then established at what is now Latham House) to Foremarke Hall, which had very basic facilities, where we were taught in Nissen huts heated by Valor oil stoves and where the staff were the usual array of unusual characters. All this in the bitter winter of 1947. Two of the more effective teachers were a Mr Spencer (History), who arrived one morning to find his beloved Austin 7 car inside his Nissen hut classroom (its widest door was a metre across), and Mr Hill, who was in a wheelchair, taught English, had a tie for every day of the year and left most of us with a lifetime enjoyment of literature.

So then, Repton and Latham House. Bernard Thomas, the Housemaster, had a taciturn manner, a wry sense of humour and a surly dog (as well as a wife and daughter). Food rationing was only just being lifted, but the food for the time was, in the main, good (though not by today's standards). There were dormitories of from four up to the teens of iron bedsteads, and football baths of the steaming hot but chocolate-coloured variety. I think that I dreamed my way through lessons with one or two distractions and eight O levels as the outcome. Cricket was – and still is – my great love, though I was probably better at

Tony Wilkinson, businessman.

hockey. Swimming was in an open-air pool, which was both murky and abrasive. Domestic matters were governed by the caste system of fagging, although the actuality of corporal punishment was rarely engaged. The Headmaster was alleged to be heavy with the cane in the most heinous instances. If there were any expulsions we rarely heard of them. Greater penalties were occasional bullying (which I somehow escaped) and peer group ostracism. I recall a Head of House who was the First XI opening bowler (and a good one, too) and an aloof individual. One day the senior students in his own house locked him in his own school trunk for some time. A lesser man might have died. It was a credit to him that he made nothing of it. At the end of my term of fagging I ended up as tip fag of the House. Latham had a yard for leisure and exercise purposes (but with plenty of ancillary sports fields). This yard was covered in gravel, which a novitiate fag who displeased might be invited to sweep. There were 7 tons of it.

Entertainment started with school concerts and plays, together with the Pedants and general release (U certificate) films – *Roman Holiday* introduced me to Audrey Hepburn – and we had had some hilarious silent films at the prep school from one of the staff's private collection. The next stage was cards, magazines and newspapers (some of which would not have had adult approval) and, of course, pop music with real instrumentation. There were no TVs in those days – they were to be a 9-inch novelty for the Coronation in 1953. Alcohol and smoking, if discovered, were indictable offences. We still wore

> *The true value of Repton for me lies not in the teaching of facts and figures but in the accumulation of lessons that will last a lifetime. I have learned to avoid prejudice, yet embrace tradition; to value achievement, but lose gracefully, and, most importantly, to be personable and polite, yet independent.*
>
> **Hannah Watson (M 2004)**

The much-loved 'Hillie'.

What recommendations might I offer? Understand that performance rules differ from individual to individual and adjust to gain support, but always within a standard of ethics. Those who fall before that standard inevitably flounder. Choose your circumstances in which to take action with care, but don't miss opportunities. Be sure that you have the confidence to do what you want to do. If you doubt your ability, so will everyone else (well, most of them).

THE HON. SIR DAVID SIEFF (H 1952)

My memories of Repton are somewhat vague, but as a slightly nervous 13-year-old who had spent the first six years of his life in America, followed by a pretty comfortable upbringing in London, I found Repton somewhat 'spartan and cold'. However, I survived – and much enjoyed most of my time, although unlike today we were not often allowed out, and when we were it seemed a long way from London.

I cannot say that I distinguished myself, either academically or on the sporting field. However, I managed to achieve my colours (so essential in the competitive environment!) in some of the minor sports, and if my memory serves me correctly I was responsible for introducing basketball.

We were all certainly very competitive both as individuals and by House. Being in the Hall with Frank Fisher as the Housemaster and T.L.T. (as he was known) as the Headmaster added a little spice to life. He and his wife Peggy made us feel at home. T.L.T. had a rather mischievous twinkle, and you always knew you were in trouble when he referred to you by your

shirts with separate collars and studs, and casual wear was not permitted. It was still a single-sex school, but ballroom dancing classes were an opportunity to meet Gloria, a vivacious blonde (and others less memorable). The large lady who managed this group and to whom we afforded an unfavourable title, used to watch Gloria (or rather Reptonian attention to her) with martinet eyes. Anyone who offended would be taken in hand by her and, where possible, carried round the dance floor as a form of ridicule.

Four exeats a term (commencing either after matins or communion and expiring at 6 p.m. on Sundays only) were the family allowance, together with forgettable half-terms. It was a cloistered existence.

Our family had summer holidays on mainland Britain, but otherwise in vacation time I worked in the family business from the age of ten. The law was lax, and the work provided me with money. School gave an altogether different dimension to my life. The family business, which has since become a powerful national player, was local to the city of Leicester in those days.

So what did this upbringing give me? Nurture in stability and security. The talent to survive indignity that some called stoicism. A thirst for knowledge in slow time to begin with but now and for many years at tremendous place. It took me much longer to grasp that everyone else does not do this the same way.

The Grubber, 1954.

144

Fire Drill.

surname. On one such occasion I had been away with the fencing team and on returning was greeted by the words, 'Sieff, I would like a word with you.' He told me there had been a strike over lunch and that everyone had downed their knives and forks to show their disapproval of the poor quality of the food. I was left with the clear impression that he felt I had had something to do with it! Well if I did, it worked, because the following term the caterers had gone and the quality had improved.

One was certainly encouraged and given every opportunity to develop whether on the sports field, in the arts or music or even academically – if one really concentrated. I remember sitting History for my entrance exam for Cambridge and thinking I had done quite well, to be told that it was an appalling paper but that my three-hour general paper was first class and if I wanted to sit it again I could. I think I knew my limitations, so decided to try my hand elsewhere – not entirely unsuccessfully!

Other memories include my time in the Corps, where I believe I was the only school prefect up to then to fail to rise above the rank of lance corporal, which raised an interesting challenge for those who did but were not school prefects! Among the many other fading memories are the importance attached to the visits to the tuck shop, the hub of school life, and the visit of the Queen and Prince Philip on the school's 400th anniversary. I had the privilege of showing Prince Philip round for part of the tour, but promptly lost him as obviously he had a

mind of his own, even then, and had other ideas of what he wanted to see. Her Majesty was rather easier to look after!

At about the same time there was the occasion when I sat between Geoffrey Fisher, then Archbishop of Canterbury, and Michael Ramsey, Archbishop of York – an interesting sandwich for someone of my persuasion! Fisher was certainly the easier, and we remained in contact for some years after I left.

Another lasting memory was being the stage manager in charge of Eric Maschwitz's specially commissioned production to commemorate our 400th anniversary. It was certainly an experience, and I wish everyone involved in the 450th every success.

My time and experiences at Repton helped to nurture many of my interests later in life, certainly my involvement with government and the community. But above all were the friendships made at the time, several of which still remain today.

THE VERY REV. NICHOLAS FRAYLING (P 1957)

An invitation to preach in the school chapel is a rare privilege, especially for a notably low-achieving Reptonian. A visit to fulfil that engagement in 2000 was made more memorable by an incident at lunchtime in the Priory. The Housemaster, Mike Stones, his wife and five senior boys entertained me in the 'private' dining room. In my day, this had been the Housemaster's study. Between courses, I asked to look behind the curtain. Sure enough, though filled-in and much painted over, was a series of holes in the woodwork. To an astonished Housemaster and five incredulous young men I explained that these were the remains of three clips, in which Dick Sale had concealed three canes of different diameter, the thickness being in inverse ratio to the severity of the presumed offence.

The Priory in my day was a 'beating house', and I endured Dick Sale's enthusiasm for what the EU now calls 'unusual and degrading punishment' four times – three, by the standards of the day, deserved; the fourth (using the thinnest cane, which drew blood) was for 'cheating in maths' – which I had not – on the uncorroborated word of a much-loved and recently deceased master. Years later, I told Dick how much I had resented this, to receive his characteristic 'Ha, ha, ha. It doesn't seem to have done you much harm!'.

Be that as it may, the Priory at the turn of the 1950s and 1960s was not an easy home for a non-athletic, late-developing boy. It was a comfort, later, to read that Repton had been no easier for its new, young Headmaster, John Thorn, as he tried to change the culture of the school, a process he described in some detail in his *Road to Winchester*.

The Repton experience was made tolerable for me by friendships, some of which have endured (and others picked up

'Part of every Tuesday and Friday was spent marching, doing drill, shooting, more marching and drill, map reading, compass bearing on bushy topped trees, marching, more drill, messing about in collapsible boats, and yet more marching and drill.'
John Blomfield (H 1955)

years later) and by the understanding and kindness of particular masters. My love of music meant that I enjoyed Chapel, though I narrowly avoided 'failing' to be confirmed, having fallen asleep and missed one of the Chaplain's mass, with a small 'm' (!), instruction sessions. Cyril Proctor described this lapse as 'an utter disgrace'.

'Harry' Hole made me Band Sergeant, which undemanding military role I combined with the post of Platoon Sergeant of the newly formed Civil Defence Platoon. This involved identifying the sorts of injuries we might encounter in the event of a nuclear attack – horrible plastic wounds, stuck on to 'unconscious' or moaning members of the Derbyshire WVS.

The greatest influence for good was the irascible Director of Music, Mervyn Williams, who appointed me Head Chorister and instilled a love of the organ, especially accompaniment, which has been an enduring joy. An occasional highlight is to meet with Martin How (H 1945), a far more gifted musician, to remember Mervyn's foibles, and to re-create, on two pianos, his improvised last verses of hymns, which were sung with great verve in our time. But chiefly we remember Mervyn's kindness.

Mervyn helped one Reptonian, at any rate, to believe himself capable of real achievement, though neither could have foreseen a career that has encompassed Harrods, Pentonville Prison, ordination to ministry in three city parishes and the Deanery of Chichester Cathedral. A psychologist would no doubt have fun working out the connections, but I can safely say that, without the privilege of five years at Repton, the story would have been very different. That's not a bad lesson for a priest to ponder.

> *Repton, like no other school I know, provides plentiful cultural activities ... Public debates, held by the Debating Society, regularly attract audiences of 70 or more; not bad after two hours of prep on a midweek night.*
>
> **Thomas Bramall (P 2005)**

THE RT HON. NICK RAYNSFORD MP (P 1958)

With the benefit of hindsight I now understand just how important a formative influence my four years at Repton proved, though at the time I often felt uncertain, confused and challenged. This wasn't just the normal process of adolescence. There were bigger changes afoot. When I arrived at Repton, so many of the school's – and indeed society's – values seemed rooted in traditions established decades, if not centuries, before. When I left in 1962 both school and country were experiencing the first shocks of what we now call the 'swinging sixties'. Iconoclastic television programmes like *That Was the Week That Was* were ridiculing traditional assumptions and lampooning the moral and political leaders of the time. Britain was beginning to look forward to a period of radical social change. My school years mirrored that process. Britain was on the cusp, and so was I.

The Rt Hon. Nick Raynsford, MP.

The Arch from the Old Priory.

government was best, and with them I applauded Harold Macmillan's 'Never had it so good' election victory of 1959.

The morning after was one of those rare life-changing moments one can recall precisely almost 50 years later. Discussing the election outcome with Michael Charlesworth I realized that there were other dimensions to politics than the certainties on which I and most of my fellow pupils had been brought up. Like any good teacher, Michael did not impose his own views, but he did question the prevailing right-of-centre assumptions, and for the first time I began to conceive the possibility that Hugh Gaitskell's alternative might have been preferable. Such is the impact that inspirational teachers can make, and I was extraordinarily lucky in that respect at Repton. Three individuals stand out.

Michael Charlesworth not only challenged me to think harder and deeper about social and political issues and values; he also enthused me, along with so many others, in literature and drama and foreign travel. My memories of Michael's productions in the 400 Hall and at the Priory are rich and varied, including the eye-gouging sequence in *King Lear* when I played Gloucester. As an antidote, I went on two eye-opening school trips Michael organized in the Easter holidays, respectively to Munich and Prague and to Venice and Belgrade. His insistence on combining one western European city with an Eastern-bloc capital was far-sighted and left indelible impressions. The tragedy of the Prague Spring a decade later was all the more poignant for me having seen this beautiful city with all its creative traditions caught in the grip of a harsh totalitarian regime.

Repton opened my eyes to the arts. There is a certain irony about this. At the time the school's ethos gave far greater emphasis to sporting than artistic prowess, and some of the writers and artists whose work enthralled me would not have been considered good influences by the more traditionally minded staff. I well recall Dick Sale, my Housemaster, looking quizzically at some of the books on my desk! But I rapidly learned how to establish a parallel universe where I could delight in the joys of literature, poetry, music and the visual arts. The Art School, presided over by the incomparable Dennis Hawkins, became my favourite bolt-hole. Not only was it a place where I could explore the creative uses of paint, charcoal, crayon and other materials; it was also a free-thinker's haven where ideas could be tested and questions raised without fear of any suspicions of 'trouble-making'.

Dennis was the kindest and most supportive teacher I have ever encountered, and I thought of him as a friend as much as a mentor. He and Heather were unstintingly generous and hospitable, and I learned as much from informal conversation in

In 1958 middle-class Britain, despite the shock of Suez, still clung to the old comfortable assumptions about the traditional order of society and our important role on the world stage. The country was still benefiting from the post-war boom, before the harsh realities of changing economic forces stripped away the complacency. Like most of my school contemporaries, I came from a background that took for granted that a conservative

their home as anywhere else in the school. As an impressionable 15-year-old I felt outrage on Dennis's behalf when the school authorities bowed cravenly to backwoods pressure to remove his fine abstract painting from the OR Room in the 400 Hall. I hope that that injustice has subsequently been made good or that it will be by the 450th anniversary.

The third inspirational teacher I encountered was Colin Davies, who transformed History for me from a subject into a passion. His teaching style was idiosyncratic – I remember him throwing out of the window a book of which he strongly disapproved and spied on one pupil's desk. Years later, when I saw the film *Dead Poets Society* and the play *The History Boys*, memories came flooding back of Colin's teaching and influence, based on his own love of the subject and desire to communicate its excitement rather than simply prepare pupils for an exam.

Of course, exams still have to be got through, and in my case this was seen as a priority as I was identified as a potential university applicant. Stuart Andrews made sure that I was properly prepared, and it was on his advice that I applied to Sidney Sussex College, Cambridge. Repton gave me the huge benefit of an opportunity to 'fast track' my O and A levels, an approach that is now being more widely advocated by educationalists. In my case it was unquestionably a good thing from the point of view of both school and pupil. By the end of my third year when I sat A levels, I was already a potential powder keg of radical social, political and artistic ideas, easily capable of blowing up if confronted with suitable provocation. An early escape, first on a gap year and then to Cambridge, was almost certainly a wise move. It was, however, a cause of some sadness that I was not able to see at first hand John Thorn's moves to reform some of the more outdated traditions in the school. John very kindly offered me a lift to Cambridge to sit the scholarship exams in his first term as Headmaster. The wonderfully stimulating conversation we had in the course of that two-hour drive was a tantalizing appetizer for a main course that I would not be around to enjoy.

My final day at Repton had a sad and in some ways surreal ending, which has also ensured that it remains indelibly etched in my memory. As we left the chapel at the end of the last service, the then Senior Master approached me to express his regret that I had declined to join the Old Reptonian Society. I tried to explain that this was not prompted by hostility to the school; on the contrary, I appreciated and valued the huge opportunities the school had given me. I had been the beneficiary of both an open scholarship and a war memorial scholarship as my father, who had also been at Repton, had been killed in the war. My family had therefore had to pay very little

for my education, and I was truly grateful for that. However, I was uncomfortable with the concept of old-boy networks, which ran counter to my emerging political and social beliefs. I wanted to make my way in the world on my own behalf and not trade on the fact that I was well connected. I could see that he simply could not comprehend what I was trying to explain but was pained at what appeared a wilful rejection of an institution he valued. Between the two of us there was an apparently unbridgeable gap, and, with the arrogance of youth, I refused to budge. But 45 years on and understanding more the processes of political compromise, it does give me pleasure to have been able to sponsor the 2007 Old Reptonian reception at the House of Commons at the start of the 450th anniversary celebrations.

PROFESSOR SIR CHRISTOPHER FRAYLING (P 1960)

The poet and critic Herbert Read wrote – in his classic book *Education through Art*, first published in 1944 – that the best kind of art education combined two separate but related approaches: teaching to art and teaching *through* art. Teaching to art, he said, involved teaching the practices and procedures and methods of art; teaching through art, on the other hand, involved teaching more general life skills – problem-solving, setting one's own brief and working to it, flexible thinking, standing on one's own two feet, preparation for a world where the goalposts keep moving, the intelligence of feeling – which

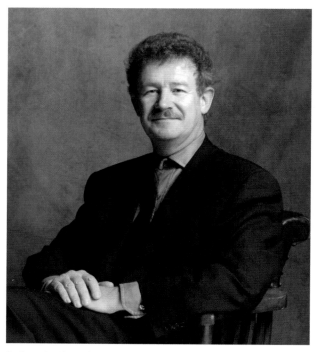

Professor Sir Christopher Frayling, Rector, Royal College of Art, Chairman of the Arts Council and Chairman of the Design Council.

could be transferred to other walks of life. Read concluded, more controversially, that art education was uniquely placed among school subjects to achieve both sets of results.

Re-reading *Education through Art* brings back vivid memories of three teachers at Repton in the early to mid-1960s: Michael Charlesworth, Stuart Andrews and Dennis Hawkins – all of whom seem to me now to have combined teaching to with teaching through. Michael it was who taught the texts of English literature (O and A level) as if they were living things rather than antiques arcadias: he encouraged communal readings, debates about interpretation and, above all, he had this double-life as teacher in the classroom and director/dramaturge in the 400 Hall, over which he seemed to have a virtual monopoly. Plays could come alive through performance, which is, of course, why they were written in the first place. Poems were there to be performed in time and space, rather than dissected like dead things. So while I was preparing for exams, I appeared (as Juliet, or rather Julia!) in the musical *Bite Your Thumb*, co-written by Michael Charlesworth and William Agnew; as a military officer in its follow-up, *Curry Favours*, and as an elderly soldier in Terence Rattigan's *While the Sun Shines*, which had been chosen, I believe, because we had a visiting scholar from America on the school's books who was ideal for the lead role; all three produced by Michael. *Bite Your Thumb* is firmly etched in my memory because at the beginning of the summer term I fell down the Priory's knotted rope during a Sunday fire practice and broke my ankle, so I had to play Juliet with my leg in plaster (the dull thump of plaster on wooden stage can still be distinctly heard on the recorded version.) Etched, too, because it was through *Bite Your Thumb* that I met my first well-known published author – Caryl Brahms, who had co-written *Don't Mr Disraeli*, the inspiration for the musical, and who attended the final performance. Thank goodness I was standing on the balcony in the famous scene rather than shinning up the ivy! All of which gave me the self-confidence to direct my own show: extracts from Sheridan's *The School for Scandal*, with James Fenton in drag as Lady Sneerwell, while I played Mr Crabtree, smoking a long wooden tobacco-pipe, which broke in half on the first night. And the self-confidence to appear in annual Priory Christmas Revues, again written by Michael, with countless in-jokes about the rivalry between Sale and Egger/Priory and Brook and clever remixes of Gilbert and Sullivan. Michael was more gently subversive in these revues than he could allow himself to be in more official entertainments. If teaching to art happened in the classroom, teaching through art also happened there – but even more in the 400 Hall. You could practise the arts as well as study them. This has stayed with me for over 40 years.

Dennis Hawkins, Director of Art, 1952-1985.

Stuart Andrews, who appeared very convincingly as Lord Snowdon, complete with camera slung round his neck, in yet another of the Charlesworth revues adopted a sterner – though never exactly solemn – approach to the History curriculum with a particular emphasis on his own research interest, the 'enlightened despots' of the mid-18th century: especially Frederick the Great, the Empress Maria Theresa and Emperor Joseph II, and Catherine the Great of Russia. In addition to the historical details, we were encouraged to reflect on politics as the art of the possible, the twin pulls of enlightened rationalism and despotic irrationalism – a live issue to boarding schoolboys in the early 1960s, believe me – the question of whether the philosophy of the enlightenment sometimes became for these rulers a form of 'spin' (although we didn't call it that yet) and the relationship between ideas and social change: a useful portfolio, in the era just after the Chatterley ban and the Beatles' first LP. It was largely because of Stuart that I came to specialize in 18th-century history at Cambridge, taking

149

> *When I arrived at Repton, I wasn't too sure where I wanted to go in terms of the arts. I soon realized that one doesn't have to choose between music or drama but can do both as both departments are so welcoming and helpful. It's so easy to get involved with productions here, and I no longer feel like a student interested in performing, but rather a performer.*
>
> **Blair Dunlop (S 2005)**

Herbert Butterfield's special subject on George III and the politicians at first degree level and a doctorate on Jean-Jacques Rousseau's ideas about art. In fact, I was in Paris – at the Sorbonne and in the Bibliothèque Nationale – when the events of May 1968 unfolded around the Boulevard St Michel. Legend has it – not strictly true – that I sat in the Sorbonne Library hissing to all comers, 'Shh – can't you see I'm trying to study the French Revolution? Can't you stop overturning cars out there?' If this were true, it would be a great compliment to Stuart and his legacy. When he was teaching, the 18th century almost seemed more alive than the 20th. The past need not be remote, after all: a foreign country, yes, where they do things differently; but not remote.

Then there was the art room – sometimes in the Undercroft, sometimes in a cluttered classroom – where Dennis Hawkins told us about – and sometimes enacted, in the round – his own very eccentric version of the history of art, while also encouraging our fumbling efforts at seeing the world through drawing and painting. He interspersed these twin projects with slide-shows of his charmingly chaotic family holidays and talks about his latest commissions. I particularly remember his textile design for Edinburgh Weavers entitled 'homage to an astronaut' – the title has a nice period feel to it – which was displayed for several weeks on an easel. This was my first introduction to the processes of design and the imagination that can go into the look and feel of everyday things. Also to the meeting of art and science, in this case space technology: everything else in the curriculum seemed to pull them apart. In out-of-school hours I had my charcoal portrait made by a fellow pupil who is now a distinguished portrait painter. Dennis didn't explicitly teach to art; rather he tested our visual ideas against his own. He certainly had strong views, and I still believe that the cardinal sin for an art educator is to lack conviction and agree with everyone's point of view. You find your own voice through having it challenged by someone who knows what they are doing and can demonstrate it. Dennis certainly did that.

These three very different educational experiences have almost eclipsed in my mind the strange, arcane rituals of the Priory, not as unpleasant as Roald Dahl recalled them in Boy, but, it has to be said, still in the early 1960s with a certain family resemblance. The 'lines' on blue paper; the 'flappings' with gym shoes by house prefects; the learning by rote of the contents of the Blue Book and of unofficial school folklore – such as all the masters' nicknames – on pain of being stripped naked and humiliated by senior boys in the bathroom; the school parade past the Headmaster on Sunday afternoons; the weird drill of 'ticking' masters with the forefinger as if one were wearing an invisible boater; having to sing a song – solo – in the dormitory, mercifully after the lights had gone out. No, rather than these *rites de passage*, which today seem much closer to the world of *Tom Brown's Schooldays* than to the early 21st century, I remember the artistic seeds that were sown. In educator and historian William Cory's words, written over a century ago, you go to school 'not so much for knowledge as for arts and habits' and in the end for understanding of yourself. This is the bit I remember.

Oh, and as I write this, two half-buried memories of Headmaster John Thorn come back to life: a seminar on film – on the Hollywood film version of *Becket* to be precise, the one with Peter O'Toole and Richard Burton, compared and contrasted with the Jean Anouilh play, my first-ever 'legitimate' discussion of the movies, which took place in the inner sanctum of the Headmaster's drawing room; and the Chapel service in November 1963 when John gave a moving address about the significance of the assassination of President John F. Kennedy, helping us all to come to terms with a semi-comprehensible event in a distant land, which seemed somehow important but we weren't quite sure why. With the benefit of hindsight this address, which sounded semi-improvised, seems also to have been about the youthful John Thorn trying to drag the school kicking and screaming into the 1960s, surrounded by an old guard who were by no means sure that this was a sensible or even an attractive idea. It wasn't bliss to be alive at that dawn –

or very heaven to be young, come to that – but my time at Repton definitely set me on course, against all the odds, for a very exciting professional career in the arts.

ROBIN MERRILL (C 1967)

Two incidents in my time at Repton really shaped my career, one a few days after I arrived, and the other shortly before I left four years later.

I arrived at the Cross House in the summer term of 1967. For the preceding five years I had been a chorister in Salisbury Cathedral choir and with puberty setting in my treble voice was faltering, so I came to Repton one term earlier than usual. Little did I know that Mr Charlesworth, Head of Drama, and Mr Agnew, Director of Music, were desperate for treble voices to play the female roles in their musical *Phineas Finn*. Within days of my arrival I was cast as Lady Laura Standish, and my voice was to have one final 'hurrah' before it descended to bass baritone. *Phineas Finn* was a huge success and set in motion my future. No, I didn't go on to dress up in women's frocks! But I did end up on the professional stage. I got my break in the West End in the original cast of the musical Evita and then spent ten years as lead singer with the Pasadena Roof Orchestra travelling all over Europe. Today I present a daily TV show on European culture for DW TV, the German equivalent of BBC World, and still sing with my own swing orchestra, the Savoy Dance Orchestra.

The second incident, when I was 17, was what finally convinced me to seek a musical career. Most of the boys in the sixth form sang in Mus.Soc., not because of a love of Bach or Mozart but rather because of the attraction of singing together with the 'ladies' of Abbots Bromley school. Repton may now be co-educational, but back in the 1960s there wasn't a female form to be seen for miles – except dear matron, of course!

One such concert was a performance of Bach's *Magnificat* at Abbots Bromley with the soloists being hired in from London. On this occasion the bass soloist fell ill a few days before the concert, and Michael Salter roped me in to take his place. Well, on the night I was very nervous but managed to acquit myself reasonably well I think. ('Quia fecit mihi magna', if I remember rightly). However I will never forget what happened immediately after the concert. I was surrounded by Abbots Bromley girls who wanted to talk to the bass soloist and was even kissed by one – surreptitiously – before we were all herded onto our bus and returned to the boys-only existence of Repton. That night a light went on in my head. Up to then I had been a music scholar on the oboe, but oboe playing didn't draw any attention from females. It appeared that singing did. Singing was sexy. I've been performing on stage ever since! Thank you Repton!

1970 Repton Sale of Work Marathon. Charles Hurtley (L 1967) and Jonathon Woodhead (L 1966).

Rob Oakley (L 1967) (on left) and Alan Longworth (L 1967) (on right).

On Sunday 8 November 1970, at the suggestion of Charles Hurtley and Chris Parker (who had recently joined the teaching staff), four Latham studyholders (pictured here) decided to undertake a marathon to raise funds for the annual sale of work. The 26 miles and 385 yards began and ended at the Arch, was accomplished in 5 hours and 12 minutes and raised just over £450, at a time when the total for the Sale of Work was roughly £850. This event, which predated the London Marathon by eleven years, was possibly the first charity marathon in Britain.

CAROLE BLACKSHAW (1970)

As is known, Sally Keenan and I were the first girls to attend Repton and, as John Gammell records, I started it off by asking him if I could be a sixth-form pupil.

To put this in context, I was in my O level year at an old-fashioned and strict girls boarding school and hoped to do my A levels somewhere more pleasant. My home was in the village of Repton, so I thought, with the optimism of youth, 'There is a perfectly good school on the doorstep. Why can I not go there?' I actually approached the then Headmaster, John Gammell, after church one Sunday in the holidays. This was quite out of the blue, and he was probably rather taken aback. He said he had not considered having girls. I then recall asking him a second time (being fairly persistent about this), and this time he told me about his daughter starting at Marlborough and said, without further ado, that if I could send my father to see him he would put it to the governors. Well, the rest is history. Looking back I feel enormous gratitude for John Gammell's brave decision. What a leap of faith!

I managed to persuade Sally Keenan to join me, as everyone agreed I should not be totally on my own in this venture. However, Sally and I were taking completely different A level subjects, so we were never together for lessons, though we had a great time comparing notes afterwards on how the boys behaved. We had a wonderful bolt-hole with our own study in the Headmaster's House where we could have a break from being in the spotlight in the early days.

At first it was all very exciting, if rather daunting. I remember that in the first Economics lesson the master asked somewhat nervously if he might call me Carole. I could not believe it. I had clearly come from hell to heaven! There I sat amongst all these boys and a very gallant male master. I soon found the lessons far more interesting and challenging than at my previous schools. There we were taught to be silent, listen and take in, without question, all we were told. At Repton there was discussion and lively debate. Early on I remember a History essay being returned to me with the comment, 'Good as far as it goes but why did you not argue with the title?' The title was a quotation from Winston Churchill, and my previous education had taught me to respect and accept what my betters told me. I would not have dared argue with Churchill! Thus, intellectually Repton was something of an enlightenment.

As we got to know more of the boys many hours followed of great debate and discussion on all manner of topics. In time a group of us would decamp, after afternoon lessons in the summer, or before in the winter, up the Burton Road to where I lived. There we would hold court while demolishing my mother's cakes and biscuits. To this day she thinks the boys must have been half-starved given their enthusiasm for food!

There was so much I grew to love about Repton, and I found myself increasingly drawn into its numerous activities. Music was always a special part of the school, and under Michael Salter it flourished to a very high standard. In Drama there was the indomitable Michael Charlesworth who was only too pleased to have the genuine article to take the female leads in school plays. I particularly recall those inspiring lessons on English literature and religion with John Billington. He could squeeze every last drop of meaning out of a line of poetry and was a real philosopher. I shall never forget his words one day when he described the world's different religions as different paths up the same mountain to the same God at the top. I often refer to these wise words in discussions with some of the influential people I have met in recent years. Whatever their religion they love that analogy.

My memories of Repton are very special, and I can truly say that those years were in many ways the happiest of my life. I also realize how very fortunate Sally and I were in being the first girls in what was probably a unique situation. Above all it was the most enormous fun!

DR KATHARINE DELL (A 1978)

I first came to Repton for music lessons when I was about 14 and spent many a happy hour with Neil Millensted in piano lessons and Tony Garton on clarinet. Tony used to make me laugh so much sometimes that I couldn't blow! When I got to sixth-form level it made sense for me to come to the school full

The Art School in the Tithe Barn in the 1950s.

A Life Class in the new Art School in the 1990s.

time. I had been at an all-girls school up to then and was quite shy of the male species. I remember, on my first day, discovering that I was the only girl in my history class and feeling so painfully shy that I didn't speak to anyone. However, at the beginning of the second lesson, one of the boys came up to me and introduced himself, and then others, and then the floodgates opened and I never looked back! When I arrived there were about 12 girls in the lower sixth and not many more in the upper, and we were housed in the Old San, now the Music School, the lower-sixth girls all in one room with a desk each. We were all day girls, but with one or two staying with families in the village as boarders.

It was during my first year that the Abbey was built, and we watched the building gradually rising. Gerry and Jill Pellow were in charge and at the beginning of my second year we moved in, and I became Head of House. I remember the Duchess of Devonshire coming to open the house and revealing, from behind curtains, the plaque that is still on the wall. We rattled around in the place a bit, being so few,

although a larger number were now joining the lower sixth. I was encouraged to board, which I did, with a palatial room all to myself.

I remember once coming back to the Abbey past John Billington's house. Bees were kept in the garden, and a number had escaped and buzzed their way into my long hair. I never ran so fast back to the house as on that occasion!

I thoroughly enjoyed my time at Repton. I did History, English and French for A level and enjoyed all my teachers, some of whom were, in retrospect, fairly eccentric. I was fully immersed in the musical life of the school and remember Mus.Soc., the Wind Band and the Chapel Choir. And I even trod the boards and played Lady Macduff in a production of *Macbeth*, one of the most memorable aspects of which was the forest of branches that emerged on stage to represent 'Burnham Wood coming to Dunsinane'. I think the banks of the Trent took some time to recover! The social life was also second to none.

I have had the privilege of returning to Repton in the last few years, after over 20 years, as a Governor. I am now a Senior Lecturer at Cambridge University and am that university's representative on the Governing Body. It has been wonderful to see the school as it has now developed, as fully co-educational, with so many extra facilities, in good heart and going from strength to strength. A couple of years ago I preached at Speech Day about having the 'wisdom' to make the most of the opportunities presented to us, especially at school. A good, rounded education is a great gift, and I certainly believe that Repton gave that to me.

> '*I thought it would be hard to join Repton and fit in because there were so many people coming from Foremarke and they would all know each other, but the warmness I received when I came was the nicest feeling I've had. There was a real feeling of acceptance and I have not encountered one snobby person yet.*'
>
> **Sam Kingston-Jones (S 2005)**

TIM TOULMIN (B 1988)

What does Iain Duncan Smith mean to you? Probably not as much as he does to me. Not that I've ever met the man, but I am thinking about how the decisions or actions of others – or seemingly small choices of one's own – can be unexpectedly important in life.

For instance, my appointment to be Director of the Press Complaints Commission in early 2004 is directly traceable to the decision by the Conservative Party to elect IDS in 2001. For had any other man won, the Tories may not have had a crisis of confidence and replaced their leader in late 2003, which would have meant no job for me to apply for at the PCC (my predecessor having been seduced at very short notice to work for Michael Howard). A little tenuous? Not to me. I am devoted to IDS for his unwitting positive contribution to my career.

Similarly, I am convinced that a decision to buy a flat in Shepherd's Bush in 1997 – rather than anywhere else in London – may have saved my life. (This one is more convoluted, so will have to remain unexplained.)

By the same token, it is important to acknowledge that decisions taken at Repton – made with the help of, and by, teachers, friends and others – while made a long time ago, are of great significance. What a responsibility for those in authority, who have the power to change pupils' minds and the course of personal histories. I am constantly telling Simon Webster (N 1988) that he has John Plowright to thank for his personal happiness, or at least for his wife and two children. I can say this with some confidence, as it can be traced to a conversation I had with John in September 1992.

> JP: 'Where do you want to go to university?'
> Me: 'I think I'd like to try for English at Oxford'
> JP: 'No you wouldn't. You want to go to Peterhouse at Cambridge to read History'
> Me: 'OK'.

He was right. As a result of this brief conversation I did as I was told and met people I would never have encountered if I'd unthinkingly pursued an alternative, including a certain rather attractive blonde with an outstanding mathematical brain who became Mrs Simon Webster some years after I'd introduced them. And the impact on me of this brief chat at the beginning of a History lesson can hardly be underestimated, directly affecting my education, circle of friends, allegiances, experiences and, therefore, identity. Of course, almost all ORs could point to a similar thing.

Such is the significance of our schooldays, regardless of whether or not we enjoyed them or thought that the decisions we took or were taken for us were any good.

Important, too, was the atmosphere in which we lived. Being educated at an expensive private school might foster a certain snootiness or exclusivity in some, which would be a terrible handicap in life. But not, discernibly, in Reptonians of my generation. People would rather have dropped dead than admit to coming from a privileged background. Such a down-to-earth environment was one of the unsung characteristics of the school and one that enabled ORs later to fit in wherever they chose.

No doubt this helped as I groped towards what was to become my peculiar niche job, running the enterprise to which you would come if you found yourself harassed by journalists, the victim of a potential or actual intrusion, or if you wanted to put the record straight over something that appeared in a newspaper or magazine or on their websites. You would be in the company of an extraordinary army of people representing a complete cross-section of society: 'neighbours from hell', petty crooks, campaigners, heads of state, serial killers, soap stars and princes, and, above all, the 'man in the street' (which is what most of us are really).

I've no idea where all this will lead. But it's likely that seemingly irrelevant decisions – or those rooted in the distant past – will have a far greater bearing on events than might initially be apparent.

Keith Workman teaching in the Audit Room.

Evelyn Perry (C 1904) was killed whilst flying near Amiens on 16 August 1914. He was probably the first British officer killed in action in the First World War. In total 1,912 ORs served, of whom 355 were killed or died on active service.

GONE BUT NOT FORGOTTEN ...

O ne does not have to subscribe to psychoanalytical theories to appreciate that memory can play strange tricks, sometimes blotting out what it would be painful to recall and even, on occasion, manufacturing events that did not occur. Childhood memories are especially problematical. Past summers never seemed so long or so hot. Friendships never seemed so strong. Unrequited love was never so bittersweet.

For some, school is justly remembered as the happiest days of their lives. For others schooldays were a trial and torment. Who is to say that the pleasured recollections of the former are merely a manifestation of arrested development, or that the bruised broodings of the latter simply denote the irredeemably thin-skinned?

The section which follows explores the darker side of Repton life, including floggings and fagging, which for a few may indeed have left emotional scars long after the physical effects disappeared. Such phenomena are still capable of exciting strong emotions and not always all on one side. All that one can say with certainty is that they belong to Repton's past. They are gone but not forgotten.

FAGGING

Looking back to his own experiences of fagging in the Hall in the early years of Victoria's reign, the Rev. Vignoles (H 1840) wrote:

I cannot bring against it any serious charge of hardship or cruelty ... On the contrary I have found it useful especially in my College Life where I brought my youthful lessons in fagging to bear on practical economy. I was always able to keep my rooms in some kind of comfort, and in particular I never neglected my fire, or tolerated an untidy hearth.

The picture over a century later painted by John Blomfield (H 1955) is similarly benign:

For the first two years we were fags for the fifth year study-holder. So the two junior boys in each study kept it clean, polished the study-holder's shoes, did his corps kit, and ran the odd errand, nothing onerous.
Each year we moved one stage up the pecking order, from bim (bottom) fag to tip (top) fag, to the intermediate position of bim second and then tip second, until the master–servant role was finally reversed for our last year when we became studyholders, or, for the more trusty senior boys, beausieurs [prefects].

However, the experience of fagging could obviously differ, not just from era to era but from House to House, and Blomfield's contemporary Rodney Knight (O 1954) would certainly be justified in describing the fagging that he performed as exceedingly onerous:

In the Orchard the main tasks that daunted fags for their first two years were cleaning Chagger and sweeping the passages and

Lunch in School House.

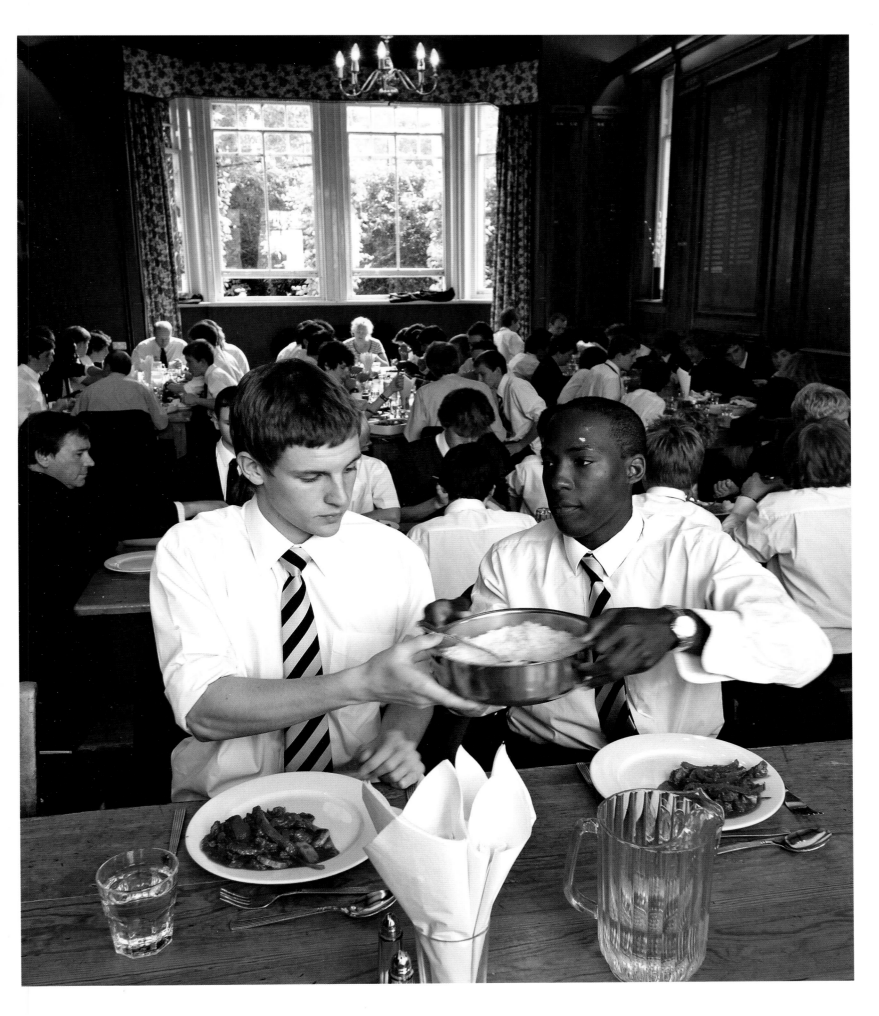

Hall fag call.

Hall fags responding to call.

boot area ... this was not cleaning as it is known conventionally ... [but] scouring and titivating to a quite unnecessary extent and the task was subjected to the scrutiny of the prefect on duty that day. In winter and spring Chagger usually looked as if a mud-typhoon had hit it! On League football days for instance three teams had changed and bathed there. Football boots were everywhere, dirty socks, shin pads, jockstraps and the dreaded towels. Towels had to be retrieved from all over the room and hung out to dry on the heated pipes. And not hung out any old how! They could only overlap by one inch and must hang without creases, all 40 or so of them! The place had to be swept and 'de-mudded' such that you could eat off the floor and all the lockers pulled out and re-packed with the boots and other gear. Clothes had to be hung up on the relevant hooks (all were named and house-numbered of course) and heaven help you if a study-holder had lost an article of clothing on your watch!

What especially galled me was the standard required of the sweeping of the passages! Was ours the only house where the beausieurs 'inspected' the work using a torch held at ground level to show up any specks of dust left uncollected by the unfortunate fag? And ... the sanctions if you did not 'pass' this fastidious inspection ... nearly always involved an unpleasantly heavy slipper!

Denys Rayner (M 1921), who possibly enjoys the unique distinction of having been beaten by two future Archbishops of Canterbury, Fisher as Headmaster and Michael Ramsey as studyholder, certainly found the latter punctilious in checking the performance of fagging duties. The story goes that to this end he put a slip of paper under a carpet to check his fag had swept there, and Rayner roused the future primate's wrath by finding the piece of paper and signing it.

Vignoles records that 'the upper form had ... the power to inflict ... a modified corporal punishment on youthful recalcitrants' and, indeed, the real purpose of fagging appears not so much to accomplish certain mundane tasks but rather to assert a pupil hierarchy. Those, like Vignoles, who showed respect to their elders and 'betters' generally found them 'reasonable, and oftentimes kind', although the corrupting nature of power certainly meant that this experience was not universal for those who were 'for all intents and purposes, the slaves of the studyholder' (Jim Furse P 1932).

Keith Stanley (H 1949), for example, records that shortly after his arrival at Repton 'when I had not had too much stuffing knocked out of me and was still rather cocky' he made the mistake of failing to keep a low profile and was as a consequence taunted throughout his time at Repton.

Fagging not only encouraged but demanded a degree of self-effacement. It also, more insidiously, encouraged deceit, as Nigel R.L. Hogg (N 1962) records:

The inevitable result of the determined attempts by the Repton system to occupy every waking moment of the inmates' time with some form of organized activity, many of them pointless and repetitive, was to promote and encourage the art of skiving. The expertise involved in skiving was to give the appearance of being fully occupied by some task whilst in fact doing nothing at all, or (even better), something not permitted.

The system itself promoted this from the outset. For example, evening fagging duties were designed to occupy all the spare time of younger boys every night in between dinner, supervised prep and bedtime. Most of these tasks could easily be accomplished in less than half the time available for them, but newcomers quickly learned that carrying them out efficiently and quickly merely meant that you had to do them all over again and repeat until the allotted time had expired. The answer was not to exert yourself at all, but to do the minimum necessary and always to have a broom or duster to hand in case anyone in authority should pass by.

By the 1960s the obvious disadvantages of fagging – and beatings – had come to outweigh the supposed advantages even in the eyes of those students who appeared to have most to gain, and Roger Noël Smith (P 1966) records that in his house 'the prefects themselves went to William Bryant to say they thought it should go' and 'fagging was abolished'.

Thus by the time Andrew Hewlett (B 1992) arrived at Repton:

Personal fagging had disappeared and there was only communal fagging … The worst jobs were the end-of-term tasks, and the worst of these jobs were reserved for the most revolting new boys who were too cocky and needed to be taught a lesson. Needless to say, I was one of them, and spent many an hour cleaning terms' worth of disgusting detritus from the bottom of the house bins. Thankfully I was never assigned the very worst job of all; known simply as 'drains', it involved scooping up the stagnant sludge from each of the elbow-deep drains into which the guttering ran. There must have been a dozen of these foul cisterns around the house for the poor Sisyphus to attempt to clear. He could never properly clear the drains – but this was the point; once he had been suitably humbled by the experience he could – after sufficient begging – be excused from the task.

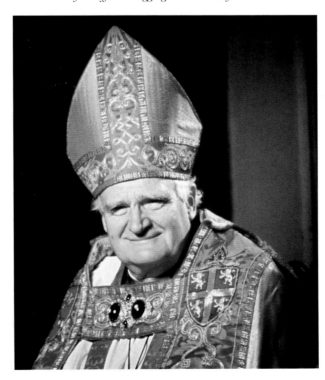

Michael Ramsey as Archbishop of Canterbury.

Andrew, like many ORs, is an advocate of fagging:

What better way of both disabusing young chaps of their cockiness, and removing the abundant spare time with which they may become troublesome, than ordering them to clean up the messes they create? It also teaches discipline and the arts of service and delegation. What a pity I didn't appreciate all this at the time.

Fagging clearly has its fans – at least in retrospect. The debate about its merits are now, however, purely academic. Fagging as traditionally understood and practised is as much a thing of the past as beating, with which it was once so intimately connected, and other ways must be found to minimize mess, instil respect and banish idleness.

BEATINGS

It's said that one Headmaster of Repton was fond of a punishment in which he'd hand a boy a copy of *Bradshaw* and ask him to find a way of travelling between Great Yarmouth and Exeter without going via London. This story may well be apocryphal. What is certainly the case is that for most of the school's history Headmasters, and many more besides, have relied on beatings or the threat of beatings to maintain order.

William Sanday (P 1858) records that 'Dr Pears was a born ruler' whose 'authority in no wise depended upon the outward paraphernalia at one time considered inseparable from the dignity of a Headmaster'. Thus, 'I believe he never made use of the flogging block, and seldom applied the cane.'

This was certainly in marked contrast with Macaulay, whose literally heavy-handed methods of disciplining Reptonians in large part explains the joy with the boys greeted the news of his impending demise.

Olinthus John Vignoles (H 1840) provides details of the sanctions meted out under Macaulay. In the case of private floggings:

the strokes of the birch rod seldom exceeded a dozen, and were administered by the Headmaster in the outer court of his study
…
At an ordinary castigation the culprit was called in by the Headmaster, who also summoned two other boys whose office was to facilitate the due administration of justice: the door was shut, and all that was heard by the outer school was the sharp cry of the sufferer. But a public flogging was much more awe inspiring, and … what I must term the cruel and almost inhuman punishment inflicted on a lad of tender years … The Master opened the study door, and almost immediately called on 'Smithers and Macaulay' (the latter was his nephew), and as

The Black Book, in which serious crimes and misdemeanours and their punishments were recorded.

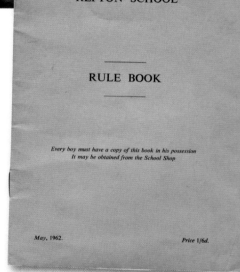

REPTON SCHOOL

———

RULE BOOK

———

*Every boy must have a copy of this book in his possession
It may be obtained from the School Shop*

May, 1962.　　　　　Price 1/6d.

The first rule is that every boy must have a copy of the Rule Book.

they approached he thundered out, 'the block in the middle of the school' ... [and] the 'gradus ad Parnassum' as some wag had euphemistically called it, was dragged out by the two lads ... only when the full 40 stripes ... had been inflicted was the poor sufferer released: he bore the marks of his punishment for months ... [In the lower forms] caning on the hand, or 'pandies' as we called it, was a pretty constant incident of the daily routine, but this we did not much mind. There was also a pretty frequent recurrence of admonitory phrase – 'Be careful or I shall send you up sir', a warning which was seldom wholly without effect even on the dullest pupil.

Lionel Ford could be almost as fearsome. Thus Norman Wallis (O 1901) described how he and two others 'had four of the very best from the Headmaster's special cane which was thickest at the business end. These we had to take on our bare bottoms, kneeling with our heads on the floor.'

However, if one was asked which Repton Headmaster used to flog boys until 'the victim was told to wash away the blood before pulling up his trousers' the answer, according to Jeremy Beadle (*Independent*, 29 July 2006) is Geoffrey Fisher. Beadle's source is, of course, Roald Dahl's *Boy*, in which it is alleged, or rather insinuated, that Fisher was a sadist and hypocrite because of the alleged manner in which he beat a friend of Dahl's.

Dahl, however, is hardly the most reliable of witnesses. He has been shown to have presented fiction as fact when dealing with other aspects of his life. For example, in *Shot Down Over Libya*, which appeared anonymously as a 'factual report on Libyan air fighting' in the *Saturday Evening Post* in August 1942, Dahl presented himself as having been downed by an enemy fighter, when in fact his crash was actually caused by a lack of fuel and wrong directions. When this discrepancy was pointed out to him, Dahl claimed that the story had been edited for dramatic effect. In fact, it had been published as written, and it was Dahl who characteristically didn't allow the facts to get in the way of a good story.

Even Dahl's biographer, Jeremy Treglown, concludes that the beating of Dahl's friend referred to in *Boy* took place in 1933 and must therefore have been administered by Christie rather than Fisher.

Ironically, Dahl himself was not opposed to beating in principle and once fantasized, like Bentham, about devising a beating machine, which could be calibrated to ensure that each blow was as severe as the last.

John Plowright

Repton's Greatest Scandal

Victor Gollancz was seconded to Repton by the War Office in 1916 in order to assist the OTC, his poor eyesight having disqualified him from active service. Shortly after arrival he joined forces with the gifted History master David Somervell with the laudable intention of educating the boys politically, so that they would know what they were fighting and, in all probability, dying for. Their chosen means for achieving this outcome were the Civics class and (from June 1917) A Public School Looks at the World *or* Pubber, *a magazine produced by the boys under their guidance.*

However, it soon came to be felt amongst some staff and boys that the magazine's policy was opposed to the vigorous prosecution of the war, particularly in the light of an article that appeared to be calling for a negotiated peace. Tempers frayed on both sides, not least because this was desired by elements of both parties, notably by the *Pubber*'s editor Amyas Ross (P 1914), who appears to have been inspired by Bolshevik rhetoric, and by H.J. Snape (Staff 1911–34), who seems to have been motivated by a mixture of unthinking patriotism, anti-Semitism and professional jealousy of Gollancz and Somervell.

The divisions within the school and Common Room were brutally exposed on 19 February 1918 when it was proposed in the Debating Society that 'it is disgraceful that conscientious objectors, whether genuine or not, should be disenfranchised'.

Moreover, the March 1918 edition of the *Pubber* was advertised as: 'Published by the Repton School Book Shop Ltd. And Henderson & Sons, 44 Charing Cross Road.' In fact, this merely meant that it was available at that address but given that the bookshop was under War Office surveillance because of its alleged anarchist sympathies, this confirmed the suspicions of those who regarded the *Pubber* as thoroughly subversive.

Fisher, who had tried to hold the ring, was now obliged to act, and he dismissed Gollancz. Somervell left the school shortly afterwards. Snape was at least as worthy of dismissal, and the affair continues to divide opinion.

Fisher may not have acted heroically, but it is difficult to see how he could acted differently.

John Plowright

Roald Dahl: professional fantasist.

BEFORE BETTING SHOPS

Betting shops were unheard of during my time at Repton. Instead bookmakers used to have runners who would collect the local bets and hand them over. The bookmaker's runner in Repton was a Mr Stoffle who had a barber's shop on Boot Hill, and who did the haircutting for certain Repton houses including New House. Boys could pop into the shop, have their haircut done and put it on the school bill. Unfortunately, the Priory, my own house, did not have this arrangement. Dick Sale had instead commissioned the Sudbury Prison barber to come every three weeks to do our hair. He was a real stylist, managing to cut sixty boys' hair in approximately three hours!

A close friend of mine, Carl Whitehead (N 1956), who was one of Repton's real characters, realised that Mr Stoffle's dual occupations provided too good an opportunity to miss. Carl used to read form avidly, especially during Latin lessons, so during morning break used to call at Stoffle's and put the price of a haircut – 2/6d (12½p) on a horse. If he won he would always take the winnings in cash, although that wasn't very often!

I always remember my first ever bet. I asked Carl to put a haircut each way on a horse called Rexequus in the 1958 Champion hurdle at Cheltenham. It romped home at 33–1 and I collected six pound five shillings (£6.25) winnings. In those days that was real money!

I also remember Carl ringing me during the Lent holidays. His father had just received the school bill and couldn't understand how he managed to have 128 haircuts in a term and still have the longest hair at Repton. He wasn't happy!

Unfortunately Carl died at a very early age and has been sorely missed.

A. P. Basnett (P 1956)

THE *450TH* CELEBRATIONS

*I*n which Brigadier Edward Wilkinson reviews the events of 2007 commemorating the school's foundation.

The programme of events for the 450th anniversary year (which had appeared in the Court Circular of 9 January) started with a thought-provoking address in Chapel on Friday 12 January by John Plowright. They continued in the House of Commons when 150 ORs and their wives attended a reception sponsored by the Rt Hon Nick Raynsford, MP (P 1958). Those present were addressed by the Patron of the Year, the Rt Hon Sir Christopher Rose (L 1950), the Headmaster, Robert Holroyd and the President of the OR Society, Robert Bond (P 1968).

The oldest OR present on Commemoration Day, John Hedley (H 1930) and Head Girl Susie Gilbert (F 2002).

Events both large and small, organized and attended by ORs, have subsequently been held in both hemispheres, in places as disparate as Auckland, Copenhagen, Ottawa, Madrid, Springwood (near Brisbane), Toronto, Dublin and Paris. The excellent Dinner at the latter, organized by the Rev James Barnett (H 1957) and held at Le Restaurant au Sergent Recruteur on the Ile St-Louis was particularly notable, being attended by over twenty ORs and their wives. The Headmaster's message – a feature of these gatherings – was read on this occasion in great style by Mike Stones as Secretary of the OR Society, which was also represented by its President and Chairman.

Commemoration Day (26 May) began when a packed Chapel heard both an inspiring sermon by a former parent, the Right Revd Michael Perham, Bishop of Gloucester, and the premiere performance by the choir of an anthem based upon the Repton hymn by the noted choral composer Bob Chilcott, who was also in attendance. The School v Pilgrims cricket match was narrowly won by the school, whilst the versatility and quality of Repton music was showcased on both sides of a buffet lunch held in the marquee on the Paddock. The Jazz Band played beforehand, on the steps of Pears School, and afterwards the school Orchestra performed a special concert in Pears School. Highlights of the latter included *Rhapsody in Blue*, with Alvin Moisey (L 1975) on the piano, and Walton's *Crown Imperial* and Handel's *Zadok the Priest* being performed in memory of the late Tony Garton.

After tours of the Houses, the day ended with tea in the marquee. The ORs especially appreciated the fact that, in addition to the special events which had been arranged, they had had the opportunity of seeing the school in session.

HRH meeting members of the Garden.

Far left: Commemoration Day 26 May 2007.

Commemoration Day, Michael Applebee (N 1947).

Celebrating the 450th in the House of Commons, Paris and Queensland.

A group portrait of those attending the Hong Kong OR Dinner.

Several generations of the Hong Kong OR community attending the Gala Dinner.

approximately 5,000 attended performances by Michael Ball and Bryan Ferry. I wonder how many of those present realized that the title track of the latter's first solo album – 'These Foolish Things'– had lyrics penned by an OR (Eric Maschwitz, H 1915).

On 14 September some 34 ORs and Staff attended the Cambridge Dinner at Corpus Christi. Those staying in College were appropriately accommodated in Beldam Hall, and reminiscences of Robert Beldam's generosity and fondness for speechmaking on such occasions were shared by many of those present. The recently retired Master of the College, Professor Haroon Ahmed, was the Guest, and Sir Nicholas Barrington proposed the toast to the school, to which the Headmaster eloquently replied.

The Garth provided a natural arena for the Son et Lumière and 250 spectators packed the stand each night, between 20 and 23 September, to witness Jeremy Bournon's production, which not only reviewed the 450 years of the school's history but also traced the history of Repton back to Anglo-Saxon times. Over 100 staff and students were involved in the spectacle which successfully combined projected light and images, live

The Old Priory becomes a screen for the Son et Lumiere.

The school's pre-history re-enacted in the Son et Lumiere.

Speech Day also had a comprehensive programme of events. The Address in Chapel at the Leavers' Service was unusually given by a young OR, namely Tom Chambers (N 1990), star of the TV series, 'Holby City'. The Guest of Honour for the day was Sir Christopher Rose (L 1950), the Chief Surveillance Commissioner and former Lord Justice of Appeal, who presented the prizes and addressed the gathering in the marquee, which was once again full.

After lunch, the rain, which had already caused the cricket match to be abandoned, meant that the Marching Display by the Band of the Light Cavalry moved into Pears School where they gave an excellent and varied musical programme. The day ended in the transformed marquee when some 350 guests sat down to dinner at the Leavers' Ball which went on until 1.00am. Unseasonable weather could not dampen the spirits of all those who attended.

The school's summer concerts took place on the Square – hallowed ground excepted – on the evenings of 7-8 July, when

The whole school assembles in the Yard.

HRH with the Lord Lieutenant, Chairman of Governors and Headmaster.

and recorded music (much of it original) and dramatic action. However, the technical wizardry was never allowed to overshadow the story's human dimensions but instead literally illuminated the tale, and the huge cast and crew having so brilliantly recounted Repton's history, thereby, in the words of the Headmaster, themselves became a part of it.

Michaelmas Half Term began with a James Bond-themed dinner party to celebrate the 450th anniversary where the staff and their spouses/guests were the guests of the Governing Body.

On Tuesday 16 October a Gala Dinner was held to celebrate the Anniversary at the Hong Kong Club, and this event was attended by the Headmaster, Mrs Holroyd and over 60 Old and current Reptonians based on the island. The wine for the occasion, a specially selected Burgundy Grand Cru, (Charmes-Chambertin 1999), was most generously donated by Richard Kan (C 1966). During the Dinner, the Headmaster spoke and outlined plans for the future of Repton, as well as thanking the current OR Hong Kong community for their continued support of the school, particularly in relation to the Studio Theatre which is now such a vital and vibrant support to the drama curriculum. It is especially heartening for the school to know that the reputation of Repton is so high on the island, and special credit for this must go to Eddie Niem, Secretary of the OR Hong Kong Branch, and to his fellow-members of the Organizing Committee for the Dinner, Robert Tam and David Poon (Hall 1985).

On 27 November HRH the Prince Edward, Earl of Wessex, and his party, including the Lord Lieutenant and

Repton Governor John Bather, arrived and were introduced to local dignitaries including the High Sheriff of Derbyshire, the Chairmen of the County and District Councils, and Jonathan Fry, the Chairman of Repton Governors.

The latter introduced the Headmaster, who escorted the Prince into the New Court Gallery where he was met by Jeremy Bournon, Ian Setterington and various students. The next port of call was the Studio Theatre, where he was introduced to Guy Levesley and witnessed a rehearsal for 'Twelfth Night'. On departing he was shown memorabilia of the Royal Visit of 1957. Walking with the Headmaster to the Paddock, the Prince spoke to members of the public outside The Arch and then discussed Duke of Edinburgh Award activities with Madeleine Court, before touring the refurbished Library, which included an exhibition of further memorabilia relating to the Queen's visit.

A group of Choristers were in attendance whilst HRH met representatives of the Governors, staff, and students at The Hall.

Head Prefects Tamsin Rees-Jones (M 2003) and Charles Sindrey (C 2003) formally thanked HRH for visiting the school and presented him with a gifts, and the visit concluded with the Headmaster inviting the Prince to unveil a plaque to commemorate the day, and with the whole school giving Prince Edward three lusty cheers.

To complete the year the traditional OR Dinner was held in Pears School on 10 November and the Young ORs organized a Christmas Ball in Pears School for 22 December.

In short, the 450th anniversary has witnessed more diverse, more numerous, better-attended and more geographically dispersed celebrations of the school than ever before. The bar has indeed been set high for 2057.

Edward Wilkinson (C 1946)

HRH and Headmaster leaving the Old Priory.

'BEYOND *450* ...'

The Headmaster reflects on recent developments and outlines his vision for the future of the school.

Roald Dahl muses in 'Boy' on how it was that he came to Repton, and all OR's will know that, when offered the choice between Repton and Marlborough he plumped for the former because of the two names it was the one he could best pronounce! I would like to claim that my own good fortune in coming to Repton could be attributed to a much more scientific approach, but any such claim would, I am afraid, be false. I had reached a stage, having run a house for ten years at another great school (which a self-denying ordinance forbids me to identify further than to say that it also begins with an 'R') when others had been kind enough to suggest that I might apply for Headmasterships, and of those that fell vacant at the time when I was looking, Repton was much the most attractive. That was not, in all honesty, to say that I had ever been to the place, but I had, of course, heard the name during my own schooldays at Birkenhead and had a great friend who was an OR, (James Wesson, H 1973), who spoke most warmly about a very special school that had clearly had a great influence on him. Thus it was that having heard that I had been long listed for the position, I found myself travelling up from Oxfordshire to Derbyshire one wet Sunday afternoon in May 2002 for my first look at the place that was soon to become my new home. Despite the showery conditions I clearly remember my first thoughts as I came through the Arch and saw The Square, in pristine condition, with lovely old-fashioned wooden waste baskets (none of your plastic rubbish) tidily positioned along The Paddock. 'If I am lucky enough to be

The Headmaster in the refurbished Audit Room.

short listed,' I gulped, 'I know I'm going to go to the interview wanting the job!' So it was a few days later that I found myself in The Athenaeum flanked by a Selection Committee who wasted no time with any looseners to allow me to play myself in. 'We know we've a great school in excellent shape' said the Chairman, 'but what are the challenges we face in the future and what would you do about them?' I had, at that point done

Inside the New Court Gallery.

enough homework to suggest an answer that was at least coherent if not comprehensive, but it was, of course, a typically good question and one that I often found myself returning to once I had been lucky enough to be offered the job.

A wise mentor had said to me, when he knew I was coming to Repton, 'read all you can', and 'listen to all and sundry…but especially the sundry'. It was good advice, and I followed it, devouring Thomas, Macdonald and John Thorn's autobiography (especially enjoying the latter and finding it less critical of Repton than I had been led to expect) and listening carefully not only to current members of the Common Room but also to some of those who had served the school with distinction in the recent past and could provide the depth and historical perspective necessary to answer the Chairman's question.

A few months into the job the core strengths of the school, the unchangeable pillars on which any future developments would need to be founded, came into sharper focus. Repton at once had a more companionable, down-to-earth feel than other schools of similarly great name and repute. Some rivals perhaps had tighter, more pressurised academic systems, whilst others were stronger magnets for the rural classes, but Repton clearly managed to sustain its sense of purpose whilst nurturing that wonderfully relaxed feel that no other school can match. It also clearly enjoyed a history of employing powerful personalities on its teaching staff who influenced generations of pupils for good in an original way without necessarily conforming to the latest educational fad. These values had to remain at the core.

It also quickly became equally clear to me what a huge debt I owed to my predecessor, Graham Jones, (a fellow Old Birkonian), who had been absolutely right in his judgements on all the big issues. I was lucky enough to be inheriting a school where the transition to full coeducation had been superbly managed – not only was the newly built and refurbished accommodation of the highest order, but the numbers were right too. Graham, with the dextrous support of Tim Collins, had managed a sometimes painful but commercially necessary task of converting the Mitre into a girls' house and transferring the Mitre boys to the Cross; he had also got the proportions spot on – at 60/40 boy/girl we had the feel and all the advantages of a fully coeducational school without any sense that the girls, who shoot ahead more quickly in the early adolescent years, were dominating. Graham was right, too, on the timing of the school day. 'End the 9pm finish for day pupils' some had said,' and you will boost numbers.' But Graham had seen that such a move would destroy the sense of family unit which was at the heart of the school, engender an 'us and them' feel between boarders and day pupils and potentially weaken the

commitment of staff to the full Repton ethos. House dining was another great Repton tradition considered ripe for change in the eyes of some (it did make sense, in their view, to reap the benefit of the economies of scale provided by central catering) but wise guidance from both Sir Richard Morris, my incoming Chairman of Governors and Jonathan Fry, his successor, ensured that this key feature of Repton life was preserved for future generations of pupils. Some have likened headmastering to producing a play – the text is set, but considerable nuance, variety and change can be achieved by the director as he gives a new shape to old values … I was now beginning to understand my text, (indeed to live, breathe and sleep it!), and this, together with the wise counsel of colleagues both senior and junior, helped give me the confidence and vision to plan for 2007 and beyond.

One of the first issues that needed to be tackled was, in my view, the confidence levels amongst *some* of the boys. A few, but too many for my liking nonetheless, felt in the shadow of the girls, and this lack of confidence manifested itself in sloppy appearance. Pat Silvey and his successor as Deputy, Sarah Tennant, together with the Housemasters, led superbly from the front supporting the message that haircuts, top buttons and general appearance mattered and that 'looking like winners' was a small but important first step in further strengthening the school. Another mark of a lack of confidence in one or two quarters was, in my view, the inability to resist the temptation of drugs and shortly into my second year a group of five boys were found to have been smoking cannabis on school premises. This is always a difficult question for a Headmaster. A strong argument exists for giving young people a second chance (one to which I subscribe on almost every

Guard of Honour in the Garth.

Big School in the Nineteenth Century, before the advent of the Library.

A fire still burns in the Common Room today but two of the other chimneys shown here have disappeared from the Old Priory.

occasion) but drugs are different – they ruin lives and destroy trust in a school. I decided the boys had to go. This policy would be backed by a full Personal and Social Education programme, and support would be offered in trying to find a new school for those involved, but a special Lists was called to remind every Reptonian where he or she stood on this matter.

Good appearance and self-discipline go hand in hand with higher expectations, and in my first address to the school I emphasised the need for inner 'steel' and a shared conviction amongst Common Room and pupils alike that 'happiness' and 'fulfilment' were not mutually exclusive. The Repton of the new millennium should be able, in my opinion, to retain its happy feel yet have even higher expectations, not least in the academic field. Repton has never been an academic hothouse and nor should it ever become one. Parents who want that are free to choose elsewhere. At the same time parents have a right to expect that the highest targets possible are being set for their sons and daughters. When I became Headmaster I felt Repton had got this question right for the top and bottom ends of its academic spectrum, but that still more could be done for those in between. I also felt that, in these days of perceived bias against the independent sector in the matter of the transfer to higher

The School Library as it used to be.

education, it was vital that we had a specialist in this role, someone of great experience whose job it was to supervise the UCAS applications and develop the relationships with the Admissions Tutors that would be so important if Reptonians were to continue to proceed to the university of their first choice. So, in September 2004 John Driver became Director of University Entrance and Tim Owen, a former city lawyer and Head of History at Cranleigh became Academic Deputy. A range of initiatives was introduced to raise academic expectations across the board: tutor groups with their own dedicated weekly session to monitor performance; electronic reporting so that pupil progress was available school wide at the touch of a button; an annual appraisal system that gave teachers the chance for a yearly review with me but also focused strategy on pupil results; rejuvenation of the academic societies and a formalisation of the exam revision process. These measures were not initially popular with Common Room and I encountered some resistance; the new focus, it was claimed, would restrict teaching freedom. However I knew the changes would be justified once the pupils began to score B's rather than C's and A's rather than B's. In 2003, our combined percentage of A★ and A at GCSE, one of the key indicators of academic performance in a school, stood at 44%. By 2004, it had risen to

The School Library. Books were not always pored over so eagerly.

57% and by 2005 to 66%, placing us 34th in the country in The Times GCSE League Table. By the same token our combined percentage of A and B grades at A level in 2005 stood at 73.4%. By 2006 it had risen to 79.1% and by 2007 it had reached 85.9%, placing us 88th in the Daily Telegraph National Table and at the very head of that group of leading Midlands boarding schools of which Repton is proud to be part.

The recently refurbished School Library.

These tables do not, of course, tell the whole story: it is important to keep them in perspective. Good teaching always goes beyond the academic syllabuses, but in the hands of the very best teachers this wider vision is not incompatible with each pupil achieving his or her maximum expectations in public examinations. Repton is fortunate indeed in having a staff able to inspire their pupils along these twin tracks, and in men and women such as Melissa Blain, Jeremy Bournon, Gary Lawrence, Guy Levesley, Ian McClary and Sandra Nield, to name but a few of many in an outstandingly talented Common Room, the school continues to be home to strong characters who influence young people for good throughout the rest of their lives.

Chapel too was a clear priority for reform as we approached the 450th anniversary of the school. It had been a source of some concern to me, when I arrived at Repton, that the pupils, so biddable in every other form of school life, were reluctant to participate in Chapel, particularly in the business of congregational singing. Confirmation numbers too were at an unacceptable low, with barely a handful of candidates being presented to the Bishop each year, this despite the unquestioned vitality of the school's Christian Forum led by the inspirational Mike Keep. The Chapel team began to work together with the

pupils on these issues, persuading them that the rousing level of singing Reptonians produced on the touchline could be reproduced in Chapel and the whole experience of the Sunday and weekly services was soon to be transformed as a result. Personnel were, as ever, key to such changes. Following the July 2004 departure of Bob Short, a much loved and respected man, the position of Chaplain was eventually filled with the arrival of Adam Watkinson in January 2006 after a series of temporary appointments. Here was a man who could take 600 pupils from a cold standing start at the beginning of a Lent term into warm laughter and praise within seconds. Careful to work with long standing members of staff such as Greg Atwood, for whom the Christian life of the school is central, Adam began to show a new generation of Reptonians the beauty and value of the Christian liturgy as we moved to our four hundred and fiftieth anniversary and beyond. On the musical side, Richard Dacey's move after twelve distinguished years' service as Director of Music to the position of Head of Performing Arts at Guthlaxton College created an opportunity for John Bowley, one of the country's leading professional tenors, to take up his first full directorship following teaching spells at Eton and St Paul's.

Sport has long been an area where Repton has rightfully reigned supreme, and the move to full coeducation naturally presented challenges to a school renowned as a beacon of success in cricket, hockey and soccer. But it also presented opportunities, and I could straightaway see that by the time of my arrival Gill Snelson had expertly built up a squad of girl hockey players capable of winning the National Championships. In 2004 we reached the final but underperformed, perhaps showing a touch of slack having steamrollered too many opposition teams 10–0 in routine school fixtures. Martin Jones (OR and GB international) was brought in to work alongside Simon Clague and Gill as Director of Hockey Coaching with a brief to toughen up the fixture list and share the newest coaching methods across the club. Though this change was not always straightforward, especially in its early days, in 2005, 2006 and 2007 we clinched a hat trick of U18 National Girls' titles, again setting a standard and a challenge for those who follow post the 450th anniversary to meet.

On the boys' side, there had, by all accounts been some relatively weak cricket played on the square in the years preceding Graham Jones' inspired appointment of Frank Watson as Master in charge of the Club, but Frank, working with stalwarts and excellent players themselves such as Peter Bradburn and Mike Stones began a steady strengthening of the sport at all levels, a process enhanced by a renewed focus on the preparatory schools with the introduction of the Donald Carr Trophy in 2006. The XI's of 2005 and 2006 have been amongst the finest to set foot on the Square, (and that, in the school of Charles Fry, the Palairets and Jack Crawford, is saying something) with two players, Chris Paget and Paul Borrington representing Derbyshire and England U19 whilst still at school, and Richard Hutton and Guy Turner's 1961 record for the opening stand eventually being broken by Borrington and James Blackwell's fine unbroken partnership of 314 against Denstone in June 2005. The foundation for the future looks bright. Pupils have risen to the standards of their beautiful surroundings, and the newly relaid Paddock and Square, together with the re-thatched pavilion, is surely one of the finest cricketing venues in the land. Equally encouraging for 2007 and beyond is the manner in which the XI are playing their cricket: the Repton XI is renowned on the circuit for eschewing multiple and meaningless appeals or witless cries of 'well bowled' to routine deliveries!

These measures, building on the foundations laid down in previous years, enabled numbers in the school to grow from around 530 to around 600 in the corresponding period, and this to me seems an excellent number in which to plan for the future – big enough to be national champions but small enough for every pupil to have their own space. At around 600 we are also full … we can all get into Chapel, (just!) and this is vitally important for the communal life of the school. 600 or so pupils also provides the economic base for Repton to continue the expansion of facilities so generously and wisely executed by previous generations. Under the expert eye of Sir Richard Morris and then Jonathan Fry a ten-year Development Plan for both Repton and Foremarke has been devised that will see the schools grow stronger in a period of overall contraction in the independent sector. 2006 saw the £750,000 conversion of the west wing of the Old Mitre into the new home of the English Department and this has paved the way for the refurbishment of the Library and Old Priory, an £800,000 project designed to preserve the integrity of that wonderful old building whilst getting more boys and girls through it on a daily basis to read and study in a way that will better prepare them for university. Indeed criticism of the Library was the only negative point in the otherwise glowing 2003 ISI Inspection of the school achieved under Graham Jones' leadership. Following the Report, a new, permanent and fully qualified Librarian, Paul Stevens, was appointed and he set about the task of reshaping the resources in the Old Priory so that pupils could learn via the new technology, discretely hidden, but also come (by stealth!) to the view that the printed word is king! Departmental Libraries have been pulled into the central orbit of the Main Library so that the experience of serendipitous discovery that lies at the heart of the best university libraries is now available to all Reptonians. The Third stage of Phase One of the Plan was the conversion of the Old Squash Courts, by 2006 a rare but real eyesore on the Repton campus, into a new Textiles and Design Studio, complete with a Sculpture Park running down to the Burton Road. This £500,000 venture will provide a wonderful stimulus to future generations of Repton artists as well as offering studio and gallery space to Artists in Residence.

The biggest challenges in the area of capital development for the school post 2007 will, in my view, lie in improving the school's academic buildings and extra curricular performance areas. The 400 Hall, a wonderfully versatile and imaginative design for 1950's Repton, now needs an expanded foyer area and permanent raked seating to turn it into a theatrical space worthy of the quality of productions it is currently staging. The vision as we advance from 450 to 500 is to extend the building out into the Precinct, creating a floor to ceiling glass frontal that will preserve the façade of the 1957 original but give us the space to modify the interior into an auditorium for the new millennium. The second strand of the Plan to lead us towards the Quinquecentenary is to rejuvenate the school's science facilities by creating a 'Science Priory' that will make Repton a national leader in the teaching of science. Of all the Repton

Repton's Headmaster and the first generation of Repton Dubai students.

An artist's impression of Repton Dubai.

buildings that call out to ORs across the years, the Old Priory, is, in my view, by far the best and most evocative, due in no small part to the building's dual identity of being both a *home* to clerics and scholars over the centuries and the *academic heart* of the school in which so many have learned to love the Classics, History and English Literature. The vision for the Science Priory is to take this principle, so integral to Repton, and develop it in a unique way by providing a first class integrative resource to support the sciences in much the same way as the Old Priory has supported the humanities for the past 450 years. Thus the hope is that the new building will be a translational Science Centre, comprising not only classrooms, a first class lecture hall, university-style 'science cave', wireless computer centre and library but also a social area where pupils and teachers can come together to discuss the key scientific issues that will shape their future whether they are to become a science specialist or not. It is my conviction, and that of Professor Alastair Buchan (H 1968), whose vision has helped shape the project, that the new building will help brand a futuristic Repton for the next fifty years as we reach towards the 500th Anniversary.

Whilst these plans, with the 450 Hall and the Science Priory at their heart, have been drawn up on the basis of buoyant pupil numbers and *not* on any spiralling increase in fee levels, the Governors are also deeply grateful for the part played in such developments by many generations of old Reptonians, parents and friends of the school over many years. Special mention must be made of Robert Beldam, now lying in peace opposite his beloved Old Priory, without whose generosity such ambition for the school would not have been possible.

Ambition, increased pupil opportunity and financial security for the school were also the key drivers behind the Governors' January 2006 decision to launch Repton's first ever sister school, 'Repton Dubai', in the Arabian Gulf.

The genesis of this project was a November 2003 conversation I was lucky enough to have with Robert Owen, (P 1953, Governor and international financier of wide experience in both the Far and Middle East), during which we

The refurbished Audit Room.

agreed that over the next decade, all good schools would have to face the challenge of preparing their pupils for the global marketplace. Robert then had the brainwave of setting this vision within the context of the rapidly expanding population of the UAE, where he was conscious of the demand for new and forward looking schools, and subsequently introduced me to Khaled Al-Muhairy, Chief Executive of Dubai-based Evolvence Capital. Mr Al-Muhairy is himself a young financier of immense talent and determination to succeed, and was at once alive to the possibility of a school being built in the UAE along the lines of a leading British public school. Such a school, would, Mr Al-Muhairy believed, appeal not only to the international day market of Dubai and the UAE but also, given high levels of imagination and investment, the wider market for boarding within the Gulf States as a whole. Thus the idea of Repton Dubai was born: our vision is to build a school with a strong boarding element and such high quality teaching staff and facilities so as to become the market leader in the region.

Subsequent to these initial conversations there then followed the long process of conducting appropriate market research and developing a business plan, which was presented to the Governing Body in successive stages from November 2004 onwards. The creation of a new school bearing the Repton name is, of course, a huge undertaking and responsibility, and the Governors were mindful of this right throughout the negotiation process. Equally, and for this I am most grateful, they also saw that here was an opportunity for Repton to become involved in an exciting and visionary project. In doing so, the Governing Body was conscious that the venture, with its very considerable levels of investment, was to be funded in its entirety by Evolvence, and not by current fee paying parents or OR donors to the Foundation. Repton will, of course, in addition to lending its name to the school, provide considerable expertise in terms of curriculum and architectural design and Robert Owen and I will have seats on the Governing Body of the new school to ensure consistency and cooperation between the two schools at all levels.

Naturally, such a venture would not be possible without strong support from the appropriate authorities within Dubai, and the next stage of the process was the granting of the land by the Dubai Educational Council, whose Secretary General, Dr Abdulla Al Karam, has been most supportive throughout. The DEC approved the establishment of Repton Dubai under its new "Dubai Schools" scheme, and following many months' examination of several sites, a plot comprising 1.4 million square feet was eventually approved some 5–10 minutes' drive from the main commercial sector of Dubai between the junction of the Emirates and Al Ain Roads. It should, at this point, also be noted that the school is extremely fortunate and honoured to have the approval of His Highness Sheikh Mohammed bin Rashid Al Maktoum, Vice President of the UAE and Ruler of Dubai, which gives us great confidence as we go forward. Following approval of the land, a full Agreement was drawn up between Repton and Evolvence Education, and this was duly signed at the Launch Ceremony held in Dubai on 24th January 2006.

The signing of the Agreement constituted a notable first for Repton. We are the first British school to open a partner school anywhere in the Middle East, and the first British school in the world to open a partner school that will have boarding at its heart. What then, are the many challenges and opportunities that face us as we plan for future success?

Key to the project, of course, will be quality and close cooperation between the two schools at all levels, from governance and management through to curriculum and architectural design and staff appointments. People are, as ever at Repton, the most important factor of all, and in January 2006 we were delighted to announce the appointment of Mr David Cook as the new Founding Head of Repton Dubai. Mr Cook, ex-Westminster housemaster and former Head of Qatar Academy took up appointment in September 2006 in order to allow him to spend a year absorbing the Repton ethos and undertaking all the appropriate planning in preparation for the opening of the school in September 2007. The Governors were also delighted to appoint Mr Mark Atkins to be Head of the Junior Section. Mr Atkins, previously Headmaster of Beech Hall School, one of our feeder preparatory schools, already knows Repton well.

September 2007 saw the Junior Section of the school open its doors to 300 pupils, who will be the first batch of 'Reptonians in the Gulf' to enjoy a new level of educational opportunity in what will be a wonderful setting. The architects' vision for the school is indeed exciting, encompassing an entrance Arch to echo the 13th Century Arch of Repton, leading on to state-of-the-art classrooms, boarding and extra-curricular facilities that include a theatre, library, covered swimming pool, extensive sports areas and gymnasia, art and music blocks, all linked by a series of covered walkways to provide much needed shade in the Gulf climate. These facilities will lead to separate boys' and girls' boarding houses at the rear of the site, separated by extensive staff accommodation purpose-built to attract the best quality teachers from the local and international market. Following hard on the heels of all this, the Senior Section will open in September 2008 and overall pupil numbers will eventually grow to Repton levels and beyond, with boarders, at maturity, constituting up to half the school's population.

The success of both the boarding operation, and by extension the provision for day pupils too, will depend on us developing the vision to tackle a number of key issues. The school will be secular in character, offering pupils of different backgrounds the opportunity to exercise their beliefs, and extensive time will be included in the curriculum to the study of Arabic language and culture. The school will follow a British curriculum, closely linked to that of Foremarke and Repton in the lower years, branching out with the international GCSE at Key Stage 4 (A Block onwards!), and thereafter offering the option of a Sixth Form programme that will prepare pupils for entry into the top universities across the world. Considerable creativity will need to be brought to the question of providing an attractive boarding day that extends beyond the traditional earlier finish of Gulf day schools, and here again quality facilities and staff will be the key as we seek to redefine and extend, rather than merely reproduce, the Repton ethos.

What, then, as we go forward, will be the benefit for Repton and its pupils in the UK? I believe the new school will present opportunities for extensive exchange between 'the two Reptons' and my vision is that within five years Reptonians of the future should have the opportunity of spending part of their own academic courses in this great economic centre. What an opportunity that will be and what an attraction to Repton parents and pupils of the next decade! As the new school grows there is also the potential for it to become a significant additional income stream for Repton UK, and I am convinced that schools such as ours will need to explore additional and imaginative sources of funding if they are to continue to widen access to the school to enable pupils from all backgrounds to attend. I, for one, and many others in the Repton family, will relish the challenge of spreading the Repton name abroad and I am sure that readers of this book will join me in wishing a glowing future to our sister school, launched 450 years after Sir John Port founded our beloved original in Derbyshire! It is my earnest hope that the two schools will be linked most closely by those values which have appealed to so many generations of Reptonians over the years, namely the lifelong comradeship and unique sense of kinship that exists between those who have been privileged to have been educated within The Arch.

Will the school last for a further 450 years? In an age that has seen the overnight collapse of an institution as ancient as Barings Bank, a complacent 'yes' is far from an adequate answer. But if we can implement the plans we have laid out with the help of all the Repton family, and carry on doing what the school does best, namely looking after every boy and girl in an individual way, then we will stand a very good chance. The gate may be empty of blame, but I am confident that its influence will remain deep, wide and sure.

Robert Holroyd

Sharing a joke on the Causey.

APPENDICES

An Anthology of Slang Currently in Use in the Hall.
Compiled March 1959 by Anthony Irwin Smyth (H 1954), edited by John Plowright

Beausieur (bow-ser) noun. Prefect, usually House. The origin of the word cannot be traced for certain, but it probably comes from mediaeval French, the constituent parts being beau, beautiful or handsome, and sieur, someone of knightly rank. [Roald Dahl in *Boy* (mis)represents this word as 'Boazer', Ed.]

Beausieuritis (bow-ser-itis) noun. An imaginary disease that can be caught by new or aspiring House and School prefects. The symptoms are said to be a tendency to be officious and too harsh in punishing minor offences. Usually the disease wears off quite harmlessly.

Bim adjective. Bottom. Can be used to denote the bottom of a form as well as the literal meaning used in 'bim floor' and similar phrases.

Bim fag The junior or first-year fag in a study. In a big study there may be more than one.

Bine verb. To smoke, usually illegally. [Presumably derived from the popular Woodbine brand of cigarette, Ed.]

Bone off noun and verb. Occurs 15 minutes after the beginning of a period if a master has failed to turn up and his form have been given no work to do by another master or a School Prefect. This may also occur on the games field if the opposing side have failed to produce a side or if the referee or umpire has failed to arrive. If one side in a game is winning 12–0 the game may be abandoned if the winning side so wish.

Bum noun and verb. Someone who rags around and causes a nuisance to the authorities. The verb is used to denote the actions of this kind of person.

Bumph noun. Paper of any kind at all, including newspaper. [John Blomfield (H 1955) specifically remembers **rear bumph** as slang relating to 'loo paper', which was then 'thin and crinkly, and smelling of antiseptic'. The word, often represented as 'bumf' or 'bumpf' is commonly taken as being an abbreviation of the term 'bum-fodder', referring to printed information which, in the opinion of the recipient, is suitable only as toilet paper, Ed.]

Bumstick A military cane about 2 feet 3 inches [68 cm] in length, metal tipped, with a Repton crest on the top end. Carried by platoon commanders and platoon sergeants.

Condescend verb. To make an effort to do one's best at something. Usually found on the games field.

Condescension noun. The act of trying to do one's best.

Non-C., noun. Not making any kind of effort to perform the job in hand.

Crack noun. Usually a place of some kind. May be found in queues, etc. – e.g., 'Keep my crack.' May be applied to buildings, etc. – e.g., 'Pears' Crack'. May be rather general and vague – e.g., 'What kind of a crack is this?' A place in a study normally reserved for one particular person – e.g., 'Put it on my tip fag's crack.' By extension, the tables in a study.

Creep noun. Someone who slinks around in soft slippers or shoes, usually with evil intent. May also be someone who gets on one's nerves a lot. Usually an unpopular person.

Dibs noun. House prayers, which normally occur at 9 p.m. every weekday and Saturday evening during the term. Possibly a contraction of the words 'House devotions'.

Flap noun. A blow with a slipper administered by a prefect for venial offences.

Flap verb. The action of delivering the blow with the slipper.

Grease verb and noun. To dodge the queue or to get off something unpleasant.

Bumsticks.

Green verb. To convince someone of something that is not true.

Grip noun. The preserving of law and order and at the same time keeping the respect and obedience of the House. Grip is lost when this no longer happens.

Gripless adjective. Corresponds to the noun above, but is the exact opposite. The noun derived from this word is griplessness.

Gut noun. A boy, who, in the opinion of his contemporaries, does too much work. Derived from the same root is **Corps gut**, which refers to someone who takes the CCF training seriously.

House spirit noun. May best be defined as a form of localized patriotism. One is expected to do one's best for the house, and if one does this, one may be said to show house spirit.

Rears noun. Lavatory.

Shift verb and noun. Same meaning as to creep (q.v.).

Syde or **side** noun. Cheek or impertinence by a junior to a more senior boy. Origin unknown. The adjective **sidy** is derived from the noun.

APPENDIX 2

Repton's Enrichment of the English Language.

Amongst its many contributions to the world over its 450 years Repton has coined or popularized a number of words and phrases. These neologisms include:

Broad Church Thomas Williamson Peile (Headmaster, 1841–54) was the author of a pamphlet entitled *The Church of England, neither High nor Low, but Broad*, which, according to Macdonald, 'is said to have originated the since popular label'. The Oxford English Dictionary (OED) merely states that the phrase 'came into vogue about 1848'.

Camp If Christopher Isherwood cannot be credited with having invented the noun or adjective denoting effeminacy, ostentatious or affected gay behaviour, he is certainly widely regarded as having been amongst the first to discuss the term and is possibly the author of the phrase 'high camp'.

Gremlin Roald Dahl didn't invent the word 'gremlin' but he certainly helped to popularize it. The word originated in RAF (or possibly Royal Naval Air Service) slang to refer to the mischievous sprite supposedly responsible for sabotaging aircraft. On one reading they were called gremlins because they were the goblins that came out of Fremlin beer bottles. Fremlin's beer bottles were certainly plentiful in the RAF messes in India and the Middle East, and this is where Roald Dahl probably first encountered them. *Gremlin Lore* (1943) was Dahl's first book, the rights of which were purchased by Disney with a view to producing an animated feature. However,

Christopher Isherwood and W.H. Auden.

because the concept of gremlins was in the public domain other studios tried to muscle in on the market and this, and the difficulties inherent in making the gremlins sympathetic characters, meant that Disney dropped the project (although a tie-in version of the book was published and Disney's gremlins appeared in comic-book form).

Rules of the game This quintessentially public school phrase was coined by Robert Molesworth Kindersley (H 1883) in 1929 in evidence to the so-called Macmillan committee on finance and industry.

Spaghetti Western Referring to a Western film set in the American 'Old West' but made in Italy or by Italians. The origins of the term are obscure but Christopher Frayling, in his ground-breaking study of the genre, *Spaghetti Westerns: Cowboys and Europeans from Karl May to Sergio Leone* (1981), has certainly done more than anyone else to popularize it.

Stig OR *Top Gear* producer Andy Wilman (P 1975) and presenter Jeremy Clarkson (P 1973) have certainly popularized this term – originally applied to first-year Reptonians – by giving the name to the show's helmeted in-house racing driver.

Welfare State This term is sometimes said to have been coined by Sir Alfred Zimmern in the 1930s, but it has not been traced in his published writings. William Temple is a strong contender for having coined the phrase and the earliest published use of the term to date, cited by the Oxford English Dictionary, is in his *Citizen and Churchman* of 1941.

John Plowright

A Speech Day Memory

My eye meets the church spire, the famous Repton landmark. Towering into the sky, its point narrowing, like the fine tip of a needle.

I see in the distance the roofs of Pears, glowing red as the oldest parts of school, hazy in the sunlight.

The sound of tennis balls being viciously hit reaches my ears. I hear happy chatter, shouts and laughter on San Hall.

I keep walking, and I view the typical English scene: cricket on the playing field; the quiet, intelligent knock of the ball as it impacts with the bat and the cheers that go up. The sunlight seems to shine perfectly on their white figures.

As I walk up to the rambling red-brick block of the Music School, a chorus of sound washes music over my brain. The spiralling, fluent notes of the piano, mingled with the slight, sharp string of the violin, and by contrast, the triumphant blast of a trumpet.

I hear my own feet resounding on the tiled square-patterned floor of the 400 Hall. The echoes are subdued by the shout of powerful voices and heavy slams from the stage. I nose in and glimpse stamping feet through the curtain, issuing a soft glow of theatre light. My heart begins to throb, as I remember what it feels like to be able to become someone else.

I enter through the cool, graceful doors of the Chapel. As I stand at the entrance, I can almost hear the hymns – that familiar tune for the 'Dear Lord and Father of Mankind'. At the same time, I remember the soft glow of candlelight at Christmas time, when we were captured in their glow, hushed by the spirit of occasion. That calm, clear carol, 'Once in Royal David's City', echoes in my head.

Further on, my steps lead through the doors of the Art School, and I instantly smell a mixture of turpentine and sawdust. As I walk in, art is happening all around me, from a small, fine etching, to a vibrant, glorious collage. The walls are an array of colour, all telling their own story. The main room – my space – is filled with light, representing a jigsaw puzzle in this moment, as every corner in the maze of construction has a different treasure. As I touch the work tables, their rough, wooden tops, I remember the patterns I made on their uneven surfaces, marvelling at the effect. So many stories in them, so much to tell.

Time is a funny thing. Sometimes it seems to storm past in a flurry of activity and events. Other times the clock travels so painfully slowly, that I wonder when it will end.

So many memories of my time at school. Every little detail has its compartment in my mind, each little memory has a place where it is kept safe, remembered, cherished. And so it is. It is Repton, Repton to the end.

Bella Denyer (G 2004)

LIST OF SUBSCRIBERS

This book has been made possible through the
generosity of the following:

Charles J. Adams	Hall 1965
Eleanor C. Adams	Abbey 1990
David H. Ades	Latham 1934
Katie Ainge	Field 1997
Timothy Alexander	Mitre 1990
George Allen	Priory 1954
R.W.J. Allen	Latham 1929
Julian F. Almond	Mitre 1974
Martin Amherst Lock	Staff 1984–2001
Bill Andrewes	Hall 1952
Stuart Anselm	Cross 1984
Michael Applebee	New 1947
David Armstrong	Brook 1967
Jess Armstrong (née Wetherall)	Abbey 1987
Michael Armstrong	Brook 1971
S.D. Armstrong	Cross 1963
Dr Eduardo Arze-Cuadros	Hall 1962
Duncan R. Ashby	Hall 1976
David Aston	Cross 1945
Andrew P. Atkins	Latham 1977
Julian Atkinson	Hall 1964
Greg Attwood	Staff 1978
Katherine Attwood	Garden 2003
Bill Auden	Orchard 1972
Edward Auden	Orchard 2001
Tom Auden	Orchard 1999
Gayle A. Audley	Abbey 1984
John Austin	Latham 1951
M.W. Bacon	Latham 1952
Katie Badger	Garden 1996
Paul A.R. Baglee	Brook 1965
P.W. Bagley	Hall 1937
Bill Bagley	Orchard 1944
R.A. Bailey	New 1946
W.F.N. Ball	Hall 1953
Robert A. Barber	Mitre 1948
G.I.A. Barder	New 194
Nigel Bark	Hall 1954
Timothy R. Barlow	Cross 1976
Alistair Morris Barnett	Hall 1957

His Honour Christopher Barnett	Hall 1949
His Honour Judge William Barnett	Hall 1950
F.A. Barnsdale	Priory 1931
James D. Barrie	New 2006
Sir Nicholas Barrington	Hall 1947
Brian Barry	Cross 1952
Alan P. Basnett	Priory 1956
James Basnett	Orchard 1983
Richard Basnett	Orchard 1986
Clive Bate	Latham 1948
John Batten	Priory 1952
Rebecca Batten	Garden 1993
Guy T. Beardsall	School 2001
Gemma K. Beardsall	Abbey 2003
John E. Beddington	New 1957
Jonathan M.T. Beesley	Cross 2001
Sqn Ldr C. Benn	Hall 1978
David Bennett	Cross 1949
J.B. Bennett	Latham1947
N.G. Bennett	Staff 1984
Paul Bennett	Latham 1975
Lloyd Berger	Priory 1971
Sarah Berisford	Abbey 1996
Tony Berner	Hall 1936
Christopher Berriman	Latham 1977
Edward Bettam	Priory 1948
W.M.A. Bewley	Priory 2003
Catherine H. Bexson	Garden 1992
John Billington	Staff 1965–97
Carl P. Bilson	Bursar 2002
Dale C. Bilson	Latham 2003
Lee R. Bilson	Latham 2004
Anthony D. Bingham	Brook 1954
John R. Binks	New 1954
J.R.M. Black	Orchard 1953
Victoria E. Black	Foremarke 2005
James W. Blackwell	Priory 2000
Sarah L. Blackwell	Abbey 2002
M.A. Blagden	Cross 1949
Terence Blain	Staff 1996
Juliette Nicola Blake (née Stevens)	Abbey 1984
D.C. Blamey	Orchard 1937
J.B.C. Blood	Hall 1948
Peter Blood	Hall 1952

R.J. Bolam	Cross 1958
John D. Bolsover	Hall 1960
Michael Bond	Priory 1999
Robert Bond	Priory 1968
Samantha Bond	Field 1999
Paul Bond	Orchard 2001
G.P.R. Boon	Priory 1956
Robin Boon	Priory 1961
Georgina Boot	Garden 1997
Hamer Boot	School 1995
William Boot	School 2001
Vanessa Bordoli	Mitre 2004
Richard J. Borrington	Priory 1990
Laurie Boswell	New 1955
John Bottomley	Cross 1952
J.F.C. Boucher	Mitre 1955
P.D. Boult	New 1952
C.M. Boulton	Orchard 1968
John Bowley	Director of Music 2006
The Boyle Family	School 2002
Richard J. Bradburn	Priory 1964
B.D.L. Bradbury	Orchard 1946
Richard Bradbury	Orchard 1981
Laura Bradley	Mitre 2005
N.J. Bradley	Latham 1964
John Bragg	Priory 1953
Peter Bray	Hall 1958
Rachel Bray	Mitre 2004
J.R. Bright	Cross 1960
John H. Brooks	Hall 1944
K. Brooksbank	New 1952
A.S. Browne	Latham 1951
Stephen James Browne	Staff 1993
Paul Brownhill	Priory 1980
Professor Alastair Buchan	Hall 1968
Kimberley Buck	Field 1997
A.J. Buckland	Hall 1971
Geoffrey Buckland	Mitre 1943
Issy Bucknall	Abbey 1999
Will Bucknall	School 1998
Alan Budge	Hall 1958
Christopher B. Bull	Priory 1958
J.C. Burgis	Hall 1946
Patrick George Burke	Hall 1957

Bob Bushby	Orchard 1974
Christopher Butler-Cole	Latham 1952
Jeffrey Butt	Latham 1984
Michael Butt	Mitre 1984
James Buxton	Cross 1957
James Bywater	Priory 1992
Stewart Bywater	Priory 1994
Mark J.A. Cann	Orchard 1979
Angus Carlisle	Brook 1977
Simon Carpenter	Brook 1988
David N. Carr	Cross 1937
Adèle E. Carter	Staff 2000–2006
Canon Paul Carter	Priory 1935
Robert and James Carter	Foremarke 2003
Noel Cartwright	Brook 1957
Martin Cashmore	Hall 1966
John Cawdron	Priory 1944
Robert Cawdron	Latham 1977
John S. Chaffe	Priory 1963
Dr Paul G. Chamberlain	Mitre 1967
Alex Chan	Cross 1994
Lee Ming Chan	Priory 1978
Alexa Chapman	Field 2007
Cameron R. Chapman	New 2007
James Robert Chapman	Hall 1983
Oliver Chapman	School 2007
Thomas M. Chapman	School 1994
Gordon Charlesworth	Orchard 1946
G.N. Charlesworth	Orchard 1953
Nicholas Charlesworth	Orchard 1953
Will Charlesworth	Orchard 2001
Reynold Charley	Orchard 1943
C.G.F. Charter	Foundation Director 1998–2006
Robert Chatwin	New 1985
John Chaumeton	New 1946
Sarah L. Checketts	Staff 2005
Alfred Cheng	Orchard 1975
Fyodor Cherniavsky	Hall 1967
Mike Cherry	New 1967
Roger Clarke	Orchard 1952
Desmond Cheung	Priory 1990
D.N.V. Churton	Hall 1963
Col G.V. Churton	Hall 1926
Simon and Fiona Clague Staff 1989 / Foremarke Parents	
Phil Clamp	Priory 1981
Andrew C.S. Clarke	Hall 1962
Hannah Clarke-Lowe	Abbey 2008
Peter Close	Hall 1955
Ben Cobb	Hall 1945
James M. Cobb	Brook 1990
Michael J. Cobb	School 1995
Nigel Cobb	Cross 1986
Alastair Cochran	Priory 1983
Rowena Cochran (née Oldale)	Abbey1987
Dominic Coe	Latham 1993
Terence Coe	Latham 1991
Douglas L. Collins	Brook 1964
Lionel F.H. Collins	Brook 1955
T.R.B. Collins	Orchard 1943
Richard Connell	Hall 1943
B.M. Cook	
The Reverend John R.M. Cook	Orchard 1974
David Cooke	Orchard 1963
His Honour Roger Cooke	Orchard 1953
Peter J. Cooper	Hall 1956
G.E. Cope	Priory 1947
P.M. Cope	Hall 1948
Richard Corbett	Mitre 1958
A.P. Corn	Hall 1948

R.P. Cotterell	New 1945
James Cottle	Mitre 1990
John H. Cottrill	Priory 1943
David P. Cousins	Orchard 2003
Andrew Cox	Staff 1976–2006
Anthony J. Cox	New 2001
Bryan S. Cox	Mitre 1944
Christopher J. Cox	New 1998
Greg Craig Waller	Hall 1966
E.A. Crane	Brook 1932
Oliver Critchlow	Priory 1994
Andrew Cross	Brook 1973
John (Charles) Crossley	Orchard 1938
David Croswaithe	Latham1981
Julian Crow	Latham 1985
Alexander J. Crowley	School 2001
Elizabeth J. Crowley	Field 2002
The Cuddington Family	
Michael Cuddington	Priory 1991
John Cursham	Hall 1942
R.G.W. Dabinett	Latham 1955
Clinton Brian Danby	Cross 1932
Eric Daniliunas	Cross 2003
Justin Daniliunas	Cross 2001
Michael D. Darby	Orchard 1950
O.C. Darby	Orchard 1948
Pat Darley	Cross 1951
Mike Davies	Hall 1962
Philip M. Davies	Cross 1972
William Davis	Latham 1966
T.J.F. Dawson	Orchard 1944
David De Piro	Hall 1964
Jacob Dean	Mitre 1984
Antony Dearden	Hall 1959
Isabella Denyer	Garden 2004
Richard Dewhirst	New 1995
Rodney Dews	Brook 1951
Nigel Dickson	Brook 1959
Group Captain R.H.B. Dixon	New 1939
B.S. Dobbs	Latham 1942
Canan Dogrul	Abbey 2004
Kudlip Singh Dosanjh	Cross 1994
J.M. Downing	Brook 1984
W.B. Downing	Staff 1961–1996
W.J.L. Downing	Orchard1983
Marcus J. Dowson	Priory 1990
J.C. Driver	Staff 1984
Simon B. Duncan	Cross 1979
John Dunham	Cross 1946
Rev. Mark Earnshaw	Mitre 1950
H.H.I. Easterling	Priory 1943
Hon. S.D. Eccles	Hall 1948
Graham Edmonds	Priory 1961
Jo Edmonds	New 1970
V.B.J. Edwards	Priory 1934
The Eldred Family	Garden 2001
E.J.H. Elliot	Mitre 1968
Michelle Elliot	Garden 1998
Malcolm E. Else	New 1945
Peter John Else	New 1940
J.B. Ervin	Mitre 1943
N. Etherington Smith	Hall 1958
Alexander Evans	New 2004
Francesca Evans	Field 2004
Lindsey J. Evans	Field 1999
Sir Richard Evans	Brook 1941
Spencer Evans	Latham 1982
Henry Everard	Mitre1954

His Honour Judge William Everard	Mitre 1962
Wilfrid Evershed	Hall 1952
Edward Every	New 1988
Sir Henry Every Bt	Governor 2003
Sheffield C. Exham	Orchard 1963
Alistair J.R. Fairclough	Orchard 1946
Alasdair Fearns	Priory 2005
Emily Fearns	Field 2003
Sarah Fearns	Field 2001
Robin A. Fegan	New 1949
Harriet Fell	Field 2004
Joe Fell	Orchard 2003
Nicole Fell	Field 2000
John Ferns	Mitre 1958
Alex Findlater	Mitre 1951
Alexander Fish	Cross 2003
Hon. R.T. Fisher	Staff 1953–69
Hamish A. Flavell	New 2006
D.C.M. Fletcher	Hall 1945
Douglas Fletcher	New 2001
Geoffrey Fletcher	Latham 1933
Henry Fletcher	Mitre 1960
Hugh L. Fletcher	Hall 1971
The Reverend The Hon. Jonathan Fletcher	Hall 1956
Natasha J. Fletcher	Garden 2003
Robert Fletcher	Hall 1967
Sam J. Fletcher	School 2005
Dr Wattle Fletcher	Brook 1947
Helen Floto (née Needham)	Abbey 1986
Andrew Forrest	Cross 1950
Liam Foster	Cross1989
Simon Foster	New 1978
Major J.A. Foulis	Priory 1943
Andrew C. Fox	Latham 1981
John Frankland	Hall 1948
Michael Franklin	Cross 1945
Katherine Franklin-Adams	Abbey 1984
Patrick Franklin-Adams	Hall 1958
In Memory of Andrew P. Fraser	Mitre 1963
Sir Christopher Frayling	Cross 1955
The Very Reverend Nicholas Frayling	Priory 1957
Andrew M. Frazer	New 1984
Andrew Freedlander	School 2006
Jo Frost (née Litchfield)	Abbey 1984
Jonathan Fry	Hall 1951
J.W.H. Fryer	Brook 1966
Le Yue Fu	Garden 2001
Toshiaki Fujii	Cross 1994
Julia Fulks (née Gladwin)	Abbey 1990
R.A. Furniss	Hall 1980
R.A. Furnival	Hall 1974
Maria Galindo	Field 1999
John Gammell	Headmaster 1968–1978
E.H. Garside	Priory 1943
George Ezra Benedict Garside	Hall 1986
John Felix Rudolph Garside	New 1997
Anthony John Garton	Staff 1974–2001
Edward Garton	Orchard 1983
David A. George	Hall 1960
Jane Gerard-Pearse (née Clarke)	Abbey 1981
Samantha Gibbons	Field 2003
Sir Sydney Giffard	Priory 1940
Benjamin L. Gilbert	Priory 1992
J.C. Giles	Latham 1962
P.N. Gill	Hall 1961
Simon Gill	New 1990
R.G. Gillard	Priory 1950
Richard Gillham	Priory 1987

Simon James Ackroyd Gilliver	Cross 1999	Brigadier P.F.B. Hargrave	Bursar 1988–1997
Tim Gilliver	Latham 1991	Dr N.A. Harker	Hall 1946
George E. Gilman	Hall 1992	Frank Harper-Jones	Cross 1946
W.J. Gleadell	Cross 1953	Mark J. Harrington	School 1996
Simon Glover	Priory 1971	David Harrison	Brook 1960
John O. Goldsmith	New 1959	Julian E. Harrison	School 2002
Matthew Goderick	Cross 1992	John Gilbert Harvey	Orchard 1964
Cathy Goodhead	Staff	A.T.M. Harwood	Hall 1942
Paul Goodhead	Staff	Claire L. Haseldine	Garden 1991
Professor C.S. Goodwin	New 1946	Christopher Haseldine	Orchard 1994
Alexander Thomson	New 1987	Olivia Haseldine	Garden 1997
A.M. Gordon	Hall 1967	Samuel G. Hassan	Orchard 1966
Devin J.G. Gordon	Priory 2002	Ire Hassan-Odukale	Latham 2003
Chris Graham	Hall 1949	Chris Havers	Cross 1963
Christopher Graham	Latham 1958	Heather D. Hawkins	Staff 1962–1985
In memory of G.M. Graham	Hall 1939	Alison Hay	Abbey 1976
J.W.L. Graham	New 1944	Oliver Hayes	Brook 1991
Jonathan Graham-Brown	Priory 1955	Alex Haynes	Priory 2004
N.J. Grantham	Hall 1947	Lois Haynes	Field 2005
Sophie Grattidge	Mitre 2003	Roger Heading	Latham1955
T.E. Gray	Brook 1988	Sian B.E. Heap	Garden 2007
Martin G. Grayshon	Cross 1961	R.J. Hedley-Jones	Brook 1951
J.B. Greaves	Orchard 1947	Staffan Hedstrand	New 1974
P.B. Greaves	Orchard 1952	Gordon Henry	Priory 1936
G. Richard Green	Hall 1952	Lt Col J.D. Hetherington	Governor 1994–2007
Jennifer Green	Abbey 2005	A.R.T. Hewlett	Brook 1992
Edward E. Greenhalgh	New 1947	Philip Hextall	Priory 1944
Steven R. Greenall	Cross 1987	Claude Heywood	New 1946
T.M. Greer	Hall 1950	James Higgins	Orchard 1999
Ben Greeves	New 1992	Thomas Higgins	Orchard 1997
Kenneth V. Gregory	Cross 1947	J.M.J. Hill	Staff 2005
H.W. Grenville	Staff 1963–1986	Paul Faulke Hill	Hall 1941
Sam Gresham	New 1951	G. Hiller	Orchard 1936
Revd Richard Lewis Grew		Nicholas Hillman	Brook 1985
	Orchard 1946, Staff 1956–1989	Christopher Martin Hills	New 2001
Derek P. Griffin	Brook 1979	Dominic Ryan Hills	New 2004
Anthony E. Griffiths	Priory 1951	Andy Hilton	Brook 1968
Patrick J .Griffiths	Staff 2000	Andrew Hine	Brook 1977
Peter Griffiths	Hall 1966	E.B. Hine	Brook 1972
Sara L. Griffiths	Field 2003	Edward Hine	Brook 1972
Sophie E. Griffiths	Field 2003	H.C.W. Hine	Brook 1969
Ian Grout	Brook 1981	John F. Hings	Priory 1955
John Grundy	Hall 1953	John Hird	Priory 1960
Katherine M. Guest	Field 2004	D.R. Hodgkinson	Mitre 1951
Michael J. Guest	Orchard 2006	David Hodgkiss	Brook 1961
C.J. Gummer	Brook 1953	T.J. Holloway	Latham 1948
Roger Gunner	New 1957	Simon James Hollowood	Cross 1981
G.D. Gyte	New 1952	R.A. Holroyd	Headmaster 2003
		Benjamin Holt	School 1998
Elisabeth Haering	Abbey 1980	Richard Holt	New 1972
J.E.G. Haigh	Mitre 1974	John Hooton	Mitre 1956
Richard J. Hale	Cross 1969	Lt Col T. Hope	Priory 1939
Daniel C.J. Hall	Orchard 1975	C.M. Horne	Mitre 1958
Ian M. Hall	New 1990	John Hosking	Hall 1979
Jonathan Hall	Orchard 1951	Tony Houghton	Latham 1951
Brigadier R.W.S. Hall	Orchard 1969	Martin How	Hall 1945
Tim Haller	Hall 1975	Rachel Howard	Mitre 2003
J.D.A. Hallett	New 1999	Louise Howarth	Garden 1996
John A. Hallsworth	Mitre 1958	Dr M.R. Howarth	Priory 1962
Peter Hamblin	Latham 1967	Daniel W.R. Howes	Latham 1998
Emma V. Hammond	Abbey 1987	Guy T. Hubball	Cross 1975
Jack Hammond	Abbey 2006	John Hubble	Mitre 1945
T.P.E. Hammond	Orchard 1961	J. Hudson	Priory 1967
Thomas Hammond	New 1998	J.R. Hudson	Priory 1935
Paul Hanson	Brook 1953	Kevin Hudson	Cross 2004
Dr David Harding	Mitre 1951	Luke Daniel Hulse	Orchard 2005
R.D. Harding Staff, Foremarke 1969–77 and 1981–2002		David Hume	Mitre 1948
Alessandra L. Hardwick	Garden 2004	Thomas Hunter	Cross 2004
Benedict J. Hardwick	Latham 2006	A.M. Hurd	Latham 1973
Lisa Hardy	Abbey 1984	Julian B. Hurst	Mitre 1982

M.C.J. Hutchings	Brook 1975
F.A. Hutchinson	Orchard 1943
John A. Hutson	Latham 1934
John L. Hutton	Hall 1959
Richard Hutton	Hall 1956
Charles William Thomas Hyde	Priory 1992
Jasper Hyde	Cross 1991
Richard John Hyde	Orchard 1941
Roger Hyde	Orchard 1941
David M. Hynes	Priory 1949
Steven J. Ingram	Hall 1990
Charlotte Ireson (née Porter)	Abbey 1993
Paolo R.A. Irvine	School 2004
H.J.S. Jackson	Orchard 1957
Simon Jakeman	Latham 1970
David J. James	Mitre 1976
Charles Jobson	Latham 1975
Ian Johnson	Priory 1949
Peter Derwent Johnson	Latham 1936
Richard Johnson	Cross 1990
Simon Christopher Johnson	Orchard 2004
Claudia Johnson-Sabine	Mitre 2005
Guy Johnson-Sabine	Mitre 1996
Thomas Johnson-Sabine	New 1998
Clare Jolliffe (née Graham)	Staff 1991–1999
Graham Jones	Headmaster 1987–2003
John D.W. Jones	Latham 2004
Neville Jones	Cross 1953
Tom Juneau	Priory 1991
Christopher Juul	Priory 1987
Sir Kit Kaberry Bt	Latham 1956
Anthony C.C. Kam	New 1974
Richard W.C. Kan	Cross 1966
Tim Karakashian	Brook 1990
Amanda Karakashian	Abbey 1989
Dr Henry H. Kaye	Mitre 1956
In memory of J.G.D. Keddie	Latham 1947
Philip Keddie	Latham 1974
Fay Keely	Abbey 1989
C.M. Keep	Orchard 1969, Staff 1978
P.A. Kelland	Brook 1940
Richard H.M. Kelsey	Priory 1958
P.H.A. Kenyon	Orchard 1936
Nigel Kew	Staff 1987
Song-Gun Kim	Mitre 1995
Matthew Kindinger	School 2002
A.J.C. King	New 1963
Andrew King	Hall 1978
Peter G. King	Priory 1951
W.R. King	New 1966
Bill Kirkham	Latham 1948
Christopher R. Kirkland	Orchard 1944
Michael J. Kirkland	Priory 1995
Philip D.M. Kirkland	Orchard 1963
Robert M. Kirkland	Orchard 1959
Tim Kirkus	Cross 1978
James Kirtland	Orchard 1988
Richard B. Kitching	New 1945
Rodney Knight	Orchard 1954
Christian Koehler	School
Jeno Kohner	Latham 1947
C.C.B. Kramer	Priory 1967
Freddy Ku	Orchard 1999
David Laing	Latham 1970
John E. Lake	Brook 1979
John W. Lake	Brook 1943

Jack Lamb	Orchard 2001	Jonathan McDonald	Hall 1988	Christopher Paget	Priory 2001
Dr Glenn Lambert	New 1948	Katie McDonald	Abbey 1989	Simon Palfreeman	Latham 1990
Tim Lambert	Priory 2001	Alastair McFarland	Priory 2006	R.W. Palfreyman	New 1944
D.W.Y. Lane	Latham 1937	Stephen J.J. McGlynn	Priory 2002	Rachael Parker	Field 2003
Commodore Michael G. Lane	Latham, 1967	Ian McHaffie	Hall 1948	Sarah Parker	Field 2002
J.F. Larard	New 1952	James McLaren	Staff 1971–2002	Louise Parkin	Field 2005
Benjamin J. Lawrenson	Latham 1992	Duncan McPherson	Priory 1992	Sarah Parkin	Field 2005
Robin Le Poidevin	Cross 1975	Dr Isabel M. McQueen (née Adams)	Abbey 1992	Stephen Parkinson	Latham 1963
J.W. Leach	Orchard 1957	Anne Meier	Foremarke 2003	Rohit Parmar-Mistry	School 2005
Jeff Leaver	Brook 1954	Robert D. Meinertzhagen	Orchard 1977	Ben Parry	Cross 1979
Tom Leaver	Priory 2005	Luisa Meller	Garden 1993	William Parsons	Orchard 1981
James T. Leavesley	New 1975	Robin Merrill	Cross 1967	S.J.R. Pattinson	Priory 1941
Harriet A.S. Lee	Priory 1960	Christopher Metcalfe	Priory 1953	Rishi D. Paul	Orchard 1995
James Fraser Lee	Orchard 1994	George Eric Mewis	Staff 1942	Doug Paveley	Priory 1970
John Lee	Priory 1960	Dr J. Paul Miller	New 1954	I.R. Payne	Latham 1955
O.J. Lee	Latham 1991	Alastair Quentin Mills	Brook 1988	R.A. Payton	Cross 1946
John C.B. Leech	Priory 1949	N. Duncan Mills	Brook 1986	J.M. Peake	Brook 1938
Ross Lemmings	Orchard 1992	Carole Milnes	Abbey 1984	Andrew Pearce	New 1978
J.M. Guy Levesley	Hall 1975	David Milnes	Orchard 1952	Lt Col R.C. Peel	Orchard 1947
J.M.T. Levesley	Orchard 1943	Paul C. Mindelsohn	New 1942	Jill Pellow	Staff 1978–1995
Frances M Lewis (née Black)	Garden 1992	E.H.O. Mitchell	Orchard 1947	Sara Pellow	Abbey 1977
The Hon. Chief Justice Andrew Li	Hall 1963	Philip Mo	Hall 1989	G.S.H. Pengelley	Hall 1968
J.E. (Tim) Lindley	Brook 1944	Francis Moll	Latham 1961	Clayton G. Penny	Priory 1997
William O. Ling	Brook 1955	Charles Molle	Priory 1963	A.N.S. Pepper	Hall 1983
Mike Linton	New 1956	David M. Moore	Cross 1964	Adrian Pepper	Hall 1983
Roger A Litchfield	Brook 1960	J. Moore	Latham 2005	C.D.S. Pepper	Brook 1990
Simon Litchfield	Brook 1989	Bruce S. Morgan	Brook 1951	D.I. Pepper	Hall 1953
Malcolm Littlefair	New 1945	Neill Morgan	Latham 1982	Colonel Edward Pepper	Hall 1951
Claire Llewellyn	Field 2001	R.B.Ll. Morgan	Staff 1962–1994	Gordon Pepper	New 1947
Marie Llewllyn	Garden 1998	Georgia Morgan-Wynne	Abbey 2004	Miss H.M. Pepper	Abbey 1990
David C.G. Llewelyn	Orchard 1963	Sandy Morgan-Wynne	Cross 2004	James Perera	Priory 2005
Jeremy Llewelyn	Orchard 1975	M.G.R. Morris	Mitre 1955	Peter Perera	Latham 2004
S.J.C. Lloyd	Brook 1972	Sir Richard Morris Chairman of Governors1997–2003		Joanna Perkins (née Haxby)	Abbey 1992
Martin Lockett	Mitre 1966	G.T. Morson	New 1936	Robert E. Perks	New 1971
John D. Lonsdale-Eccles	Hall 1959	R.T. Morson	New 1965	Dougal Philip	Cross 1966
Mark Loosemore	New 1986	J.R. Muir	Staff 1968–2000	Adam D. Phillips	Brook 1979
Andy Lord	New 1984	Alexander Mullarkey	Priory 2000	Timothy F Phillips	Hall 1949
Tom Lovell	Cross 1997	James Mullarkey	Priory 1997	Sarah Pickard	Abbey 1997
David Loy	Latham 1940	Richard Murrall	Orchard 1992	Edward Pickard	Latham 1997
A.E. Loyd	Hall 1934	Edward J.A. Myhill	Cross 2001	Geoffrey Piper	Brook 1957
Fraser Ludlam	Orchard 1982			Tim Piper	Brook 1952
Peter M. Ludlam	Priory 1997	Roderick T. Newal	Cross 1960	Charles Platts	Priory 1989
Dennis Lui	Cross 1985	Julie Needham (née Pepper)	Abbey 1984	Benjamin R. Politowski	Orchard 1999
Geoffrey Lui	Brook 1990	Christopher Needler	New 1958	Lucy E. Politowski	Field 2001
Joe Lycett	Orchard 1944	Martin Needler	New 1956	Sophie A. Politowski	Field 2004
		Paul Needler	New 1991	Nick Pooler	Mitre 1997
John G. Macartney	Brook 1978	Dr James P. Nelson	Cross 1954	Matthew R. Pope	Latham 1985
Andy Maguire	Mitre 1969	Robert C.J. Nelson	Latham 1949	Claire Popham	
Benny Xinyi Mai	School 2003	J.A. Nelson-Jones	Brook 1948	D.H. Popham	Brook 1945
Baktash Manavi	Hall 1982	Andrew Neville	Hall 1968	James Porter	Latham 1959
David J. Mansell	Orchard 1954	R.A.K. Nevitt	New 1938	Michael S. Potts	Cross 1955
Helen Mansfield	Abbey 1986	M.H. Newbould	Cross 1954	Steven Potts	Cross 1970
A.J. Marden	Priory 1952	John M. Newell	Priory 1947	Michael Powell	Latham 1978
J. Marcus Marsh	Priory 1966	Amanda Newton (née Leamon)	Abbey 1980	A.G. Pratt	Cross 1947
Dr Robin Marsh	Cross 1947	James Nicholls	Priory 2000	G.L. Pratt	Cross 1947
Harry John Marshall	Priory 1942	Sandra Nield	Staff 1991	Joe Pratt	Latham 1970
Tony Marshall	Hall 1974	E.Y.F. Niem	Latham 1966	Michael Preston	New 2001
Bradley James Martin	New 2003	Mark R. Norton	Mitre 1986	M.W.H. Prettejohn	Hall 1950
Nick Martin	School 2005	Rex Norton	Hall 1936	Henry A.S. Price	Priory 1985
John Ross Martyn	Latham 1957	D.P. Norwood	Staff 1960–1991	Peter Prickett	Priory 1964
Patrick Masefield	Hall 1956			Air Marshal Sir Charles Pringle	Priory 1933
David Matthews	Hall 1957	Dr Rob Oakley	Latham 1967	Jonathan Proctor	Orchard 1976
Saskia Matthews	Garden 2004	Simon Oborn	Orchard 1989	S. Harnwaak Purewal	Priory 2005
Simone Matthews	Abbey 2006	W.G. Odell	Staff 2005	S. Terjinder Purewal	Priory 2001
Adam A. Maxwell	Mitre 1980	Nicholas Ogden	Priory 1971	Victoria Pym	Field 2002
R.G. Maycock	Priory 1948	J.D.M. Olsen	Cross 1989	T.J. Pywell	Brook 1963
Bob McArthur	Mitre 1956	Peter Osgood	Mitre 1953		
Ian William McClary	Staff 2002	Anna Ostersprey	Garden 2001	Daniel Quarshie	New 2001
Patrick Michael McConvey	New 2002	Moritz Ostersprey	Orchard 2003	David Quayle	Hall 1949
Ryan Alexander McConvey	New 2004	T.C. Owen	Staff 2004		

G.R.H. Ralphs	Hall 1971	Tim Scorer	Orchard 1954
Catherine E.J. Rang	Abbey 1996	Kenneth Scott	Orchard 1938
Quentin Rappoport	Mitre 1957	Philip D. Scott	New 1955
Harun Adil Rauf	Cross 2004	M.A. Seaford	Cross 1964
Mateena Zarah Rauf	Field 2006	Calum Setterington	School 2006
Edward S. Raynor	Latham 2003	Lucy Setterington	Abbey 2007
Helen K. Raynor	Garden 2005	Ian Setterington	Staff 2005
Dr John Reddington	Brook 1942	Shelagh Setterington	Staff 2005
Harry J. Redmond	Priory 2003	R.H. Sexton	New 1946
Diana Rees-Jones (née Soper)	Abbey 1971	David Stamford de Rede Shale	Hall 1944
Franco Reine	School 2006	William S. Shand	Orchard 1950
Repton Village History Group		John Sharp	Hall 1956
B.L.L. Reuss	Priory 1929	Benjamin John Sharpe	Brook 1989
David Reynolds	Hall 1966	Richard James Sharpe	Brook 1987
E.R.U. Rhodes	New 1995	Nick Sharrard	Cross 1975
R.P.B. Rhodes	New 1998	Christopher Shaw	Orchard 1958
Robert Rhodes	Priory 1961	Matthew D. Shaw	Brook 1981
J.A. Richardson	Hall 1945	Ruth E.S. Shaw (née Fletcher)	Garden 1992
Jeremy Richardson	Hall 1980	Andrew Sheard	Mitre 1970
Nigel G.R. Richardson	Hall 1976	John B. Sheldon	Brook 1949
Alistair John Riley	Priory 1997	Tessa Sheldon	Garden 1997
Philip Neil Riley	Priory 1995	David J.T. Shentall	Orchard 1953
Adrian George Ringer	Brook 1948	Min Hee Shin	Garden 1998
David Brian Roberts	Mitre 1949	Rosalie Shin	Garden 2002
Emma Elizabeth Roberts	Abbey 1999	Camilla M. Shires	Field 2000
Jane Roberts (née Bossons)	Abbey 1973	Edward T. Shires	School 1999
Megan C.H. Roberts	Garden 2005	James M. Shires	Foremarke
Michael Guthrie Roberts	School 1995	J. Andrew Shires	Mitre 1947
Dr Iain Robertson	Mitre 1960	Rev'd R. Short and Family	Staff 1993–2004
C.J.T. Robey	Latham 1982	Anthony Shuttleworth	Priory 1962
M.N.T. Robey	Latham 1986	Ronald J. Sichel	Latham 1954
N.W.T. Robey	Latham 1955	Sir David Sieff	Hall 1952
Andrew Robinson	Cross 1951	Sunil Sikka	Latham 1965
Dr K.F. Robinson		Lauren Silk	Garden 2003
Noah T. Robinson-Stanier	Cross 2005	Ronnie Silk	Bursar 1997–2002
J.O.M. Robotham	New 1942	Gary Simmonds	Brook 1966
J.G. Rodger	Hall 1933	Jay Simnett (née Ellerton)	Abbey 1981
Dr Peter W. Rodgers	Hall 1990	Thomas Simpson	Orchard 2004
Mike Roff	Orchard 1946	Darrel Sinclair	Priory 1982
Peter William Rolfe	Hall 1956	Charles Sindrey	Cross 2003
P.F. Rollinson	Latham 1948	Claire Slater	Abbey 2006
Michael Rolt	Brook 1957	Hannah Slater	Abbey 2006
K.V. Rose	Orchard 1939	Nick Slater	Hall 1978
Philip G. Rose	New 1985	Tom Slater	School 2006
James Ross	Hall 1968	Henry Slesenger	New 1941
Dr Peter Dallas Ross	Orchard 1935	Edward Sloane	Priory 1997
Kate Rotheroe	Garden 2005	Quentin R. Sloper	Latham 1997
W.N.K. Rowley	Governor 1972–1997	A. John Smith	Latham 1948
A.A.V. Rudolf	Staff 1961–1976	Anton J. Smith	Staff 1993
J.E. Rushton	Brook 1950	Jasmin L. Smith	Field 1997
Michael N. Rushton	Mitre 1961	Jeremy C.A. Smith	Priory 1971
Ian Russell	New 1953	In memory of Mark J. Smith	Orchard 1975
J.F.S. Russel	Orchard 1935	Nicholas R.S. Smith	Brook 1969
J.S. Russell	Brook 1944	Nick Smith	Mitre 1989
Victoria Russell	Garden 2000	Nigel G.L. Smith	Hall 1957
C.I. Rutherford	Cross 1932	R.A.S. Smith	Brook 1943
John Rutherford	Latham 1952	Rebecca Smith	Abbey 1993
James S. Ryan	Hall 1979	Roger M. Noël Smith	Priory 1966
		Simon Andrew Smith	Mitre 1986
C.L. Sale	Brook 1970	Stephen C.D. Smith	Priory 1979
Tim C.H. Sale	Cross 1953	Thomas A. Smith	Mitre 1991
Jeremy R. Samways	Hall 1977	Victoria H. Smith	Abbey 2000
Mark Sanderson	Cross 1978	Robin Smitherman	New 1957
R. David Sands	Cross 1946	The Revd Anthony Smyth	Hall 1954
David Sanford	Priory 1964	Gill Snelson	Staff 1991–2005
William Sankey	Priory 1957	Mark Snelson	Orchard 1987
David Sarson	New 1939	Alexander Sohn	Orchard 2003
Matthew Saunders	Priory 1997	Paul Anthony Spence	Orchard 1951
C.G.C. Sayer	Latham 1952	Edward Spencer	Orchard 1985
Matthias K. Scumacher	Priory 1993	Emma Spencer (née Dollamore)	Abbey 1988

J.D. Spencer	New 1956
Ralph Spreckley	Cross 1946
J.F.N.Stanier	Hall 1941
Christian J.W. Stanley	Latham 1990
John Stanley	New 1952
Christabel Stanton	Garden 1992
Jeremy Stanton	Brook 1989
Melissa Stanton	Abbey 1993
Simon Blunt	New 1979
C.M. Staveley	Priory 1943
Richard Steele	Priory 1944
Roger Stephens	Brook 1957
A.R. Stephenson	Staff 1953–1959
Ben C.W. Stevenson	Hall 1989
Michael F. Stevenson	Hall 1976
Robin Steward	Brook 1948
Jessica C. Stewart	Abbey 2007
Susanna Stiff (née Postlethwaite)	Abbey 1983
Maurice Stockdale	Hall 1927
Andrew Stockman	Hall 1967
M.J.R. Stockman	Hall 1940
Chris Stokes	Hall 1964
Mike Stones	Staff 1982
Christopher N.R. Strange	Priory 1970
M.N. Stretton	Hall 1975
I.D. Stretton	Hall 1980
Tim Strevens	New 1947
Professor R.C. Stuart Harris	Cross 1964
A.C. Stubbs	Brook 1971
J.W.S. Suckling	Orchard 1939
Dr Lionel J.D. Sully	Priory 1957
Richard Sutton	Cross 1989
Julian Swann	Mitre 1950
Graham Swerling	Brook 1944
Lt Col Andrew Swindale	Orchard 1959
C.J.N. Sykes	Hall 1953
Gerald Sze	Priory 1991
Kin Tung Robert Tam	Latham 1970
Maurice K.W. Tam	Latham 1966
Miss Teen Wing Veronica Tam	Abbey 2003
Miss Teen Wun Alicia Tam	Abbey 1998
Miss Teen Yut Jennifer Tam	Abbey 1999
J.K. Taplin	Brook 1933
R.W. and S.J. Teroni	Foremarke Parents
Emma Tate (née Downing)	Abbey 1982
Ken Tatham	Cross 1959
David Taylor	Latham 1947
Harriet A.A. Taylor	Field 2005
Jonathan P.A. Taylor	Orchard 1999
L.C. Taylor	Staff 1950–1954
Mark James Taylor	Mitre1994
Sarah R.E. Taylor	Field 1998
Sarah Tennant	Staff 1992
Edward ter Weeme	Priory 1997
J.T.D. Thomas	Priory 1983
Jim Thomas	Brook 1948
M.J. Thomas	Priory 1945
Stephen A. Thomas	Mitre 1974
Ralph R.J. Thompson	Priory 1999
Roger Thompson	Staff 1975
Rosemary Thompson	Staff 1994
Ross Thompson	Hall 1946
A.F. Thomson	New 1989
A.S. Thomson	New 1987
Alistair F. Thomson	New 1989
Richard David Thomson	Hall 1944
Julian W. Thornhill	Mitre 1991
Cassandra Thorpe	Abbey 2006
T.A. Thwaites	Latham 1937

Gordon Tickler	Orchard 1948	W.P. Warburton	Latham 1942
Richard Tillett	New 1977	John A. Ward	Brook 1946
Hugh Tilly	Hall 1958	Chris Warmoth	Hall 1973
Jessica Titcumb	Garden 2002	Clive Warrington	Hall 1982
WO1 (RSM) M.F. Todd	Staff 1989	Dr R.A.H. Washbrook	Friends of Repton
J.J.W. Tomlinson	Brook 1954	Peter T.A. Watson	Mitre 1950
H.S.L. Tottenham	Hall 1936	Greville Watts	Hall 1948
Daniel Townley	School 2000	Alison Webb	Staff 1975–81
Oliver Townley	School 2004	Stephen Webb-Jones	Orchard 1952
Adarsh Trivedi	Latham 2002	Mark Webster	New 1960
Nishant Trivedi	Latham 1998	Robert J. Weir	New 1951
Dr Constantine Tsang	Cross 1994	Charles Wells	Brook 1955
Rev'd Peter A. Tubbs	Cross 1935	Robert William Wells	Latham 1987
J.S. Tudsbery-Turner	Orchard 1956	Richard Wendell Jones	Hall 1944
Toby A.R. Turl	Cross 1950	George J.A. Wenger	Cross 1953
G.C. Turner	Priory 1956	J.M.C. Wesson	Hall 1940
Julian Turner	Cross 1991	W.A.S. Wesson	Hall 1943
Trevor Turton	New 1975	George H. West	Cross 1945
Charlie Twigg	Latham 2005	K.C. West	Brook 1959
Georgie Twigg	Field 2003	Anne Elizabeth Weston Smith	Field 2002
		Catherine Hay Weston Smith	Field 1998
David Van Beesten	New 1963	Mark William Weston Smith	Orchard 2005
P.H. Vaughan	Cross 1952	Rebecca Clare Weston Smith	Field 2000
Darren Vickers	Latham 1983	Ben Whitehead	Priory 1996
J.E.G. Vivian	Cross 1933	Lucy Alice Whitehead	Mitre 2004
		Stuart Whitehouse	Latham 1978
James Waddilove	School 2004	R.J.H. Whittaker	Priory 1988
Professor O.L. Wade	Cross 1935	Paul Whitworth	Hall 1963
Paul Wade	Orchard 1973	Nick Wilcox	Orchard 1998
John F. Wadsworth	Orchard 1958	Richard G. Wilkes	Orchard 1942
J.F.M. Walker	Hall 1946 and Staff 1957–1997	Mike Wilkins	Latham 1990
M.J.H. Walker	New 1949	Andrew Wilkinson	Priory 1982
Dr James Walkerdine	Brook 1990	Samantha Wilkinson (née Braddock)	Abbey 1986
Jonathan Craig Waller	Hall 1976	Brigadier Edward Wilkinson	Cross 1946
Geoffrey I.A. Wallis	Priory 1941	Fraser Wilkinson	Orchard 2003
John Wallis	Latham 1971	Lydia Wilkinson	Field 1999
Stephen Walwyn	Latham 2002	Alex Willcox	Priory 2005

A.J.T. Williams	Hall 1942
Chloé Williams	Mitre 2005
H.B. Williams	Staff 1949–1959
Jack Williams	Orchard 2003
Jack T. Williams	School 2004
T.R. Williams	School 1995
Professor Andrew Wiliamson	New 1959
Ashley George Williamson	New 1995
Jonathan Stewart Wills	Priory 1979
Anthony M. Wilson	Hall 1942
Neil Wilson	Brook 1953
Nicholas Wilson	Latham 1949
Edwin Wilton-Morgan	Latham 2007
Megan R. Wilton-Morgan	Mitre 2004
T.S. Winslow	Latham 1960
A.M. Winter	Cross 1950
Ken Winterschladen	Pirory 1958
Peter J. Wood	Latham 1988
Richard J. Wood	Hall 1971
Mark Woolgar	Hall 1954
Alistair C. Wright	Orchard 1986
David Allan Wright	Mitre 1943
David H.T. Wright	Mitre 1946
Mark Wright	Mitre 1973
Jeremy Wyld	Brook 1989
Gerard Wyllys	Cross 1952
Huseyin Yardimci	Hall 1983
Allan Yates	Latham 1985
Paul Yeats	Cross 1973
D.M. Young	Mitre 1954
Neville J.E. Young	Hall 1937
Christopher Zeuner	Hall 1991
Jiahui Jackfy Zhao	Priory 1999
Jiaxin Eric Zhao	School 2001

INDEX OF NAMES

PICTURE CREDITS

Unless an acknowledgement appears below, the illustrations in this volume have been provided by Repton School. Every effort has been made to contact the copyright holders of all works reproduced in this book. The publishers invite those whose images appear but who are not listed below to contact Third Millennium Publishing.

The editor wishes to express particular thanks to Peter Ashley (for TMI), Johnny Blomfield (H 1955), Robert Blomfield (H 1951), Tom Boot (H 1977), Molly Carstairs, Chris Charter, Terence Coe (L 1988), John Cursham (H 1942), Richard Frase (M 1969), Richard Grew, Heather Hawkins, Ian McClary, Eddie Niem (L 1966), Rob Oakley (L 1967), David Pepper (H 1953), Chris Sale (H 1957), Andy Weekes, Mick Wolford, Burns Graphics, for providing many of the photographs reproduced here.

Peter Ashley: pp 48, 50, 64, 65, 67, 69, 89, 90, 129, 131, 132, 133, 167, 168, 169, 179
Neil Burkey: pp 116, 117, 118
Andy Weekes: pp 9, 51, 87, 156, 163, 164, 169, 177
Matt Wilson: pp 13, 47, 122, 160

BFI: Cabaret poster, p 92
Corbis: Harold Abrahams, p 96; C.B. Fry, p 100, 113; Chris Adams, p 101; Bunny Austin, p 109; Lord Fisher, p 120; Michael Ramsey, p 159; Roald Dahl, p 161; Christopher Isherwood and W.H. Auden, p 180
Getty Images, Hulton Archive: 'Goodbye Mr Chips', p 34
Mary Evans Picture Library: Hubert Murray Burge, p 27; C.B. Fry, p 112
National Portrait Gallery: Willam Bagshaw Stevens, p 20; John Traill Christie, p 33; Aldous Huxley, p 49; Denton Welch, p 72
Roald Dahl Nominee Limited: Roald Dahl with camera, p 73
The Estate of Anthony Gross, courtesy of The Redfern Gallery: Anthony Gross, p 72

TO ALL REPTONIANS.

Repton.

A. C. B.

Not fast, but in strict time. ♩ = 108.

C. H. L.

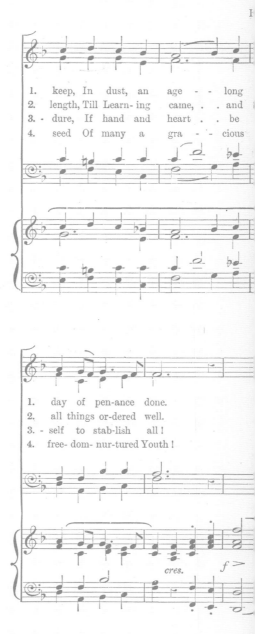

STANZAS 1, 2, 3, 4.

1. Where staid and sil - ver Trent Once wound, in deep . . in - dent, . . By
2. How far our fame ap - pears A - mong the dim - - orbed years! . . First
3. Glad Hill of Reap - ing, dear To all who, breth - ren here, . . Pass
4. Ah, pure and gold - en gleam Of har - vest— 'tis . . no dream— The

1. these rich fields that Hot - - spur claimed . . and won, Where kings and war - riors
2. flame and smoke; then choir . . and ves - - per bell, Still strife! but peace at
3. in and out by Prior - - y, Arch . . and Hall: Your glo - ry shall en -
4. gar - nered grain of vir - - tue, hon - - our, truth; The har - vest, yet the

1. keep, In dust, an age - - long
2. length, Till Learn - ing came, . . and
3. - dure, If hand and heart . . be
4. seed Of many a gra - - cious

1. day of pen - ance done.
2. all things or - dered well.
3. - self to stab - lish all!
4. free - dom - nur - tured Youth!

Stanza 1 may be sung in Chorus
   ,,   2   ,,   ,,   by Trebl
   ,,   3   ,,   ,,   by Teno
   ,,   4   ,,   ,,   in four-p
In any case Stanza 5 should be sung in Unis